Snapshots Of Welsh History – Without The Boring Bits!

Snapshots Of Welsh History – Without The Boring Bits!

Phil Carradice

Published by Accent Press Ltd – 2011

ISBN 9781908192431

Printed and bound in the UK

Cover design by Madamadari

Acknowledgments

Thanks are due to many people, notably BBC Wales who commissioned the series of Blogs on various aspects of Welsh History and have subsequently given permission for them to be re-produced in book form. Thanks in particular to Suzanne Morrow for her help and encouragement.

Thanks also to Hazel Cushion and Accent Press for agreeing to take on this project.

Most of the photographs are taken from my own collection. However, certain images have been provided by other individuals. For these, particular thanks to Margaret Colley, Roger McCallum, Mike Edwards, Bob Priddle and Trudy Carradice.

Thanks to all my teachers and lecturers from the past who managed to instill in me a sense of history – in the main, by studiously ignoring all "the boring bits" until I was well and truly gripped by the subject. History as it should be taught.

As ever, thanks to Trudy, my wife, for her assistance, particularly on the computer – I remain a 'Luddite' and I could not have done it without you, Trude.

Introduction

I have always found history fascinating. Perhaps I have been lucky. Early on, my father – to whom history was a living, breathing thing – and my teachers at the old Pembroke Grammar School in west Wales imbued me with a love of the subject. Further study at college and university served only to add to my enthusiasm.

And yet, for many people history remains a dry, sterile topic. As a man once told me, he would rather have his teeth pulled without anaesthetic than read a history book! That attitude is such a shame – the gentleman concerned just doesn't know what he is missing.

Unfortunately, many people feel the same. And much of the blame for such feelings or attitudes has to come down to bad teaching – not to mention bad writing. But if history teachers had only managed to catch the imagination of their pupils in the first place, had enthralled them with stories of the past, things would have been very different.

I think it was Rudyard Kipling who said that history would be far better remembered if it was taught through the medium of stories rather than as a simple litany of dates and information. And history has to be remembered if we are not to repeat the mistakes of the past. That, really, is its only purpose. As a writer and as a teacher I have always tried – in my books, in my lessons, in general conversation – to weave the story-tellers web.

So when the BBC asked me to write a series of weekly history blogs, I was happy to take on the project. But I was determined that each blog I wrote would be a story in itself – in effect a little piece of fascinating history, well known or obscure. As far as I was concerned this was to be history like your teachers would never have taught you. Effectively, what I wanted to write was history without the boring bits. I hope I managed to do that with the blogs in our wonderful, new electronic world – now it is the turn of the printed page to throw out the same degree of fascination, to catch the imagination of the reader.

The blogs or articles – give them whatever terminology you will, they are really snippets of historical fact – are presented here in a roughly chronological order. It was not possible to run them strictly in date order as several span the centuries and historical periods. But wherever and whenever possible they do run chronologically and can therefore be read as one continuous book or dipped into whenever the mood or interest takes you.

If the blog articles – I don't know what else to call them – in this book manage to catch your interest then their purpose will have been achieved. It is then up to you, the reader, to go and find out more about the topics covered.

Read the book, then go on to uncover a new world of fact, fantasy and imagination. You won't be disappointed.

Phil Carradice, St Athan, 2011

1 – The Celts

Every autumn and winter, with the prospect of the forthcoming Six Nations Rugby Championship looming large in people's minds, many red-blooded Welsh men and women (and Irish and Scots, too, come to that) become suddenly conscious of their Celtic roots.

We are all of us proud of our heritage. That applies whatever nationality we are – English, Irish, Scottish or Welsh. And rightly so. But how many of us are aware of the origins of the Celtic people of Wales? It is a fascinating story.

The Celts first arrived on our shores and began living in Britain – all of Britain, not just the extremities like Wales, Ireland and Scotland – in approximately 1000BC. Originating in the Danube area, they gradually moved northwards, a process of migration that took many hundreds of years. They were an adventurous and curious people and it was inevitable that, standing on the shores of what later became the English Channel, they should be attracted by the mysterious land they could see on the horizon.

The Celts came to Britain, first, as explorers, sailing their flimsy coracle craft across the waters of the Channel and the western seas, and landing on the southern coasts of the island. Over the next two hundred or so years they came to settle and stay. They were skilled workers in metals like bronze but they were also farmers who soon began to clear the forests and cultivate crops.

By the time the Romans arrived, between 43 and 85AD, the Celts were the dominant influence in Britain. These Celts were a fierce and warlike people, Julius Caesar himself commenting on the blue-painted warriors who attacked without fear, time after time, not knowing when they were beaten. However, faced by superior fire power in the shape of the Roman Legions, the Celts were gradually pushed back, out of the rich farmlands of central and southern England, to find refuge in the wild and rugged mountains of the west and north.

Ireland, Scotland and Wales were never fully integrated into the Roman Empire and Wales, in particular, was seen as something of a frontier zone. At one time over 30,000 legionary and auxiliary troops were stationed around the edges of the country, in bases like Caerleon and Chester. There were many bloody campaigns and battles in Wales, events like the killing and destruction of the Druids by Suetonius Paulinus on Anglesey in 61AD, but in general the Roman occupation of Britain had little long-lasting effect on Celtic art, language and culture.

When the Romans left in the years after AD410 Celtic culture was strong enough to resist that of the in-coming Saxons. By now the Celts spoke a language known as Common Celtic, a language that was divided into two strands – Goedelic which was spoken in northern Scotland and Ireland, and Brythonic which was the language of Wales and Cornwall. Brythonic was also spoken by the people in the areas around modern day Carlisle, Edinburgh and in Strathclyde.

While there were, to begin with, strong links between the Celts in Wales and those in the north of Britain, Saxon advances into the west were soon causing problems. Saxon victories at Dyrham in Gloucestershire and at Chester (AD577 and 615 respectively) isolated the Welsh from other Celtic peoples. And when King Offa of Mercia built his dyke in the middle years of the eighth century – an attempt to define the frontier of Mercia, not Wales, as many believe – it gave Wales, for the first time, an eastern frontier.

A recreation of a typical Celtic village. Roofs are thatched, houses are round and the village is protected by a wooden fence.

Secure, now, behind this 150 mile ditch and palisade, the Celtic people of Wales were free to continue their lives, untroubled by what was going on over the border.

Iron Age Celts lived in round houses that were grouped together inside a series of circular ramparts. There was also a protective ditch, far more effective at keeping out wild animals than any attacking enemy force. They also had hillforts – over 500 of them having been discovered in Wale alone – but these were places of refuge, used only when a community was in danger or under direct attack.

It has been claimed that the Celts had over 4000 different gods and deities. Usually these gods represented crucially important elements such as the sun, sea, stars and wind.

The only people who could talk to the gods were the Druids, the Celtic priests, who had immense power in Celtic society. As there was no written language at this time, their knowledge and ritual was remembered in verse form and as a consequence the Druids were part of the privileged circle of poets, story tellers and musicians who surrounded the tribal chiefs.

After AD61 and the brutal killing of many, if not most, of the Druids on the shores of the Menai Straits, the power of these strange, intense men declined. Not until the modern incarnation – the Gorsedd – was created in the nineteenth century did the significance and importance of the Druidic order come to the forefront of Welsh society once more..

However, the Celts of the west and north retained their love of poetry and music, celebrating victory and lamenting defeat down the years. They have remained fiercely proud, independent peoples who are conscious of their heritage and their past history.

Small wonder, then, that battles – on the sports field these days, not in war – bring back feelings of belonging. Small wonder that they stir the pride of nationhood.

2 – Prince Madoc and the Discovery of America

Who discovered America? It's a simple question and one that usually brings the standard response – Christopher Columbus. But here in Wales we have our own theory. And that theory says that America was actually discovered three hundred years before Columbus sailed "the ocean blue" in 1492 – and more importantly, that it was discovered by a Welshman.

The man in question was Prince Madoc, the son of Owain Gwynedd, one of the greatest and most important rulers of north Wales, and while the legend cannot be corroborated there are many who believe it implicitly. Owain Gwynedd certainly existed, his reign being marred by long and hard-fought disputes with Henry II, king of England.

The story goes that in 1170 Owain died and, almost immediately, a violent and very bloody dispute arose between his thirteen children regarding the succession. Madoc and his brother Rhirid were so upset and angered by events that they decided they wanted no further part in what was happening. Indeed, they wanted nothing more to do with their family or their homeland. They duly took ship from Rhos on Sea (Llandrillo) and sailed westwards to see what they could find.

What Prince Madoc found, so the legend runs, was America. He and his brother managed to cross the Atlantic and land on the shores of the New World. Madoc apparently then returned to Gwynedd for more men, before sailing off again, this time never to return.

Madoc supposedly settled in North America where his sailors, naturally enough, inter-married with local Native Americans and for years the rumour of Welsh-speaking Native American tribes was widely believed. It is, of course, the stuff of legend but like all good legends it has at least a grain of truth about it.

As America was explored and colonised several Native American tribes were discovered, speaking a language that did actually sound quite like Welsh. All right, so it may not have been Welsh but it certainly sounded like it. That was not the only connection.

The Mandan Indians used Bull Boats for transport and fishing, vessels that were identical to the famous Welsh coracles that are still used today in some parts of west Wales. It was all too good for storytellers and poets to ignore.

The legend lasted well into the nineteenth century and even the explorers Lewis and Clark, two of the early pioneers who trekked off into the American hinterland, were instructed to keep their eyes open for these "Welsh-speaking Indians" while they were searching through the interior of the country. They found, of course, precisely nothing!

The earliest reference to such a Welsh-speaking people in America can be found in a Welsh poem by Maredudd ap Rhys who lived and wrote in the years between 1450 and 1483. However it was during the Elizabethan period, the first great age of discovery, that the story gathered momentum and grew.

There was, however, a political agenda behind the spreading of this legend – it was a ploy, used to assert the right of England to the lands of the New World. Put quite simply, Welsh colonisation of America, many years before, was a convenient justification for Elizabethan settlement in a territory that had already been claimed by Spain.

Starting with Humphrey Llwyd in 1559 the story was embroidered and developed – the detail of the Welsh-speaking tribe comes from this period – and even recognised experts in the field of navigation and exploration, men like Richard Hakluyt, consciously and deliberately wrote about the legend as if it were the absolute truth. Sadly, there is no absolute historical or archaeological proof – even Lewis and Clark, try as they might, were unable to find that – but it remains a great story, one that we in Wales have taken to our hearts.

Perhaps the very lack of evidence, one way or another, is what makes the story so fascinating. It lies in that strange and indefinable gap between fact and legend and like all good stories relies on listeners or readers to make their own judgements about where the truth actually lies.

Many people have not been quite as happy to believe the story of Prince Madoc as the Welsh. In 1953 the Daughters of the American Revolution set up a plaque on the shores of Mobile Bay in Alabama. On the plaque it stated that it had been erected "In memory of Prince Madoc", who was, in the opinion of the Daughters of the Revolution, the original discoverer of America. The plaque did not last long and was soon removed by the Alabama Parks Department.

For Welsh men and women, however, the story of Madoc's discovery of America remains special – even if, in our heart of hearts, we know that it is probably not true. And as the man once said, why let the truth get in the way of a good story?

3 – Hywel Dda – the Lawmaker of Wales

Wales is certainly not lacking when it comes to stories and tales of kings or great warriors. Ranging from the mythological heroes of the Mabinogion, where legend mixes easily with fact and reality, to genuine historical figures like the Lord Rhys or Llywelyn the Great, there are so many to choose from.

Yet one of the greatest is remembered, not so much for his prowess as a warrior, but from the laws and statutes he commissioned and put into practice in a time of peace and security.

That man was Hywel Dda, Hywel the Good as he might be called in English. And it could be argued that his laws and reforms, laid down in the mid-tenth century, have had more effect than any of those of most Welsh rulers, either before or afterwards.

Hywel Dda was the son of Rhodri Mawr, another great Welsh prince who, during his period in power at the end of the ninth century, managed to unite large parts of the country under his dynamic and thrusting leadership. As a result of this the Saxon attacks or incursions into Wales were restricted for many years.

While Rhodri's efforts kept the Norsemen at bay, the modern-day country of England began to take shape as the various kingdoms across Offa's Dyke gradually developed and merged into something like a unified state.

In Wales, it was a different matter. Everything was fine while Rhodri was alive but, once he died, his lands were divided amongst his six sons, as custom demanded. Unable to stand alone, most of these Welsh territories or kingdoms soon declared homage to the English kings and, theoretically at least, the Welsh people became subjects of the English monarchy.

Hywel Dda became king of Seisyllwg – roughly speaking the modern-day counties of Ceredigion and Carmarthen – in the year AD 900. Through a marriage alliance he quickly acquired the area known as Dyfed and this, along with his original possessions, created the kingdom of Deheubarth. Hywel did not stop there and, in time, seized Gwynedd and Powys so that until his death in AD 949 a huge portion of Wales was once more united under a single ruler.

With his kingdom secure from raiding Saxons – and from the power of England – Hywel set about reforming or at least codifying the customs and practices from the various regions of Wales and turning them into a single law. These were the famous Cyfraith Hywel Dda, the Laws of Hywel Dda.

The traditional story is that Hywel had a mind to change some of the long-accepted laws of Wales. He therefore called representatives from all his cantrefs to a convention, held at one of his hunting lodges. This was Ty Gwyn in Whitland.

The date of the meeting remains a little unclear although it probably took place over the Lent period sometime in the late 940s. The meeting lasted for six weeks while the laws were proposed, discussed and then set down. The old laws were studied, the useful ones retained and the inappropriate ones discarded. And, of course, new ones were written.

How true that story is, remains a matter of conjecture. The earliest existing copies of Hywel's Laws date from the twelfth century, two hundred years later. They are copies of the original documents in existence, eighty manuscripts in Latin and Welsh – and two of them, Gwentian Brut and Brut Ieuan, might even have been copied or written as late as the eighteenth century. Certainly all of the Laws, as they are seen today, contain additions made many years after Hywel's death.

Despite these reservations the Laws, as we know them, do contain much material that was written during Hywel's reign. And many of them are extremely enlightened. According to the Laws marriage was considered an agreement, not a holy sacrament and divorce was permitted by common consent. Precedence was to be given to a woman's claim in any case of rape.

There was to be no punishment for theft – provided the sole purpose of the offence was to stay alive. Under these Laws compensation for the victim was felt to be far more important than any possible or potential punishment of the offender. Illegitimate children received exactly the same rights as legitimate sons and daughters. There were many more, covering the whole range of Welsh life and society.

There is no doubt that the Laws of Hywel Dda were insightful and enlightened. Quite how much Hywel had to do with their compilation will never be known but he was a well-read and intelligent man and so it is quite likely that he had more than a little involvement. He was on good terms with Alfred the Great, the king of Wessex, and. inspired by Alfred's example, Hywel had undertaken a pilgrimage to Rome long before he began codifying

Welsh Laws. Clearly, then, this was no petty prince, concerned only with his own local glory. This was a man of vision and integrity.

After Hywel's death in AD 949 Wales quickly fell back into being a disparate and warring state, threatened by the growing power of the Saxons on the one hand and by the gathering might of England on the other. The one thing that did remain, however, was the series of Laws that the king had brought into use.

Hywel Dda's Laws were enforced in Wales for several centuries. Not until Henry VIII passed the Acts of Union in the sixteenth century did they finally disappear. They are remembered, now, as a series of legal documents that provided justice and compassion for all. Modern day enthusiasts or historians can visit the Hywel Dda Heritage Centre in Whitland where extracts and examples have been mounted on slate and stone. It is a fitting tribute for one of Wales's most renowned rulers.

4 – Giraldus Cambrensis and his Journey Through Wales

Most of us could probably be excused for failing to note 14th April 1188 as a date of particular importance or significance. It's hardly one that springs to mind when you consider great moments in the calendar of Welsh history. But this was the day when Giraldus Cambrensis finally finished his mammoth 600 mile trek around Wales, a trek that led to him writing "Descriptio Cambriae," one of the earliest of all travel books.

Giraldus Cambrensis in Latin, Gerallt Cymro in Welsh, Gerald of Wales in English – the man had as many names as he had careers. Born in Manorbier Castle on the south coast of Pembrokeshire in approximately 1146, Giraldus came from a mixed Norman-Welsh background. His father , William de Barri, was one of the leading Anglo-Norman barons while his uncle, David Fitzgerald, was Bishop of St David's.

Manorbier Castle was the birthplace of Giraldus Cambrensis. For some reason the castle managed to avoid the rigours of war and looks now very much as it would have looked in the days of Giraldus.

Manorbier and its castle remained important places for Giraldus. They were, he later wrote, "the pleasantest spots in Wales". When the sun shines and the wind blows, cool and gentle from the sea, there are few who would disagree with his assessment.

Giraldus was the grandson of Gerald de Windsor, constable of Pembroke Castle during the early years of its existence, and of Princess Nest, the daughter of Rhys ap Tewdr. So his pedigree as a well-to-do nobleman left nothing to be desired. However, with an uncle as Bishop of St David's it was, perhaps, inevitable that his education should have a religious bias.

He went, first, to school in Gloucester, then to Paris to finish his education. He returned to Britain somewhere around 1172 and was immediately employed by the Archbishop of Canterbury on a number of ecclesiastical missions in his native Wales.

When his uncle, the Bishop, died, Giraldus was proposed by the chapter of St David's Cathedral as by far the most suitable man to succeed him. The king and the Archbishop of Canterbury refused the nomination, however. The king, Henry II, certainly did not want a dynamic and energetic man in charge at St David's – such a man could only give extra importance to the people of Wales. In effect he was not appointed simply because he WAS Welsh!

As it happened, Giraldus was again nominated for the Bishopric of St David's in 1198. The king, by then, was John, the son of Henry. Although he allowed an election amongst members of the chapter, an election that Giraldus won and then went on to serve four years as Bishop elect, in the end it was a position that went to someone else. Giraldus was bitterly disappointed and even left the country, fleeing because the ports were being watched and patrolled, to try to present his case to the Pope – all to no avail.

Failing to gain the Bishopric at St David's did not mean Giraldus was totally out of favour with the monarchy. As early as 1184, for example, he had been appointed Royal Clerk and chaplain to Henry II and the same year he accompanied Prince John on his military conquests in Ireland. This led to his first book, "Topographia Hibernia" (1188), an account of the campaign and one that stressed the barbaric nature of the native Irish.

As something of a reward for his services, in 1188 Giraldus was nominated to accompany the Archbishop of Canterbury, Baldwin of Exeter, as he rode through Wales on a recruiting drive. The purpose of the journey was to enlist men for the 3rd Crusade but as far as Giraldus was concerned the trip gave him the ideal opportunity to study his fellow countrymen and to develop his literary skills.

The books that Giraldus produced after the journey, "Itinerarium Cambriae" and "Descriptio Cambriae," still stand as valuable historical documents but their real importance lies in the fact that they set the tone for all travel writing ever since.

The books do not just record places visited and sights seen but are full of Giraldus's unique take on Welsh life, prejudiced and vain as they are – a style that so many travel writers had emulated over the years. "This is what I saw but this is what I think," Giraldus seemed to be saying. The personal opinion, something so vital in good travel writing, was shown to its best advantage in these two books. If the best advice of travel writer Jan Morris is "Never divorce the I" then it is something that Giraldus Cambrensis understood and used long, long before:

"Merioneth – is the rudest and least cultivated region and the least accessible. The natives of that part of Wales excel in the use of long lances, as those of Monmouth are distinguished for their management of the bow."

As a chronicler of his times and as a travel writer Giraldus Cambrensis was unsurpassed. He went on to become Archdeacon of Brecon and visited Rome three times – no easy task in the twelfth and thirteenth centuries. He was offered the Bishoprics of places like Wexford and Bangor but refused them. St David's was what he wanted but was never offered.

Critical, prejudiced and self-opinionated, Giraldus still managed to retain an open mind about many Welsh customs:

"No one in this region ever begs, for the houses are common to all. And they consider liberality and hospitality amongst the first of virtues."

The date of Giraldus's death is not totally clear but it was probably about 1223. He died disappointed in his main ambition but as the provider of one of the earliest pieces of travel writing – and for that we should be grateful.

5 – Welsh Christmas and New Year Traditions

Like most other parts of Britain, Wales has long had its own Christmas and New Year traditions, practices and superstitions that have now largely died out – which is something of a shame as they are fascinating examples of social history. Some, however, have managed to linger on, remaining as wonderful examples of a world and a society that have now passed into memory.

In the days before Christmas it was always customary to decorate your house with huge swathes of mistletoe and holly. Mistletoe was supposed to protect the family from evil while holly was there as a symbol of eternal life. When you consider that mistletoe had always been regarded as the sacred plant of the ancient druids it is not too difficult to see its importance as a symbol for people living in isolated parts of rural Wales.

The old Welsh custom of plygain has almost died out – almost but not quite – and there are still parts of the country where it has clung tenaciously to life. In fact, many people believe it is currently undergoing something of a revival.

Plygain was originally an early service in either church or chapel, sometimes beginning as early as three in the morning. At this service men – always men, never women – would sing Christmas Carols for three or four hours, unaccompanied and in three part harmony. In some parts of Wales plygain has now developed into an evening service, in others it has either disappeared or has remained an early morning event.

While waiting for plygain to begin families would occupy themselves in taffy making. Toffee would be boiled in pans over the open fire and then, when it was almost cooked, huge mounds of the toffee would be dropped into ice cold water. The moment it hit the water the "taffy" would curl into strange and unusual shapes. Some of these shapes closely resembled letters and were thought by younger family members to indicate the initials of any future love.

One less than palatable tradition on Boxing Day was that of holly beating. Boys and young men would take sprigs of holly and roam the streets looking for young women. When they encountered them they would hit out at their arms and legs, beating them with the holly – sometimes until their victims bled.

One variation of this violent tradition – which probably had its origins in the scourging of Christ on his way to the cross – was for the last person out of bed on Boxing Day morning to be beaten with the holly sticks. Thankfully for all concerned, this tradition seems to have died out towards the end of the nineteenth century.

As with Scotland, the tradition of "first footing" was always important in Wales. There were differences, however. If the first visitor across a Welsh threshold was either a woman or a red-haired man it was considered terribly unlucky for the household.

Never lend anything on New Year's Day was another important Welsh tradition in the Victorian Age. A person's behaviour on that auspicious day was usually considered to be an indication of the way they would behave or conduct themselves for the rest of the year.

The most renowned of the New Year traditions in Wales, however, was that of the Mari Lwyd, the phrase meaning the Grey Mare. There have been attempts to revive the tradition in certain parts of the country – not entirely successfully, although the custom has been revived in a few places. The Mari Lwyd was a horse's skull covered with a white sheet and ribbons. It had false ears and eyes and was carried on a long pole.

Gangs of men and young boys would carry the Mari Lwyd from door to door. They had usually consumed copious amounts of alcohol and the procession would be accompanied by a growling cacophony of noise. When a door was opened the householder would be assailed by poems and insults – in Welsh – and to this they were expected to reply in like form. When the verbal battle had been won or lost the Mari Lwyd and her followers were invited inside for yet another drink.

In the nineteenth century the churches and chapels began to object to the violence and drunkenness that invariably accompanied a visit from the Mari Lwyd and, gradually, the singing of carols began to replace the poems and insults. There are many who say this "watering down" of the tradition led to the eventual decline in the popularity of the Mari Lwyd.

Calennig is another Welsh custom that died out at the end of the nineteenth century. From dawn until dusk on 1st January small parties of boys would pass from house to house in the village or town, carrying twigs of evergreen plants and cups or jugs of water. They would use the twigs to splash water at people and, in return, would receive the calennig – small copper coins.

Christmas, of course, did not end until Twelfth Night and in

Wales the custom of hunting the wren was something that took place on this last night of festivities. Men would catch a wren, put it in a wooden box and carry it from door to door. Householders would then pay a penny for the privilege of lifting the lid of the box in an attempt to see the tiny bird.

These days there are very few traditions that have survived. Time, of course, changes everything and many of the old customs were politically very incorrect. Yet they remain an important part of our history.

6 – The First Eisteddfod – Christmas 1176

These days we are used to our main or major eisteddfodau being held in the summer months – the Urdd in the week of the Whitsun holiday, the International at Llangollen in the first week of July and the National in the first week of August. It hasn't always been like that and, even now, in many parts of Wales the "winter eisteddfod" is still an important part of the cultural year. Yet the three main events remain very much a part of the summer programme of festivities.

It is interesting to note, therefore, that the very first eisteddfod actually took place, not in the summer but over the Christmas period of 1176. The term "eisteddfod" was not used for this first event and did not achieve common parlance until the fifteenth century. When this first cultural gathering was called it was known simply as a bardic tournament.

Following the victory of Duke William – William the Conqueror as he became known – at the Battle of Hastings in 1066 there took place a piecemeal division of England. The great lords and warriors who had been persuaded to help William in his campaign greedily accepted their payment or prizes – prizes that invariably meant huge parcels of land previously owned by the Saxon earls.

Wales, however, was left untroubled for some time. It was a wild and ferocious country where for many years, both before and after the Normans began their incursions, the King's writ truly "did not run". Only in the late eleventh century, when the great Marcher Lords of Chester, Shrewsbury and Hereford finally felt strong and powerful enough, were the first attacks made across Offa's Dyke.

The next two hundred or so years saw a period of intense warfare and bloodshed as the Norman barons and the Welsh princes clashed in battle after battle, campaign after campaign. It was a see-saw period with, first one side, then the other, gaining the upper hand.

However, by 1155 Rhys ap Gruffydd had, through military strength and cunning, managed to bring all of Deheubarth – the western parts of Wales – under his control.

It had been a long and powerful struggle and Rhys had been forced to submit to the power of Henry II, the English king, on no fewer than four occasions. Such was the Welsh determination, however, that no sooner had Henry withdrawn his troops, thinking that the war had finished, Rhys rebelled and rose up in defiance once again. Henry was finally forced to come to terms with Rhys, formally granting him the title "Lord of Ystrad Tywi". He immediately became known, and has been ever since, as the Lord Rhys.

There were to be further campaigns and battles in the years ahead but, for now, the Lord Rhys felt sufficiently secure to turn his mind to matters other than warfare.

What Rhys wanted was to organise and run a cultural event that would underline his position as the most important Welsh chieftain in the country. He had seen and enjoyed many aspects of Norman culture or lifestyle but knew also that he could not afford to alienate his native Welsh followers. He was fond of music and poetry and, like most of the Welsh princes, patronised bards who, in return, wrote long odes or verses extolling the significance of the Lord Rhys.

What he now decided to do was to hold a bardic tournament over the Christmas period of 1176/77, a festival of music and poetry – for prizes – that would celebrate the arts and ensure the supreme position of the Lord Rhys as a far-sighted ruler and as a major supporter of artistic endeavour. Such a gathering of poets, singers and musicians probably owed more to Norman than Welsh influences as, up to that point, there had not been any similar event in Wales. In France, however, they were a common occurrence.

It was a significant moment in Welsh history as all of the eisteddfodau since held in the country owe more than a little to this first event.

Perhaps even more important, however, was the statement Rhys was making by holding the tournament in Cardigan Castle rather than at Dinefwr, the traditional seat of rulers of Deheubarth. Cardigan, recently restored, was a stone-built castle and both it and the surrounding Borough of Cardigan had been recently acquired from the invading Normans. Rhys was clearly showing his power and position to Normans and Welsh alike.

This first eisteddfod had many of the aspects of the modern event. The tournament was announced a year in advance and minstrels and bards from places as far-flung as Ireland and France were invited to come to Cardigan to compete. Two bardic chairs were to be awarded to the victors in poetry and music.

A bard from Gwynedd in North Wales duly won the poetry chair while the son of Eilon the Crythwr, from Rhys's own court, claimed the prize for music. Now regarded as the first eisteddfod ever held in Wales, it does not take much imagination to conjure visions of the festivities, the singing and dancing, the feasting and flirting, that undoubtedly took place at Cardigan over that Christmas period in 1176.

Bardic tournaments continued to be held during the fifteenth and sixteenth centuries until the Acts of Union in the reign of Henry VIII saw eisteddfodau decline in importance. From that point on it became more important to look to London if you wanted financial and political favour and Welsh noblemen and the emerging middle classes turned their backs on Welsh culture.

Not until the Gorsedd of Bards held a special ceremony at the Ivy Bush Hotel in Carmarthen in 1819 did the eisteddfod once again become a significant factor in Welsh life. But, in one form or another, the eisteddfod survived and the Lord Rhys, by calling his first bardic tournament at Cardigan in 1176, had begun a tradition that continues in the present day.

7 – The Last Prince of Wales

On 11th December 1282 a small skirmish took place close to the River Irfon in Mid Wales. The battle – if it can be called that – was fought between a party of mounted English knights and a group of unarmoured Welshmen who were clearly travelling on foot. The encounter was soon over, an uneven contest if ever there was one.

The significance of the event, however, is not that the battle took place but in the simple fact that one of the casualties of that minor and otherwise insignificant skirmish was none other than Llywelyn ap Gruffudd, the last true Prince of Wales.

Llywelyn was the grandson of Llywelyn the Great, the man who had effectively kept the English kings out of Wales for many years and greatly reduced their influence in the Principality.

But by the time his grandson achieved manhood things had changed. The young prince inherited a country that was now under constant threat from its more powerful eastern neighbours. Wales was divided, the Treaty of Woodstock ensuring that Llywelyn's native Gwynedd was partitioned between him and Dafydd, his younger brother. Such partition was, the English kings reasoned, the only way to keep the Welsh nation weak and so protect their vulnerable eastern border.

It was a situation that could not last. Chafing against such humiliation, Llywelyn first fought against his brother, then imprisoned him and finally declared himself sole ruler of Gwynedd, in direct contradiction to the Treaty of Woodstock. The punitive and harsh treaty was something that Llywelyn and most Welshmen considered to have been unfairly forced upon them.

In 1258, with Henry preoccupied with his warlike and rebellious barons, Llywelyn demanded that the lords of Deheubarth and Powys should swear allegiance to him rather than Henry, the English king, and formally adopted the title "Prince of Wales". He then set off on a series of campaigns against the English and quickly regained lost territory in Gwynedd and Powys.

Llywelyn even found time to take Eleanor, daughter of Simon de Montfort, as his bride, sealing a powerful alliance with the English baron. Llywelyn was now at the pinnacle of his fame and popularity. He had a degree of ability and personal charm that meant the Welsh people, always looking for a charismatic leader who would bring them freedom from their English overlords, took him to their hearts. As if bowing to the inevitable, Henry III formally recognised Llywelyn as Prince of Wales at the Treaty of Montgomery in 1267.

Although he was still expected to pay homage to the English king, Llywelyn had effectively created the Principality of Wales and for a few years an uneasy peace descended across the land. When Henry died in 1272 he was succeeded by Edward I and for some reason – something that has never been made totally clear – Llywelyn refused to attend his coronation. On five occasions he was summoned to pay homage to the new king and each time he refused.

There may have been personal animosity between the two men. Certainly Edward, before he succeeded to his father's throne, looked on with bitterness and increasing frustration as the Welsh prince moved from one successful campaign to another. At that stage he did not have the strength or the experience to match Llywelyn – but he could wait. And when he became king and his repeated summons to appear at Westminster was ignored, everyone knew there would have to be some sort of reckoning between the two monarchs.

Llywelyn's refusal to pay homage was a deliberate snub that could, eventually, have only one result and in 1277 Edward lost patience and invaded. Despite their earlier successes, the Welsh armies were no match for the better-armed, better-equipped English.

The winter of 1277 was a hard one and Llywelyn's forces were pushed steadily back by the powerful war machine of Edward's England. Soon Llywelyn was forced to ask for peace and by the terms of the Treaty of Aberconwy he was deprived of all his lands except those in Gwynedd that lay to the west of the River Conwy.

The next four years passed peacefully enough but Llywelyn was seething with resentment and, like the rest of his countrymen, was determined to end English influence in Wales. When, in March 1282, his brother Dafydd rebelled against Edward, a series of linked revolts broke out all across the country. Llywelyn had little choice other than to join a rebellion that was clearly going to be a fight to the death.

To begin with the Welsh did well. Edward's army was soundly defeated at Llandeilo and an English seaborne force was destroyed in the Menai Straits. Yet Llywelyn knew that the longer the war went on the more the balance of power would shift to Edward. He knew he needed more troops.

He went south to recruit soldiers and just outside Builth Wells learned of the presence of a large English force in the area. It was while he and a few followers were reconnoitring the English positions that he was surprised and attacked on the morning of 11th December.

The English knights charged the defenceless Welsh prince and his party. Llywelyn had no option other than to make a run for cover but, in the confusion, with horses screaming and men straining to reach the safety of cover, Stephen de Francton plunged his lance into the unarmoured body of what he then thought was a simple Welsh foot soldier. Only when he returned to the scene of the skirmish later in the day did de Francton realize he had killed the Welsh prince and war leader.

Llywelyn's head was cut from his body and sent to London where the grisly object was displayed at the Tower for many months, a warning to all those who dared to defy the might of Edward I.

In the wake of Llywelyn's death the rebellion quickly fell apart and within a few years Edward had mercilessly ground Wales beneath his iron foot. The last Prince of Wales remains, now, as a symbol of a proud and determined people – and of the fight for freedom against oppression, from wherever it might come.

8 – Castles of Conquest and Oppression

When we have visitors come to stay, friends or relatives who have, perhaps, never been to Wales before, one of the first things many of us do is take them out to see some of the majestic ruined castles that still dominate our landscape. This is Wales, we say, these are part of out heritage. And they are – but most of us remain unaware that the majority of these great stone edifices aren't Welsh at all. They are English and were built with the sole purpose of grinding down the populace, of keeping the Welsh people in subjugation.

That doesn't make them any less magnificent – as pieces of architecture, as weapons of war. But it is good and only right that we should know and pass on their original purpose.

When Dafydd, brother of Llywelyn, the last true Prince of Wales, was captured and executed at Shrewsbury in 1283 it left Edward I of England in total command of Wales. The Statute of Rhuddlan, signed in 1284, set out the principles on which Edward intended to rule his newly acquired territories.

From the beginning it was clear that he intended to rule as an autocrat, a conqueror who had little or no concern for the Welsh people and their traditions. Boroughs on the English style were created at places such as Aberystwyth and Caernarfon and new Marcher Lordships were brought into existence in border regions like Chirk and Denbigh. A system of courts in the English style or format was also introduced, along with the imposition of English criminal law.

In order to ensure adherence to the new systems Edward built castles, huge stone monsters that were power bases for English Lords and English arms.

In the south several stone-built castles were already in existence. These included fortresses such as Caerphilly, Cardiff and Pembroke. They had been built by the early invaders of Wales, the Norman barons who originally arrived with William the Conqueror in the years after 1066.

The very earliest Norman (or English) castles in Wales had been earth and timber structures, motte and bailey castles with a wide courtyard (the bailey) and a motte or mound some thirty or forty feet high – both Cardiff and Pembroke had, originally, been motte and bailey forts.

The first stone-built castle in Wales was Chepstow, built by

Baron William FitzOsbern in approximately 1067. It retained the motte concept of the early earth and timber castles but added rectangular and, eventually, round or circular towers and keeps. The Welsh chieftains had quickly copied the castle concept and built a few of their own. After Edward's successes in the thirteenth century these castles, places like Dinefwr and Drystwyn, were taken over and adapted by the victorious English.

It was in the north, however, traditionally the centre of Llywelyn and Dafydd's power, that Edward built his strongest castles. By 1282, before the Statute of Rhuddlan had even been contemplated, the enormous stone portals of Rhuthun, Denbigh and Holt Castles were beginning to take shape. The following year work began on places such as Harlech and Conwy. Beaumaris – arguably the most perfect concentric castle in the world – began to take shape late in 1295.

Building castles at the rate Edward demanded did not come cheaply. By 1301, when work had been completed on the majority of his planned fortifications, it was estimated that the king had spent over eighty thousand pounds on the building programme. This was a truly incredible figure, one that would now translate to a sum in the region of sixty million pounds.

Carew Castle, the northern section, modified into a Tudor gentleman's residence. The southern section remains pure Norman.

Building materials such as stone, lead and iron had to be transported to Wales from various parts of Britain and Edward, always conscious of the need to make the castles both defensively effective and, at the same time, emotionally dramatic, employed only the very best craftsmen on each project.

James of St George, the Master of the King's Works in Wales, was the man who designed fortifications like Caernarfon and Beaumaris. In those two fortresses, in particular, this amazing architect and craftsman created military masterpieces, works of beauty that took the art of castle building to its zenith.

Caernarfon and Beaumaris are concentric castles, complete with two lines of defence, making them almost – almost but not quite – unconquerable. Caernarfon, with its polygonal towers and lines of coloured stone, the low symmetrical lines of Beaumaris – they might be weapons of oppression but, even now, they remain incredible works of art.

The castles of Wales, most of them English, were powerful units of military occupation. They were the physical manifestation of totalitarianism, the symbol of a dictatorial regime. Without them Edward could never have established and maintained his hold over the Welsh people. We need to celebrate them for the superb pieces of machinery that they are but we should never forget their original intention.

9 – Henry Tudor, the Welsh King of England

The date 28th January 1457 will probably mean very little to most people. But this was the day when, at mighty Pembroke Castle in west Wales, the only Welshman ever to become king of England was born. There are those who claim Henry V, born in Monmouth, as a Welsh monarch but his pedigree and lineage are tenuous and pale into insignificance when compared to the man from Pembroke.

That man, of course, was Henry Tudor who ruled for over twenty years as Henry VII and, perhaps more importantly for the history of this country, founded the Tudor dynasty, a dynasty that effectively created modern Britain. He came to the throne at a troubled and chaotic time but in his twenty-three years at the helm he brought peace and stability to a realm that, for thirty years, had known only bloodshed and mayhem.

Henry's grandfather came from Ynys Mon, Anglesey as the English knew it, and had served with honour and bravery in the French wars with Henry V. He fought at the Battle of Agincourt alongside the young king and was well respected by the royal family. Indeed, legend declares that he secretly married Henry's widow Catherine some time after the king's untimely death. His son, Edmund, was later declared legitimate and made Earl of Richmond in 1452.

The years after the death of Henry V saw the eruption of the Wars of the Roses, the great baronial houses of York and Lancaster fighting for control of the country and the throne. The trouble lay in the person of the new king, Henry VI. He was, initially, under age but when he did take over the trappings of kingship he was soon revealed as a weak and unstable leader who might well have had problems with his mental health.

With both York and Lancaster vying for control of the king – and therefore the right to rule or run the country – this was a period of confusion and terrible destruction. Battle followed battle, execution followed execution, with first one side, then the other, achieving superiority.

Henry Tudor's father, a Lancastrian, was heavily involved in the campaigns and the fighting. He was eventually captured by Yorkist forces and was executed at Carmarthen some three or four months before his son was born. Edmund's brother, Jasper, Earl of

Pembroke, then became protector of Edmund's widow, the thirteen year old Margaret Beaufort. She was ensconced in Pembroke Castle, the strongest and most prestigious castle in the country, and there she gave birth to Henry.

The actual birth place of the future king has been identified as a tower on the south-west wall but this identification is largely due to a coat of arms above the fireplace in the room and it remains a matter of some conjecture.

When the Yorkist Edward IV came to the throne in 1461, Jasper Tudor was forced to flee, taking sanctuary on the continent. William Herbert was given control of Pembroke Castle and the young Henry lived in his household until 1469. When, thanks to the wiles of Warwick the Kingmaker, Edward was briefly deposed and Henry VI returned to the throne, Jasper also came back, bringing the young Henry to court with him.

It was a brief sojourn as Edward was soon back in control and Jasper – and Henry – were forced to flee once more. Henry spent the next 14 years in exile in Brittany, albeit as the last and most significant opponent of the Yorkist cause. He made one attempt to invade but this failed dismally. And so, in 1485, it was with a degree of trepidation that Henry decided on a final throw of the dice.

Backed by a small force of French soldiers he landed at Mill Bay in Milford Haven and called all of Wales to rally to his banner. By now Edward had died and his brother Richard had seized the English throne. He was not unduly popular in Wales and so many noblemen and foot soldiers did quickly join Henry's growing force, notably the king's main functionary in this part of Wales, Sir Rhys ap Thomas.

Legend and fact do blur somewhat at this time. There is a wonderful story of Sir Rhys – who had sworn to the king that Henry would land only "over my body" – lying under a bridge so that Henry could march his army over his prostrate form and thereby keep his word. A great story – but probably only that, a story!

Henry Tudor duly defeated Richard at the Battle of Bosworth Field and established his dynasty. During the build up to the battle he had unashamedly played on his Welsh origins, making great capital out of the old Welsh story of Y Mab Darogan – the son of prophesy – who, people believed, would lead the Welsh out of oppression. He, Henry claimed, was that man

Yet once he became king Henry neatly turned his back on Wales, leaving the control and governance of the country to men like Sir Rhys ap Thomas. Sir Rhys ruled Wales well – in Henry's name – taking time to begin the rebuilding of the northern section of his great castle of Carew, in the form of a gentleman's country residence.

And Henry? Did he ever revisit Wales? The answer, sadly, is no. Again, it is only a story but many believe that Henry's old nurse at Pembroke Castle, the wife of Philip ap Howell of Carmarthen, actually taught him to speak Welsh. He certainly remained fond of her and when he became king one of his first acts was to award her a pension. It was something of a shame that he did not think so highly of the country of his birth.

Yet Henry's main concern was to bring stability and peace to all of Britain so it is perhaps understandable that Wales, safe in the capable hands of Sir Rhys ap Thomas, should be left alone. Over the next twenty or so years Henry VII destroyed the power of the barons, outlawed private retainer armies and made the country wealthy once more.

Henry's claim to the throne may have been weak – it was, ultimately, little more than the power of the sword. But this previously rather obscure nobleman, whose roots lie in an island off the north coast of the country, remains one of the most influential Welshmen in British history.

10 – Where Did That Come From?

Have you ever wondered where some of the words, phrases or sayings that we now use on a daily basis actually originated?

For example, many of us often light bonfires in our gardens. But where did the word come from? In the Middle Ages it was quite normal to dig up people's bones after 30 or 40 years in order to make room in the churchyard. Initially, the bones were put in a charnel house and when this became full they were burned on a "bonefire". The word has, over the years, been shortened to bonfire.

Several of our common phrases or sayings have a Welsh origin. Welsh rabbit – or Welsh rarebit as it is known when served in posh restaurants – is, of course, melted cheese on toast, the cheese sometimes being mixed with eggs, milk and ale. The dish dates from the sixteenth century when only rich landowners could afford to eat deer or birds from the Welsh game preserves. Many ordinary Welsh people were never able to taste delicacies such as rabbit in their entire lives. But they could afford cheese on toasted bread and jokingly referred to it as their Welsh rabbit. The term stuck.

Those same huge estates also gave us the saying "to eat humble pie". The rich squires and landowners ate the flesh of the deer they had hunted and disdainfully threw away the innards, the 'umbles as they were known, the liver, kidneys and so on. The poor took those 'umbles, baked them into a pie and so "ate 'umble pie". Over the centuries the letter h has been added to the word and it has come to mean admitting inferiority.

The phrase "spooning" dates from sixteenth-century Wales when men courting young girls would have to sit with their beloved under the watchful eye of the family. There was no possibility of being left alone, unchaperoned, or going for a walk in the early evening air. While sitting there, undoubtedly bored and fed up, they would carve a wooden spoon, complete with intricate patterns, which would be presented to the girl on the wedding day. Thus the Welsh Love Spoon and the term "spooning" came into existence.

One symbol, not a phrase but a gesture, that was always thought to originate with the Welsh has little credibility – which is sad, as it remains a good story.

Welsh archers, particularly those from Monmouth, were considered to be the best in the world. The French, with whom the Hundred Years War was being fought, feared their accuracy.

To keep captured prisoners was both time-consuming and expensive as they had to be guarded and fed. So when the French captured a Welsh archer they simply cut off the first two fingers of the hand that drew the bowstring and then sent the mutilated archer back to the English forces where such wounded men would be useless. After the Battle of Agincourt, runs the story, the Welsh archers simply stood on a mound and waved their two fingers at the French prisoners in a gesture of defiance and, of course, as a warning.

Unfortunately, the story has little substance. Although the gesture, the V sign, has been identified on the Macclesfield Psalter of 1330 and, according to some writers from the time, even though Henry V referred to the French practice of cutting off the fingers of soldiers in his pre-battle speech before Agincourt, there is no evidence that such mutilation was ever carried out. Nor does anyone record the Welsh archers waving their two fingers in the air as a gesture of defiance.

11 – Welsh Witches

Stories about witches are found all over the world. During the sixteenth and seventeenth centuries a "witch craze" in Europe saw over 100,000 people, mainly women, accused of witchcraft and executed, both by secular government and by the church.

Yet, despite this witch mania, there were relatively few witch trials in Wales, only five Welsh witches being executed for their supposed crimes. It is relatively easy to see why this should be. With great reliance placed on the power of the wise man or the wise woman, witchcraft in Wales had long been connected, not to the black arts but to healing.

"The term witch has meant many things to many people over the years," says Dr Kathleen Olsen of the University of Wales, Bangor. "But for most of the Middle Ages the word really meant the local healer, someone who made poultices and medicines and perhaps had charms or spells for healing cattle and other farm animals."

Be that as it may, the powers of darkness certainly had an appeal to some people. When, in the early years of the sixteenth century, a woman by the name of Tangwlyst ferch Glyn was accused by the Bishop of St David's of living in sin, she fashioned a figure of the Bishop and called down a curse upon him. The Bishop fell ill but the affair fizzled out – the only known instance of a poppet doll being made and used in Wales.

Tangwlyst was lucky, a few years later witchcraft was a matter for the State and had she been accused then, her fate would have been considerably different. A Statute in 1563 made witchcraft a capital offence and from that point on more and more people, right across Britain, were called out as witches.

Often this "calling out" was little more than a handy way of labelling some unfortunate woman who was different from everybody else – or, sometimes, as a way of exacting revenge when the wise man or wise woman failed to cure an ache or heal a hurt animal.

"Witchcraft comes into the historical record in 1594," comments historian Richard Suggett, "when Gwen ferch Ellis from Bettws is indicted and subsequently executed for witchcraft. It's the first recorded instance of what, I suppose, you can call black witchcraft. She was a healer but for some reason she was persuaded by another woman, called Jane Conway, to leave a charm at Gloddaeth, the home of Sir Thomas Mostyn, a sworn enemy of Jane Conway."

Gwen was imprisoned and convicted of murder by witchcraft. She was duly hung. There were many other accusations of witchcraft – but proving them was another matter. Most of the women spent brief periods in prison before being released when the case against them collapsed. The National History Museum at St Fagan's has a fascinating collection of witch-related artefacts – including a bottle that is filled with pins and was intended to turn the witch's curse back on herself.

"The bottle would have contained urine," says Lisa Tallis of the museum, "urine from the victim. The idea of the pins was to cause the witch, who had put on the curse, to suffer excruciating pain and thereby break the spell."

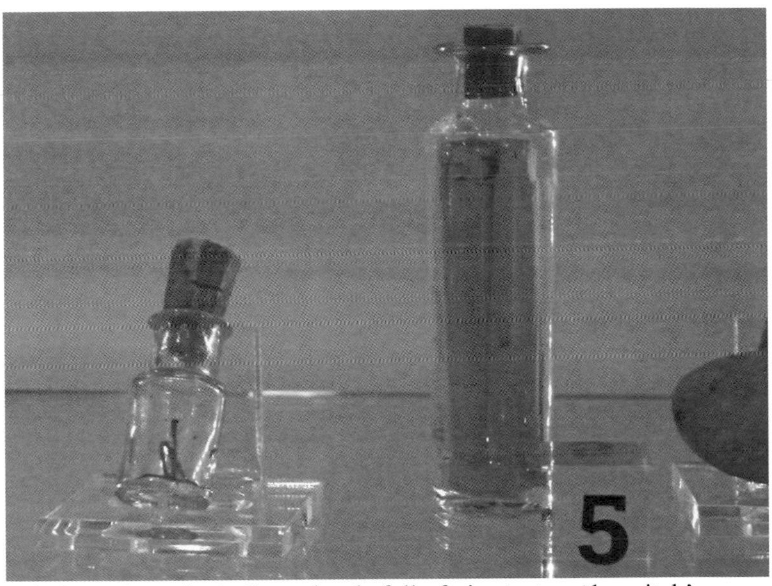

Witch artefacts, including a bottle full of pins to turn the witch's curse back on herself, on display in St Fagan's Museum.

The laws against witches were repealed in 1736 but the very name witch still has the power to cause a shiver of apprehension and fear in many people – particularly on dark winter nights when the powers of darkness might just be wandering abroad!

12 – Royal Weddings – the Welsh Connections

During the early months of 2011 there began to develop an enormous media and public interest in the royal wedding of Prince William and Kate Middleton. The event duly took place on 29th April, over a million people crowding into London to watch and enjoy the celebrations.

This particular wedding remained very much an English affair but here in Wales we, too, have had our involvement in Royal Weddings of the past. And very often they have been events or occasions with more than a few political overtones.

Although not technically a "royal" affair Gerald de Windsor was at the forefront of things back in the twelfth century. In 1105 this Norman knight was appointed Royal Steward and Constable of Pembroke Castle. He was the man who held control of all the King's lands in west Wales and, in Pembroke Castle, commanded the most powerful military fortress in the country. By marrying Princess Nest, the daughter of Rhys ap Tewdwr, the most important Welsh prince south of Gwynedd, Gerald brought the region to an uneasy but ultimately rewarding truce.

Almost exactly a hundred years later another royal marriage brought a degree of peace and stability to Wales. By 1199 Llewelyn Fawr had become the acknowledged ruler of Gwynedd, in effect the northern part and most powerful part of the country. In various campaigns he drove the Normans back beyond Offa's Dyke and made great inroads into Powys. He then turned his attention the southern part of Wales.

Llewelyn was so successful that in 1204 the English king, John, was forced to acknowledge him as Lord of Gwynedd. To seal the acknowledgement or the bargain John gave Joan, his illegitimate daughter, to Llewelyn in marriage. The union did not end the various disputes but it was, by all accounts – and against all the odds – a loving relationship. Joan proved to be a more than useful ambassador for Llewelyn, dealing frankly and openly with her father and, later, her half brother Henry III on his behalf. When, in 1237, Joan died she was buried at Llewelyn's manor of Llanfaes in Ynys Mon and he even built a monastery to commemorate her life.

Perhaps the most significant Welsh connection with royal weddings came in 1501 when Arthur, Prince of Wales, the son of

Henry VII, was married to the Spanish Princess Katherine of Aragon. Born in 1486, Arthur was undersized and sickly but he was heir to the throne and everyone, King and courtiers alike, had a vested interest in keeping him alive and well. A return to the chaos of the Wars of the Roses was not to be countenanced.

Henry – of Welsh descent and born in Pembroke Castle – deliberately named his son after the legendary King Arthur who, many supposed, was himself a Welsh chieftain or cavalry leader. After a "proxy" marriage to Katherine in 1499, the real wedding took place two years later when Arthur was fifteen years old. He and his new bride then left London for Ludlow where Arthur was serving as head of the Council of Wales and the Marches.

And that was when British history changed. The young Prince of Wales and his Princess fell dangerously ill, their fevers being attributed to the unhealthy climate of the Welsh border regions. Katherine soon recovered but Arthur, always an underdeveloped and wasting boy, grew steadily worse and died.

He was succeeded as heir – and as Prince of Wales – by his far more robust younger brother Henry. Rather than renegotiate the alliance and valuable dowry that Katherine had brought from her native Spain, Henry VII simply re-married her to the new heir.

When, years later, Henry VIII, as he had become, decided to divorce Katherine in favour of the younger Anne Boleyn, the whole divorce issue rested on one simple question – had Katherine and Arthur actually consummated their marriage? The Pope had only approved the marriage between Henry and Katherine on the understanding that Katherine and her first husband, Henry's brother, had not been intimate during the brief three or four months of their relationship.

It was a complicated affair that took several long months to sort out but it eventually led to the break with Rome, the English Reformation and the establishment of the Anglican Church – and all because of the weddings of two Princes of Wales.

Another Prince of Wales whose marriage caused great interest for the general public was that of Victoria's son, Edward VII. He was a great rake and philanderer, including women such as Lillie Langtry and Alice Keppel in his list of acquaintances. Soon after the death of his father, Prince Albert, Edward was married to the Danish Princess Alexandra. How would Edward and Alexandra – Bertie and Alix as they were affectionately known – cope with the restrictions of marriage, people asked?

As far as Bertie was concerned it hardly affected him and he carried on much as before. Alix did better than anyone could have ever imagined. When she had wed Bertie at St George's Chapel in Windsor in 1863 she came from the Danish Royal family, a family that was impoverished and almost penniless. Indeed, her father was so poor that he could not even afford to come to the wedding. But Alix took to her new role, enjoying the trappings of royalty and turning a blind eye to most, if not all, of her husband's indiscretions.

Queen Victoria did not attend the ceremony either. But in her case it was because she was in mourning for her recently deceased husband, Albert. She watched the wedding, however, peeping through a hole in the door of Katherine of Aragon's closet, where she sat concealed.

When Prince Charles married Lady Diana Spencer on 29th July 1981, she became the Princess of Wales. He had been invested as Prince in 1969, an event marked by more than a little nationalist unrest but, with marriage to Diana, new-found popularity seemed to fall over the royal couple and they subsequently made many very successful visits to Wales.

Divorce and disclosures about their private lives unfortunately smashed away much of this popularity and now people have seen the new Royal Wedding, hoping it will bring happiness and enjoyment, not just to the royal couple but to all the population of Britain.

13 – Welsh Islands

It is hard to believe but there are somewhere in the region of 100 islands or islets around the coast of Wales. These range from substantial landmasses such as Ynys Mon to tiny and little known places like the St Tudwal's Islands off Abersoch on the Llyn Peninsula. And most of them have fascinating histories.

Sully Island is a low hump of land in the Bristol Channel, situated between the small towns of Penarth and Barry. There is a prehistoric fort on the island and in the eighteenth century this was home to several bands of smugglers. These days you can walk out to the island at low water but you need to be careful. When the tide turns the sea comes racing in over the causeway. Visitors are often cut off by the tide and people have been drowned trying to get back.

Barry Island is now a popular holiday destination but long before Welsh businessman and millionaire David Davies built a huge dock in the area and, thereby, changed the whole layout of the region, it was an actual island. It was only connected with the mainland by a causeway after Davies built his dock in 1884.

Even before that date, however, Barry Island was immensely popular with visitors. In the year 1876 alone, for example, over 12,000 visitors made their way out to the island, either by boat or, at low water, by carefully negotiating a series of stepping-stones.

Most visitors to the Mumbles, outside Swansea, take a walk along the pier. But they give little thought to the two small islets a few hundred yards to the west that give the area its name.

Always a dangerous place for shipping, a lighthouse was built on one of the islets and in 1883 the daughters of the lighthouse keeper rescued two lifeboat men who had been thrown into the sea. The girls simply knotted their shawls together, waded into the raging waters and used them as a lifeline – a rescue that, in its own way, was as worthy as anything the famous Grace Darling ever achieved.

Many islands guard the county of Pembrokeshire. Several of them have Viking names as Norse raiders visited and pillaged the region on many occasions.

Caldey is perhaps the most famous of these islands, having been inhabited by monks since the sixth century. The island has always been a farming community and these days about sixty people still live there. Yet most visitors fail to realise that Caldey is actually made up of two islands, Caldey itself and, off its western tip, St Margaret's, now home to thousands of breeding cormorants.

Sheep Island, off the Pembrokeshire coast

Grassholm is Wales's most distant island, lying seven miles west of Skomer. These days it is famous as a gannetry and visitors are not allowed. However, you can visit some of the other Pembrokeshire islands, places such as Skomer, Skokholm and Ramsey.

St Justinian, always the most intractable of Welsh saints, supposedly met his end on Ramsey when he accused his followers of idleness. They were somewhat put out by the slur and, in retaliation, cut off his head. He simply picked it up, put it under his arm and walked across Ramsey Sound to the mainland to the place where his church can be found today, looking out over the Sound and Ramsey Island. Such is the stuff of legend.

Little known Cardigan Island is situated off the mouth of the Teifi Estuary. When the old steamer *Herefordshire*, on her way to the breakers yard on the River Clyde, ran aground there in 1934, hundreds of rats escaped from the bowels of the ship and made their home on the island. For years they wantonly destroyed birds nests and eggs before being finally killed off in experiments on the drug Warfarin in 1968.

Bardsey lies two miles off the Llyn and, according to Arthurian legend, was once the home of the magician Merlin. The remains of a thirteenth-century abbey can be found on the island and, it is said, 20,000 saints were buried there. In the Middle Ages this was an important place of pilgrimage, three visits here equalling one to Rome.

The steamer *Herefordshire*, ashore on Cardigan island.

You rarely associate the Menai Straits with islands but in fact there are many of them sitting in the waterway. Perhaps the most interesting is Ynys Gorad Goch, sometimes known as Whitebait Island. The Maddoc Jones family lived on the island from the 1820s until the 1920s, selling visitors who rowed or sailed out from Bangor or Menai Bridge "Whitebait Teas" for a shilling.

Ynys Mon, or Anglesey to give the place its anglicised name, is the largest Welsh island. It used to be the granary of Wales and was known as Mon, Mam Cymru (Anglesey, Mother of Wales).

These days it is perhaps better known for the ferry port of Holyhead – located on Holy Island at the northwest tip of Ynys Mon – and for the village of Llanfairpwllgwyngyllgogerych-wyndrobwllllantysiliogogogoch. A name made up to entice and beguile tourists, it remains the one place that every visitor to Wales has heard about.

14 – What Else Happened on St David's Day?

March 1st is arguably the most famous and important day in Welsh history and culture. It is, of course, St David's Day and all over the country celebrations – usually in the shape of eisteddfodau or arts festivals – take place. They are held in schools, in colleges, in chapels and churches, even in hospitals.

The celebrations are held each year to mark the death of St David, patron saint of Wales. Traditionally, the saint died on 1st March 589 AD, having been born at what is now called St Non's Chapel in Pembrokeshire around the year 520. Such are the bare facts of the man and the legend. But 1st March is more than just a commemoration of our patron saint. It has, in Welsh history, many other significant and interesting events attached to it.

On St David's Day 1827 the appropriately named St David's College, Lampeter was opened, one of the earliest seats of learning in Wales. The College is still functioning in the tiny town to the north-east of Carmarthen. Also on this day in 1918 the Order of St John of Jerusalem established the Priory of Wales in Cardiff. It was the first new priory established on the authority of the old king, Edward VII, and its creation had obviously been delayed by the First World War.

On 1st March 1927 a crippling explosion at Marine Colliery, Ebbw Vale, killed no fewer than 51 miners. There had been worst mining disasters in Wales but this one, coming so soon after the tragedy of the First World War, was a particularly painful event for a community that thought it had managed to get over the worst that could happen.

On a somewhat lighter note, on 1st March 1965 singer Tom Jones hit the Number One spot for the first time with his single "It's Not Unusual". It was the start of an amazing career for the Pontypridd boy, a career that continues to this day. Songs like "The Green, Green Grass of Home" and "Delilah" remain a poignant memory for most Welsh people and no rugby international would be complete without at least one rendering of "Delilah". And to think it all began on St David's Day.

St David's Day 1979 saw the rejection of devolution in a referendum held right across the country. The result of the vote, rejecting the concept by the huge margin of 4 to 1, was totally unexpected and was a major setback for supporters of nationalism.

The idea of devolution disappeared from the Welsh political agenda for over ten years; only in September 1997 was a second referendum held, this time resulting in a narrow victory for the supporters of devolution.

Dylan Thomas, in many respects the traditional national poet of English-speaking Wales, was honoured on 1st March 1982. On that day a memorial to the boozy bard of Cwmdonkin Drive was unveiled and dedicated at Poets' Corner in Westminster Abbey. Dylan, who always loved the idea of being a poet – perhaps as much as the art of writing poetry – would surely have felt highly pleased by the accolade.

St David's Day 1986 saw the death of one of Wales's great sporting heroes. Tommy Farr, the Tonypandy Terror, might have resisted the fists of Joe Louis but he could not escape the clutches of his greatest opponent and died at the age of seventy-three.

Born in Clydach Vale on 12th March 1913 Tommy fought, first, as a light heavyweight, then as a full heavyweight. He became British and Empire Champion in 1937 and in August of that same year was matched against the great American world champion, Joe Louis, in a bout at Yankee Stadium, New York. Louis had carried all before him, knocking out the nine opponents before Tommy Farr and nobody gave the Welshman much of a chance.

In a brutal and close contest Tommy Farr lost on points and earned the respect of Louis and all the spectators. Indeed, when the decision was announced many of the crowd booed to show their disapproval.

Tommy's later life did not run smoothly. He lost virtually all of his money in various ill-advised business deals and, having retired in 1940, he was forced to return to the ring to try to recapture some of his lost fortune. He tried singing in the Music Halls and on stage and actually was not that bad a performer. He even ran a pub in Brighton for a while but his moment of triumph (even though it was, in reality, a defeat) had come years before in his contest with Joe Louis.

Clearly, then, St David's Day is about more than just the death of Wales's patron saint. But however we remember it, we should never forget the emotional and cultural significance of 1st March. It is a day to wear your leak or daffodil with pride.

15 – The Milford Haven Waterway

No feature on the entire Welsh coastline is more remarkable or more fascinating than the sunken valley of Milford Haven. Shakespeare, while he may not have visited the area, certainly knew of it. In "Cymbeline" he wrote about the ria (to give the waterway its correct geological name):

> "Tell me how Wales was made so happy
> As to inherit such a Haven."

The area around Milford Haven has felt and seen the presence of human beings since man first trod upon the earth. Evidence of early people has been found in many of the caves that nestle into the carboniferous limestone outcrops around the Haven and it does not take the greatest imagination in the world to conjure a vision of hunting people from the Mesolithic and Neolithic periods paddling or sailing up the estuary in their simple skin boats, boats that were not dissimilar to modern Welsh coracles.

Milford Haven, once supposedly called by Lord Nelson "The finest natural harbour in the world." Whether or not he actually said it is a matter of conjecture.

Later, the Romans also knew the Haven and probably used it as a temporary base for their patrolling fleets from what is now the Cardiff area of Wales. When the Romans left Britain in the years after 410 AD the early Christian missionaries used the estuary as a route into mainland Britain but it was the raiding Vikings that left a really indelible mark on the waterway.

Between AD 844 and 1091 they raided the Pembrokeshire coast many times, burning the nearby cathedral at St David's on no fewer than eight separate occasions. Milford Haven was a safe anchorage for the Norsemen and the Chieftain Huba almost certainly gave his name to Hubberston, a small village at the mouth of the estuary after he spent the winter of AD 877 sheltering in the Haven. Huba was apparently accompanied by a fleet of over 20 ships and nearly 2000 warriors. The effect on the local birth rate can only be imagined.

Several other locations in and around the Haven have names of Viking origin. Carr Rocks off the town of Pembroke Dock derive their name from the Norse word "scare", meaning rocks, while Skokholm and Skomer Islands, just outside the Haven, are clearly names of Norse derivation.

With the coming of the Normans – themselves a people of Norse origin – the area of Milford Haven began to assume even greater political and military significance. A series of strong stone castles across the centre of Pembrokeshire created a line or barrier, the Landsker, with the Welsh to the north and a mixture of Flemish, Welsh and English to the south. Milford Haven lay within the English-speaking region to the south of this Landsker and was, therefore, hugely significant for the early Norman kings in their campaigns against the Welsh and Irish.

The Haven has often been a centre for invasion, both outwards and inwards. In 1171 it was the base for Henry II's invasion of Ireland, over 400 ships gathering in the estuary before the assault. In 1397 Richard II also left for Ireland from the Haven, as did Oliver Cromwell in 1649. Coming the other way, the Haven saw the arrival of a large number of French mercenaries, journeying to support Owain Glyndwr, in his rebellion in 1405. Henry Tudor, born in Pembroke Castle just off the waterway, also landed in the Haven when he came to challenge and defeat Richard III in 1485.

The Haven had been used as a significant port since the Middle Ages but the modern-day town of Milford did not exist until 1790 when Sir William Hamilton, husband of Nelson's Emma, founded the place. His nephew, Charles Greville, invited seven Quaker whaling families from Nantucket and New England to settle in the town and start a whaling fleet.

The whaling venture was short lived but Milford did become an important fishing centre. By 1906 it was the sixth largest fishing port in Britain with over 500 people working either in the industry itself or in related trades. The fishing fleet continued to thrive throughout the first half of the twentieth century, only really beginning to decline once fish stocks in the Atlantic started to vanish in the 1950s.

The importance of the Haven as a port had been noted by Admiral Nelson during his visit to the area in 1802, the Admiral apparently declaring it one of the finest natural harbours in the world. Considering his relationship with Emma Hamilton – and Sir William, with whom they lived in a bizarre menage a trois – if Nelson did make such a statement then its objectivity has to be questioned.

The town of Milford did, briefly, serve as the base for a naval dockyard between 1797 and 1814 but it was too close to the mouth of the estuary and the land was privately owned. As a consequence the Navy Board of the Admiralty transferred its yard a few miles upstream to what soon became Pembroke Dock.

Lying on the southern shore of the Haven, the yards at Pembroke Dock were in existence for just over a hundred years. In that time they produced 263 warships and four Royal Yachts, becoming one of the finest dockyards in the world. When the yards closed in 1926 it caused widespread unemployment in the area. The RAF created a flying-boat base in the old dockyard in the years after 1930 and for many locals and visitors the sight of giant Sunderland flying boats on the waters of the Haven was a remarkable and welcome experience. When the base closed in 1959 it was a sad day for Pembroke Dock and for the Milford Haven waterway.

With the Suez Crisis of the early 1950s and the loss of the Suez Canal as a trade route (temporarily as it turned out) Milford Haven again assumed a strategical importance when the construction of large, deep-water oil tankers – to bring oil from the Middle East around the tip of Africa – became an imperative. Such giant vessels needed a secure base and Milford Haven, with plenty of deep water, was the site chosen.

In 1960 the Esso oil company opened their refinery just outside the town of Milford, closely followed by other refineries and pumping stations such as BP, Regent (soon renamed Texaco), Gulf and Amoco. Within a few short years both sides of the Haven were encrusted with the derricks, tanks and jetties of the oil industry. It seemed as if long-term prosperity had come again to the area. By 1970 Milford Haven was the leading oil port in

Britain, the second largest in Europe.

It was a brief flourish, however, as the "oil boom" finally stuttered to an end in the late 1970s and early 1980s. Esso closed down in 1983 after just twenty years of operation. Gulf lasted a little longer before finally shutting down in December 1997. The BP pumping station at Popton on the south shore of the Haven also soon closed.

Nowadays the Haven is still in use as a base for the leisure industry. Milford docks function as a marina and there are other centres for watersports at Neyland and Pembroke Dock. The Irish ferry operates out of the old dockyard at Pembroke Dock and the sight of ships, small and large, sailing up and down the Haven remains relatively common.

As Nelson may or may not have said, the Milford Haven waterway is one of the finest natural harbours in the world. It is an essential destination for anyone who wishes to see and experience all of Wales, not just the industrial heritage of the south east.

16 – Welsh Pirates

Our image or impression of pirates has, in the main, been shaped by our reading or film watching. Say "pirate" and you immediately think of Long John Silver from *Treasure Island* or one of Errol Flynn's dramatic film creations. Reality, however, is far removed from these idealized versions of piracy. Real pirates were vicious and deadly – and a large number of them were Welsh.

Perhaps the most famous of these men was Sir Henry Morgan who was not so much a pirate as a licensed adventurer for the British government.

Born about 1635, his origins remain unclear. What is known is that he came from the county of Monmouthshire and before he was thirty he had sailed off to the Caribbean where he quickly made a name for himself as a bold and ruthless sailor who was as likely to be working for the good of Oliver Cromwell's Commonwealth as he was for himself. When the monarchy was restored in 1660, Morgan simply switched his allegiance to Charles II and continued his piratical career.

Fighting against the Spaniards, he plundered the Mexican coast and the Caribbean islands on a regular basis. One of his most famous escapades involved him capturing, looting and putting to the sword the supposedly impregnable town of Camaguey on Cuba in 1667.

In 1671 he burned and sacked Panama, the richest of all Spanish colonies. Unfortunately, a treaty had recently been signed between Spain and Britain and Morgan was brought back to England in disgrace to answer for "his crimes". He was able to prove that he had no knowledge of the treaty and, instead of being punished, he was knighted and sent back to the Caribbean as Governor of Jamaica.

Other Welsh pirates were not so fortunate. John Evans was originally an honest enough seaman, sailing out of the Caribbean island of Nevis. In 1722, when he lost his job, he and some colleagues decided to try piracy, starting out by raiding rich houses on the north shore of Jamaica, operating out of a small dug-out canoe. After capturing several Spanish ships, his career as a pirate was short but decidedly successful.

Sailing out of Grand Cayman he made several voyages. Then,

one day, he found himself embroiled in a dispute with his Bosun and was challenged to a duel. When they reached port Evans reminded the Bosun about the challenge. The Bosun refused to fight, whereupon Evans beat him with a cane. He turned away just as the Bosun drew his pistol and shot him in the head. In retaliation the crew promptly killed the Bosun and decided to disband. To their amazement they found that they had a total of £10,000 to share between them.

John Callis operated not, like so many pirates, in the Caribbean but along the Welsh coast. He was hugely successful for many years, terrorising the shipping lanes around the Severn estuary and the Bristol Channel. He used several houses and inns as his base but most notably the Point House at Angle in Pembrokeshire. When he was finally captured in 1576 he was an old man and tried to buy his freedom by informing on other pirates. It was no use. He was tried and hung at Newport that same year.

Howell Davis came from Milford Haven and in a piratical career of just one year was hugely successful. His end came when he attempted to seize the Governor of the Portuguese island of Principe with the aim of holding him to ransom. The Portuguese had recognised Davis and his men, however, and ambushed them as they came ashore. In the skirmish Howell Davis was shot and killed.

When Howell Davis was killed his crew promptly elected the best navigator on board their ship to the position of captain – pirates were nothing if not democratic, at least among themselves. This man was Bartholomew Roberts, Black Bart as he is known, and he was undoubtedly the greatest of all Welsh pirates – if you can use a word like "greatest" when talking about such abject villains.

Like Davis, Black Bart had a short career as a pirate. Originally an honest sailor who had been captured by Howell Davis, he quickly turned to piracy and in his two short years of terrorising the Atlantic sea lanes he captured nearly 500 ships. He knew what his eventual fate would be and declared that what he wanted was "a short life and a merry one". He got his wish.

A teetotaller, a man who wore flamboyant red coats during battle and tried to stop his crew swearing, Black Bart was killed when the Royal Navy sloop "Swallow" ran him to ground on 10th February 1727. He was cut down by grapeshot to the throat and, before the Navy sailors could get aboard the pirate ship his crew had weighted his body, wrapped it in sail cloth and dumped it over board.

With the death of Black Bart Roberts the great age of piracy came to an end. There are still occasional outbreaks, particularly in the Far East, but these days – one hopes, at least – Welsh involvement remains minimal.

17 – The Welshman who Gave London Clean Water

On 10th December 1631 Sir Hugh Middleton, a truly unsung Welsh hero, died quietly at his home in London. Sir Hugh came from Galch Hill outside Denbigh in North Wales. He was the sixth son of Richard Middleton, MP for the Denbigh Boroughs and Governor of Denbigh Castle, and spent his childhood in the beautiful Clywd countryside.

He was born in 1560, right in the middle of Queen Elizabeth's traumatic and glorious reign, an age when Britain first achieved world, as opposed to European, significance. His name is often spelled Myddelton, such variations in spelling being quite common at the time – no less a person than William Shakespeare even spelled his name in at least half a dozen different ways.

Hugh Middleton, in the fashion of most younger sons, had to leave home to make his way in the world and he decided to try his hand in London. There he was apprenticed to a goldsmith – presumably his father paid the necessary fees for indentures – and in time became so successful that he was appointed Royal Jeweller to Elizabeth's successor, King James I.

As a successful businessman Hugh Middleton moved easily between London and Denbigh, becoming an Alderman and, eventually, succeeding his father as MP for the Welsh town. He was not just a goldsmith, his interests and business concerns stretching into many diverse areas. He also traded as a cloth maker, a banker, a mine owner and as an engineer.

It was in this last capacity that Middleton really made his name. London had been, for many years, a stinking and filthy community where the infrastructure was incapable of dealing with or supporting the thousands who flocked to the city every year. The lack of clean water – for drinking and for washing – was a major problem. The Thames was, literally, a floating sewer. Small wonder that disease was rife and that the plague visited almost every year.

Hugh Middleton became the driving force behind the plan to create a clean water supply for London. It was not his idea and he only became involved once the original designers found themselves in financial difficulties. However, once he was part of the project Middleton drove it forward with an almost raging intensity.

The plan was to construct something called New River, a culvert that would bring water from the River Lea at Ware to what was soon being described as New River Head in London. This "new river" was dug out and constructed between 1608 and 1613, being 38 miles in length and used by people who lived on its route as well as householders in the city.

The project took both time and money. Much of this was provided by Hugh Middleton although the King (who had always been a supporter of the scheme) was also induced to lend a financial hand in 1612. New River was finally completed and officially opened on 23rd September 1613, giving Londoners their first clean water for dozens, perhaps even hundreds, of years.

Hugh Middleton was truly a real Renaissance Man with so many interests and hobbies. He enjoyed art and literature and collected a well-stocked and wide-ranging library. Also, as well as his traditional business interests in London and his community work in Denbigh, he developed and ran lead and silver mines in Ceredigion.

Middleton also found time to sire ten sons and six daughters, their survival into adulthood – always a perilous process in the seventeenth century – undoubtedly being helped by the clean water supply that their father had created.

Sir Hugh Middleton was created Baronet in 1622, a clear sign of the position he held and his significance in Stuart England. He died on 10th December 1631 and was buried in London.

There is a memorial to Sir Hugh on Islington Green and several streets have been named after him in the capital – and in the small Hertfordshire town of Ware.

Yet surely the greatest memorial to this Welshman of drive and vision has to be the fact that, thanks to his efforts, the people of London finally got decent drinking water. The system he created kept the capital supplied until the middle years of the nineteenth century. A far-sighted man indeed.

18 – John Dee, Magician to Queen Elizabeth

Of all the many important and influential Welsh men and women, people who undoubtedly influenced the course of British life over the centuries, none is more mysterious or, arguably, more powerful than John Dee.

A mathematician and teacher of navigation, an astrologer and astronomer, an alchemist and, by all accounts, a magician too, John Dee occupies that mysterious middle ground between science and folk lore. He sits, a fascinating figure, somewhere between the canting spells of Macbeth's witches and the epoch-forming discoveries made during the sixteenth century's voyages of exploration.

Born on 13th July 1527, both of Dee's parents were Welsh – the family name derives from the Welsh word "Du", meaning black – but, as with many ambitious young men, from an early age his eyes were set on London and the court. Educated at St John's College, Cambridge, he was later Founding Fellow at Trinity College and quickly became renowned in the fields of mathematics and navigation.

While still in his twenties Dee was invited to lecture on algebra at the University in Paris and, as a young man, he travelled widely on the Continent. Such wanderings were rare, almost unheard of in those days but perhaps it was this period of travel, combined with his love of mathematics, that led him to the art of navigation. It was not long before Dee was renowned as both a scholar and as a navigator, even though his travels were, in the main, confined to Europe.

As his reputation grew, many of the sea rovers and explorers, men who were beginning to carve out new territories and lands for Elizabeth and England, came to him for advice and instruction. Dee had a practical side to his nature and as well as being the first person to apply Euclidian geometry to navigation, he also contrived to build many of the instruments the early navigators needed on their journeys.

There are those who believe John Dee was also the first man to use the phrase "British Empire". He certainly had a vision and a dream of creating a standing British navy and of establishing a realm of interest and power for Britain (England would probably be a more accurate word) that stretched right across the Atlantic

Ocean to the New World.

John Dee continued to travel widely for most of his life. From 1553 to 1559, for example, when he was already thirty years old – an age when men were expected to settle down – he once more set out to journey where the will took him. He roamed central Europe and later journeyed to Hungary to present the Holy Roman Emperor with a copy of his book "Hones Hieroglyphia".

His life was not without troubles, however. In 1555 he was charged with "calculating" – casting horoscopes for both Queen Mary and for Princess Elizabeth. This charge was quickly increased to one of treason and for a while his life was in serious jeopardy. He appeared before the Court of Star Chamber but, with some brilliance, he managed to exonerate himself. Despite this he was, thereafter, subjected to regular abuse and accusation – powered, undoubtedly, by fear and jealousy – and, as a result, he developed a lifelong penchant for secrecy.

When Princess Elizabeth became Queen Elizabeth she offered Dee a considerable amount of patronage. Quite apart from his skill in navigation, the Queen believed in his magical powers and consulted him on a regular basis. He chose her coronation date and even cast a spell on the Spanish Armada in 1588 – presumably the Queen was suitably grateful. He continued to advise both her and her influential ministers and spy-masters like Walsingham and Cecil.

Always hovering, perhaps uneasily, in the area between science and magic – a phenomenon of the age as much as anything else – John Dee spent the last twenty or thirty years of his life trying to communicate with angels. What he was doing was, in fact, searching for divine forms. He believed in them implicitly – along with many other men and women of his age – and he was even to claim that angels had dictated several of his books.

In 1595 Queen Elizabeth appointed Dee to the position of Warden of Christ's Hospital College in Manchester. It was almost her last act of patronage as Elizabeth died a few years later. Her successor, James I, had little or no time for magic or superstition and Dee declined in influence from that point onwards.

He spent the final years of his life in poverty, dying in either 1608 or 1609 – the date is unclear. He was buried in Mortlake but his gravestone has since disappeared and it is not possible to verify the exact date of his death. He was 82 years old, a considerable age for the sixteenth and seventeenth centuries.

John Dee was married twice and had eight children. He was a writer of considerable skill but, despite his interest in magic and his influence over the Queen, it is as a mathematician and teacher of navigation that his legacy really lies – yet another remarkable Welshman who influenced a whole generation.

19 – Rawlins White Goes to the Stake

The reign of Henry VIII was significant for many reasons, not least the break from Rome. This abandoning of Catholicism and the creation of the Anglican Church – fuelled by nothing more than Henry's need to sire a son – ushered in a period of religious and social discord that, ultimately, lasted for over a hundred years.

Henry's religious settlement was, at best, a lukewarm affair – his interest was not theology, only to secure the Tudor succession – but during the short and tempestuous reign of that son, Edward VI, the Protestant religion was firmly established in Britain. So when, after Edward's early and untimely death in July 1553, the Catholic Mary Tudor came to the throne it was clear that great troubles lay ahead.

Mary quickly re-established the Catholic religion, re-introducing the Catholic mass and requiring everyone to acknowledge the authority of the Pope in Rome. Committed Christians, many of whom had only really known the Protestant religion, were faced with a terrible dilemma – a dreadful death, burnt at the stake for failing to recant, or the death of their immortal souls for accepting a creed in which they did not believe.

During Mary's reign nearly 300 were burnt, including 55 women and a number of children. Many more died in prison while awaiting trial or execution. The queen's revenge touched everyone, rich or poor alike. Archbishop Cranmer, architect of Henry's religious reformation, was one of them. And so, too, was a poor fisherman from Cardiff, by the name of Rawlins White.

White was executed on 30th March 1555, the fire that took his life being built outside Bethany Church in the centre of Cardiff. The site of the old church is now occupied by James Howells Department Store, a plaque on one interior wall of the shop marking the spot where White breathed his last.

Rawlins White was a fisherman who had little reading and probably spoke only Welsh. However, he was extremely religious and with the aid of one of his sons read the Holy Scriptures every night. He was also profoundly influenced by the itinerant preachers who travelled the country and regularly came to Cardiff during the reigns of Henry and Edward. He certainly had a good memory and happily passed on the stories and doctrines that had been given to him by these preachers.

Once Mary had instituted her reforms, the Bishop of Llandaff, now strongly Catholic once again, tried to prevent Rawlins White from talking to the people – preaching to them would be too strong a word. White refused to stop, believing he was doing God's work. And, more importantly, he refused to accept the authority of the Bishop in Rome.

Faced by such a refusal, the Bishop had little alternative, although it has to be asked if, over time, White's nuisance value would simply have gone away. Rawlins White was arrested and imprisoned, first, at Chepstow and then in Cardiff Castle. He languished there for a year, the authorities clearly hoping he would change his mind and recant his Protestant views. The Cardiff fisherman did nothing of the sort.

Eventually, White was sent to a prison in Cardiff called the Cockmarel where conditions were at best primitive, at worst appalling. He still refused to recant and was eventually convicted of heresy and of spreading such heresy to others. His fate was to be burnt alive.

On 30th March 1555 White was conducted to the site of execution. He was escorted by many soldiers and apparently commented that they were not needed, he was not proposing to go anywhere. He showed no fear as he was chained to the stake but asked the jailers to make sure that the chain was tight in case his flesh was weak once the flames began. As preparations continued, White carefully arranged the wood and straw around his body in order that the flames should do their work as quickly as possible.

He wept when he saw his wife and children in the crowd but not once did he show signs or give any indication that he recanted his views.

The fire was lit, to cries of "Burn him, let the fire be lit" from the hundreds of watchers. It must have been a terrible death, the pain and anguish only too easy to imagine. White's legs burned quickly and his body slumped forward over the chain into the fire. Whether or not he was already dead will never be known.

Rawlins White was one of only three Welsh heretics burnt at the stake during the reign of Bloody Mary.

The others were Robert Farrar, Bishop of St David's, who died in Carmarthen on exactly the same day as White and a young man by the name of William Nichol who was executed in Haverfordwest in April 1558. Little is known about Nichol. He may have been a priest but, dying in April, just seven months before Mary's own death in November 1558, he was probably one of the very last martyrs of her reign. Like Rawlins White, this unknown man from Haverfordwest also has a memorial, the inscription reading "Burnt at the stake for the Truth, April 1558."

The memorial plaque to Rawlins White on the wall of James Howells Department Store in Cardiff.

The three executions mark an appalling and dreadful period in Welsh and British history when religion and the belief of many were used and abused to further the ends of the state and of those with the ultimate power – the power of life and death over their fellow men.

20 – Robert Recorde – the Man who Invented the Equals Sign

We've all used them, countless times, in Maths lessons, in the bank, in working out our weekly bills. But, strangely, they didn't exist until 1557 and the man who invented them was a Welshman from Tenby.

We are talking about the equals signs, the ubiquitous = mark that we all take for granted. And the man who invented them and used them for the first time was called Robert Recorde.

Recorde was born in Tenby in the year 1510, the son of Thomas Recorde from the Pembrokeshire town itself and of Rose Jones of North Wales. He was a gifted child, receiving his early instruction in the small school that was then based in the town church.

However, when he was just fifteen years old Recorde left Tenby to make his way to Oxford where he began a course of studies in mathematics. It must have been a terrifying experience for a young man from the far west of Wales, suddenly thrust into the bustling academic life of Oxford, but he persevered, gained his degree and in 1531 was elected Fellow of All Souls.

In 1545 Recorde went to Cambridge where he studied for a degree in medicine and it was in this field that he first made his mark in the world.

He became physician to the young king Edward VI and, after his death from TB, to the Catholic Queen Mary as well – despite his clear Protestant leanings. Recorde even dedicated some of his books to this catholic monarch who quickly earned the accolade of Bloody Mary due to the number of Protestant martyrs she caused to be burned at the stake.

Recorde's life in public service was far from easy. As well as being a royal physician, he was, at various times, controller of the royal mint at Bristol and Comptroller of Mines and Monies in Ireland.

He was, perhaps, not very skilled at public affairs as by 1553 the mines and mints in Ireland were showing a loss and were, consequently, closed down. There is a certain irony in Recorde's failure in business. He was, after all, one of the most notable mathematicians of his age.

Perhaps more important than business failures, he quarrelled with Sir William Herbert, later the Earl of Pembroke, and made the stupid mistake of trying to sue him for defamation of character. The Earl of Pembroke was one of the most powerful noblemen in the land, someone who had the ear of many important government and royal officials. Recorde may have been a mathematician of note but he obviously chose his enemies very unwisely.

The Earl of Pembroke counter-sued, Recorde lost and ended up being ordered to pay a fine of £1000, an enormous sum for those days. He couldn't – or wouldn't – pay and was sent to the Kings Bench Prison in Southwark where he languished for many months and finally died in 1558.

However, it is as a mathematician that Recorde will be remembered. He wrote several seminal books, works such as The Grounde of Artes in 1540 and The Urinal of Physic in 1548. Interestingly, Recorde wrote in English, not the Latin that was usual for academic tomes at this time. He wanted everyone to be able to read his works.

His most influential work, written in the classical style of a dialogue between master and scholar, was The Whetstone of Witte. This book appeared in 1557 and is credited as being the book that first introduced algebra into Britain.

The Whetstone of Witte is also the work that used, for the first time, the equals sign. Unlike our modern version, Recorde's equals sign consisted of two long parallel lines that could, if necessary, be drawn right the way around the globe and still not join together. As he said:

> "noe 2 thynges can be moare equalle."

The concept was not immediately popular but by 1700, in a shortened or abbreviated form, the equals sign had become accepted throughout the country – for working out bills, for academic study, even as a method of speech.

There is a memorial to Recorde in St Mary's Church in Tenby but, other than that, most people will never have heard about this remarkable and far-sighted mathematician.

21 – Death of Bishop Morgan, Translator of the Bible into Welsh

On 10th September 1604 Bishop William Morgan died in relative poverty at his home parish of St Asaph. He is, these days, largely unremembered by most people in Wales but he holds significance in Welsh history that is second to none. For this was the man who translated the Bible into Welsh and by so doing helped a dying language to survive and grow.

When Henry VIII broke with Rome to create what became the Anglican Church it brought about widespread objections, even revolt, in many parts of the kingdom.

When, years later, Henry's son Edward VI introduced the Book of Common Prayer into the churches of Wales it left many Welsh men and women bewildered. They could no more understand the service in English than they could the old one in Latin. But the old Catholic services had at least been familiar. They knew what they were going to get. They liked the rhythm of the words and found security in the traditions of the past. English was a harsh, alien language that many of them could not understand or come to terms with.

The security of Wales was always a concern for the Tudors. After all Henry VII had himself come ashore at Milford Haven in 1485 and then marched through Wales to his victory at Bosworth Field. Both Edward and Elizabeth knew how critical it was to keep this turbulent region calm and at peace.

As a consequence an Act of Parliament in 1563 commanded the Welsh bishops to allow and encourage the translation of the Bible and the Book of Common Prayer into Welsh because, in the words of the Act:

> "the English tongue is not understood by the greatest number of Her Majesty's obedient subjects inhabiting Wales."

William Salesbury, a lawyer from Denbigh, produced the first translation in 1567 – but only of the New Testament. And the words of his translation were very formal and stiff, hardly calculated to ensure the acceptance of the Welsh people.

Enter William Morgan. He had been born in 1545, the son of a farmer in the Conwy Valley. Educated at Cambridge, he became vicar of Llanrhaedr-ym-Mochnant in 1578 and, realising the inadequacies of Salesbury's translated Bible, spent the next ten years making his own translation into Welsh. He was encouraged by Archbishop Whitgift and by several Welsh language poets, thus ensuring that his Bible was lyrical and passionate at the same time.

When the new Welsh Bible appeared in 1588 it was clear that this was a classic Welsh text, a work of great beauty that appealed to the gentry and the ordinary man or woman in the fields.

In the eyes of many Welsh scholars, Morgan's Bible literally saved a language that, at the end of the sixteenth century, was beginning to fragment into a number of different dialects and styles. By going back to early sources, texts such as the Mabinogi and other early bardic poems, William Morgan managed to avoid the corruption of the Welsh tongue and produce a work of magnificent power and style.

When, fifty years later, Griffith Jones began his Circulating schools, this was the text he and his teachers used. Over 250,000 people were taught to read and write using Morgan's Bible. The spoken language also benefited from Morgan's translation with the result that the language did not die away, as had been feared, but grew in strength and power as the years rolled by.

In 1595 William Morgan became Bishop of Llandaff and began to revise his great work. He also produced his translation of the Book of Common Prayer at about this time.

In 1601 he was made Bishop of St Asaph, a position he held for the next three years. He died in 1604, not quite a pauper but with few material possessions and was buried somewhere in the grounds of St Asaph Cathedral. Bishop Morgan's grave remains unknown but a memorial in the Cathedral grounds marks the achievement of the man who, more than any other single individual, did so much to defend, protect and develop the Welsh language.

22 – Victory by Cow!

Many things can bring about victory in battle or war, not least a liberal helping of luck. But victory thanks to a herd of cows? Now that really does take some beating.

The English Civil War began in 1642 and was, amongst many other things, the culmination of a series of long-running disputes between the King and his Parliament. They were disputes that, essentially, centred on a single question – who held the ultimate power in the state, King or Parliament?

The Civil War was a bloody and violent interlude that, like any conflict within a country, saw brothers fighting against brothers, fathers against sons. It ended with the execution of the King and the setting up of a Commonwealth in Britain – a relatively short-lived Commonwealth, to be sure, but the only time the British state has run without a monarch at its head.

The Civil War in Wales was a confused and troubled time, people changing sides on a regular basis. One of the hotbeds of Parliamentary support and effort was South Pembrokeshire where men like John Poyer, the Mayor of Pembroke town, and the outstanding Welsh general of the war, Rowland Laugharne, led by example.

In December 1643 and the early part of 1644 Poyer and Laugharne were holed up in the town and castle of Pembroke, not quite under siege by the King's forces but with their movements curtailed and the very real risk of death and destruction hovering in the wind. Help was at hand, however.

During that winter a feeling of resentment began to grow amongst the people of the region regarding the behaviour of many of the Royalist troops and, banking on local support, Laugharne decided it was time to take action. He sallied out from Pembroke Castle and quickly set about reducing the enemy forces wherever he could find them.

On 30th January 1644 he took the fortified manor house at Stackpole and four days later moved on to Trefloyne, outside Tenby. After four or five hours of artillery bombardment his forces charged and took the house. Now all that remained were the Royalist bases in the northern part of the county.

On 23rd February Laugharne crossed the Cleddau River and laid siege to the Royalist fort of Pill, just outside the modern town of Milford. Four ships from the Parliamentary fleet aided Laugharne's artillery bombardment. They moored below the fort and added the weight of their broadsides to the battering.

The fort surrendered the following day, 300 officers and men, 18 large guns and 160 smaller weapons falling into Laugharne's hands. In return Laugharne's casualties amounted to just one man killed.

Rowland Laugharne now decided to march on Haverfordwest. As well as being a vital market town, Haverfordwest was the centre of Royalist support north of the Cleddau and Laugharne knew that it must be taken. The town and its castle were well supplied, well armed, and he expected a fierce fight.

However, when he and his soldiers approached the town they were met, not by a hail of gunfire or by a phalanx of soldiers ready to give battle but by local dignitaries who were happy to surrender the town and all its supplies.

The garrison in Haverfordwest had, simply, run away. They had heard the sound of the cannonade from the south and knew that they would be next. Then, as they waited, tense and frightened, a lookout saw dust on the horizon. Laugharne and his victorious troops were coming.

Panic seized the garrison and they abandoned their positions and fled. Only later did they realise the dust was not caused by advancing soldiers but by a herd of bullocks, running in frenzy, frightened by the firing and by the sudden appearance of dozens of armed men. Rowland Laugharne did not care what had caused the garrison to flee. Haverfordwest was his, that was all that mattered.

Over the next few days Laugharne moved on to take the castles of Roch, Picton and Wiston. By the beginning of March not a single Royalist stronghold remained in North Pembrokeshire – and all because of a herd of frightened cows.

23 – The Battle of St Fagan's

On Monday May 8th 1648, at the village of St Fagan's to the west of Cardiff, over 10,000 men clashed in a life or death contest that was, quite probably, the largest battle ever to take place on Welsh soil. It was one of the final acts in the long-running English Civil War, a conflict that eventually saw King Charles I executed and a republican Commonwealth under Oliver Cromwell established in Britain.

The Battle of St Fagan's was, from the beginning, an uneven contest. By 1647, with the King defeated in battle and held in virtual captivity, it seemed as if the Civil War had come to an end but rows and disputes over unpaid wages, as well as Parliament's demand that the various generals should now stand down their armies, meant that a new conflict – sometimes called the Second Civil War – was inevitable.

Many Parliamentarian generals, upset and dissatisfied with the way things were going, soon changed sides, among them Rowland Laugharne, John Poyer and Rice Powell. They all now declared their loyalty to the king, despite having spent the previous five years trying their best to defeat him in battle.

Parliament was taken by surprise and the king's new supporters quickly gained the upper hand in Wales. It was a short-lived success although, for a while, it seemed as if they were unstoppable and Laugharne, the most renowned and successful of the turncoat generals, found himself at the head of an army marching on Cardiff. By Sunday 7th May his forces had reached the tiny village of St Fagan's, about three miles to the west of Cardiff. And here he found the enemy waiting.

Laugharne was reluctant to press too far, too quickly. He knew that his position was not as strong as it seemed and the bulk of his army, though large, consisted mainly of 4000 eager but amateur volunteers. They were referred to as "clubmen" – quite literally, untrained soldiers armed only with clubs and billhooks. Opposing him were the highly professional and well-equipped Parliamentary forces of Colonel Thomas Horton, men of the New Model Army that had been created by Oliver Cromwell who defeated the King's forces at battles such as Naseby.

Knowing he had to seize the initiative, Laugharne decided on a surprise attack. Shortly after 7.00 on the morning of 8th May he hurled 500 of his infantry against the Parliamentary outposts. It was something of a forlorn hope and the well-trained Parliamentarians quickly threw them back.

Major General Rowland Laugharne, defeated Royalist leader at the Battle of St Fagan's.

Thereafter the battle degenerated into a hit and run affair, the Royalist forces trying to make stands behind the high hedges and the ditches of the area. Gradually, inexorably, the Parliamentary infantry and dragoons advanced and panic began to set in amongst the Royalist forces.

It was inevitable that the makeshift Royalist troops would break and within two hours, despite a desperate cavalry attack led by Roland Laugharne himself, the battle was over. Approximately 300 Royalists were killed, over 3000 were taken prisoner. Laugharne and his senior officers fled west where they barricaded themselves into Pembroke Castle, enduring an eight-week siege before Cromwell himself battered them into surrender.

Visitors to the modern museum at St Fagans can still walk the fields of the battle, even though the topography has changed somewhat over the years. Historical artefacts such as musket balls and buttons have been found in the area but the speed of the Parliamentarian victory and the nature of the battle, one of movement rather than a set piece slogging match, has meant that they are few and far between. Don't let that stop you looking as you walk the field of battle – you never know what you might find.

24 – John Poyer, the Forgotten Hero (or Villain) of the Civil War

When you think of the Civil War, the great rebellion against the crown that took place in the seventeenth century, you tend to think only of famous men like Charles I and Oliver Cromwell. Yet the war was organised and fought by dozens of less well-known individuals, all of whom contributed, in lesser or greater degrees, to the success or failure of the war.

In Wales there was one man in particular who seemed to symbolise the turmoil of the age, supporting first Parliament and then the King. He was the Mayor of Pembroke, John Poyer.

Initially at least Poyer was devoted to the Parliamentary cause. He was a rumbustious and temperamental man who, unfortunately, created a large number of enemies for himself in his relatively short life. As well as being Pembroke's Mayor, in the years running up to the outbreak of war he also commanded one of Pembrokeshire's Trained Bands, the groups of ordinary citizens who made up most of Parliament's forces during the early months of conflict.

Parliament needed people like Poyer and his Trained Band because by 1642 all of south Wales had come out in favour of the king – apart from the towns of Pembroke and Tenby. Over the next few years the war in Pembrokeshire was chaotic with first one side gaining the upper hand, then the other. John Poyer was in the thick of it all, manipulating, bribing and fighting to advance the Parliamentary cause.

Many of his actions were high-handed and, sometimes barely legal. At Michaelmas 1642, for example, Poyer, his term of office as Mayor of Pembroke at an end, refused to stand down. The new Mayor had decidedly Royalist leanings and there was no way Poyer was going to let him take control. He duly retained and held the position of Mayor for the next six years.

Pembroke castle and town, under the command of Poyer and General Rowland Laugharne, quickly became a serious thorn in the side of Royalist forces in Wales. So serious was the threat that the local Royalist commanders declared that when they captured John Poyer they would put him in a barrel pierced by nails and roll him down the hill into Milford Haven. John Poyer merely shrugged and commented that they would have to catch him first.

Thanks to the military skill of Rowland Laugharne and the adept political manoeuvring of Poyer, the Parliamentary forces in Pembrokeshire were ultimately successful and in May 1646, with the surrender of Charles I to the Scots, the Civil War came to an end. Parliament had clear control of the country and now, it seemed, men like Poyer could enjoy the fruits of victory.

In Pembrokeshire, however, bad feelings continued to simmer. Poyer was called to London to answer charges of appropriating land and property in the county, to the value of six thousand pounds. The charge eventually came to nothing but John Poyer was incensed that he should be called to task by Parliament, the very people he had risked his life to champion.

For some time Laugharne's soldiers – like many other armies across the length and breadth of Britain – had been refusing to disband until they were paid arrears in wages. Sir Thomas Fairfax, General of all Parliamentary forces, now ordered Poyer to appear once more before a Committee of Accounts and to give up control of Pembroke and its castle. Poyer, an unruly and, probably, very dishonest man, refused and used the excuse of the unpaid soldiers. He would vacate the castle, he declared, when Laugharne's men had been given the wages they were owed.

And so the country slipped towards a second Civil War. There were many other causes of this second eruption of civil war but men like Poyer and Laugharne – who had been solid supporters of Parliament – were now declaring for Prince Charles, the king's son. When Parliament sent a large force under General Thomas Horton to deal with the south Wales rebels John Poyer simply declared:

> "He, who feared neither Fairfax, Cromwell or Ireton, would be the first man to charge against Ironsides."
> (Quoted in *Pembroke: For King and Parliament* by Phil Carradice)

Unfortunately for Poyer and Laugharne, their army was defeated at the Battle of St Fagans on 4th May 1648 and the pair fell back on the fortress of Pembroke to lick their wounds and to take stock.

Parliamentary forces under the same Colonel Horton who had defeated Laugharne at St Fagan's soon appeared outside the town walls and a seven-week siege began. Little headway was made against the town walls and the rugged might of Pembroke Castle and, eventually, no less a person than Oliver Cromwell himself arrived to take command of the besieging troops.

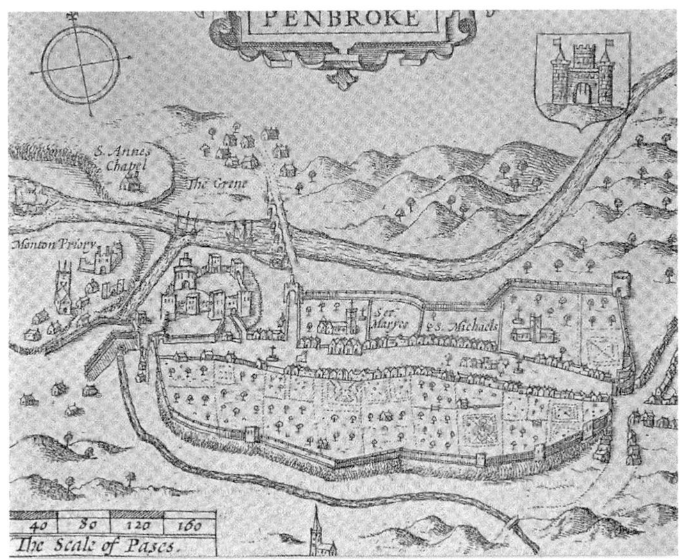

The town of Pembroke is shown here on John Speed's 1610 map – both town and castle were defended by John Poyer and Rowland Laugharne against the might of Oliver Cromwell and his Ironsides.

Poyer, like Rowland Laugharne, was tireless in the defence of the town, appearing on the walls, leading out sorties against Cromwell's troops. But inevitably, food and water began to run short and at the end of July the town surrendered. John Poyer, along with Laugharne and Colonel Rice Powell who had garrisoned Tenby against Cromwell, were sent to London for trial as traitors to the state.

A military court sat from 4th to 12th April 1649 and, at last, returned a guilty verdict. All three men were condemned to death for their part in the rebellion. However, the Council of State decided on leniency – only one man must die, his fate to be decided by a child who would draw lots to discover who would face the firing squad. Perhaps inevitably, the unlucky man was John Poyer.

Poyer had certainly created his fair share of enemies over the years and whether or not it was "a rigged ballot" will never be known. But it does seem strange for Puritans, who hated all forms of gambling, to be playing a game of chance with that most precious of commodities, a man's life.

Poyer's execution took place at Covent Garden on 25th April 1649. Led to the place of execution by two troops of horse and three companies of foot, he made a short speech, confessing to having led a "loose life" but insisting that his loyalty to Parliament had never changed. He was then shot, dying with the same courage and spirit he had displayed all his life.

John Poyer was a charismatic, contradictory and self-destructive character. His final words were later taken by his family and used as a motto – "Son est contra me" (Fate is against me). It was a suitable epitaph, even though it could be argued that Poyer's fate was, ultimately, controlled by no one other than himself.

25 – Griffith Jones and the Circulating Schools

Most people who drive west from Carmarthen on the road to Pembroke pass through the village of Llanddowror, blithely unaware that this quiet backwater spot was, in the early eighteenth century, the centre of an educational movement that was taking Wales – perhaps even the world – by storm. For this was the base of Griffith Jones and his famous Circulating Schools.

In an age when there was no compulsory education, when the vast majority of working-class people could neither read nor write, Griffith Jones created a system of schooling that by the time of his death in 1761 had taught almost 200,000 people to read. Jones, arguably more than anyone else, helped to make Wales into a literate and literary nation.

Griffith Jones was born in Carmarthenshire in 1683. He was educated at Carmarthen Grammar School and was ordained into the Church of England in 1708. After early curacies in places like Penbryn (Cardiganshire) and Penrieth (Pembrokeshire), he became curate and master of the SPCK (the Society for the Promotion of Christian Knowledge) School in Laugharne.

At one stage Griffith Jones did consider going to India to carry out missionary work for the SPCK. It would have been a bold and challenging move but eventually he decided against it and in 1716 became rector at Llanddowror, a post he was to hold for the rest of his life.

As an active member of the SPCK, Jones was concerned about the illiteracy of his parishioners and when he began his Circulating Schools in about 1731 he was clear that one of his main aims was salvation. He wanted people to read but only so that they could read the Bible and the catechism of the Church of England.

What Griffith Jones created was a series of schools that would rotate or circulate around the rural parishes of Wales, mainly in the winter months when farm work was relatively slack. The schools would stay in one place for approximately three months and then move on to another location.

Almost from the beginning the movement was an amazing success. Dozens of men, women and children flocked to the schools where they used the Bible both as a means of instruction and as a training manual or reading book.

By 1737, just six years after they began, there were 37 such schools in existence with over 2500 pupils or scholars attending the classes. For those who had to work during the day, evening classes were set up and Jones himself, from his base in Llanddowror, was instrumental in training the teachers. He had powerful support from wealthy landowners like Madam Bevan, the woman who continued to run and oversee the schools after his death in April 1761.

The system attracted the interest of reformers and educationalists from all over Britain – and from further afield as well. In 1764 Catherine II of Russia commissioned a report on the activities of the schools, with a view to creating a similar system in her own country.

Griffith Jones was not without critics, however. Many people disagreed with teaching ordinary working men and women to read, particularly reactionary clergymen who felt that their position at the centre of the community was being undermined.

Jones was a powerful preacher, someone who would hold the attention of mass gatherings, whether they were in the church or in the open air. He was called to account on several occasions by his bishop for ignoring church rules and customs and, particularly, for things like preaching on the weekday! It did not stop Griffith Jones who was determined to proceed with what he felt to be his mission in life.

While not being a reformer himself, he can be seen to be something of a forerunner to the Methodist revival that was soon to hit Wales and all of the United Kingdom. By creating a literate and educated populace, men and women with a deep and focussed interest in the gospels and all scriptures, he had certainly paved the way for ministers like John Wesley.

More significantly, Griffith Jones and his Circulating Schools had created a people for whom education was crucially important, not just as a way to better oneself but as an aim and an end in itself. That is a stance that has never left the Welsh people.

26 – Jacobites in Wales

The summer of 1715. James, the Old Pretender, almost the last of the Stuart claimants to the throne, is about to return, landing with his army in Scotland and rallying supporters of the Stuart cause to his flag. George I and the whole Hanoverian dynasty appear to be resting on the edge of disaster. Discontent is rife everywhere and in the north Wales town of Wrexham, as the summer progresses, more and more signs of anti-Hanoverian anger are to be seen.

Rioters break windows in the Dissenting Chapels (Dissenters being fervent supporters of the new regime) and crack open more than a few heads as they roam, unchecked and unhindered, through the streets of the town. Jacobite songs are roared out and for several weeks the place is almost besieged by mob violence.

It is a picture that is rarely conjured by anyone other than academic historians. For most of us, when we think about the Jacobite rebellions we think of that 1715 landing of James and, usually, of the more famous rebellion of 1745 when, for several months, James's son, Bonnie Prince Charlie, held the whole country in the palm of his hand.

And, thanks to the romantic novels of people like Sir Walter Scott, we tend to associate Jacobitism only with Scotland. Not so – witness the events in Wrexham. In these difficult and dangerous years, Wales, too, was a hot bed of Jacobite fever.

Jacobitism had its origins in the Glorious Revolution of 1688 when the Catholic King James II fled before an invasion by William of Orange. Desperately unpopular, James had seemed secure enough while he had no heir but after a visit to the Catholic shrine at Holywell in north Wales, where he supposedly prayed for a son, his wife suddenly conceived. The thought of another Catholic monarch was too much for a now staunchly Protestant Britain and James had to go.

James had his supporters, however, and once the last of the Stuart monarchs, Queen Anne, died in 1714 many expected there to be something of a restoration with Anne's half brother James, the Old Pretender, returning to take the throne. Instead, his claims were ignored and George, the German-speaking Elector of Hanover, became king. Jacobite supporters immediately began to plot, plan and pray for a restoration of the Stuart monarchy.

The riots in Wrexham were probably orchestrated by Sir

Watkin Williams Wynn, the most powerful and prestigious of all Welsh landowners and squires. He was a member of a secret political club known as the Cycle of the White Rose, an organisation that had been founded on the birthday of the Old Pretender in 1710. It was called The Cycle club because, quite simply, its members met in turn at each others' houses. They would dine, sing Jacobite songs, toast "The King Across the Water" and probably engage in secret rituals which, ultimately, meant very little – just a group of "boys" having a good time.

The amazing thing about the members of Cycle Club is that, despite its potentially treasonable purpose, they kept minutes of their meetings and even had special glasses made from which they would drink their toasts – the National Museum in Cardiff actually owns several examples!

The club might sound like a vehicle or an excuse for romantic, landowning gentry to eat, drink and be safely treasonable but, potentially at least, it was a very powerful base for men such as Sir Watkin Williams Wynn. Every significant landowner within a ten mile radius of Wrexham was a member of the Cycle Club.

The difference between the Jacobites of Wales and Scotland, however, was that when the Old Pretender did finally arrive, those north of the border quickly took up arms in support. Welsh Jacobites sat silently by, meeting to drink and talk treason but not actually to perform it – which was probably just as well, for them, as the rebellion ended in utter disaster.

Outbreaks of violence like the Wrexham riots were a rare occurrence. Despite the fact that the disturbances went on well into 1716, Sir Watkin never revealed his hand and, as a result, he was never caught up in the aftermath of the failed rebellion. And the Cycle Club? It continued to meet, usually in the Eagles Hotel in the middle of Wrexham, for the next 150 years, a more than merry dining club – but one spiced with a fair degree of treason.

The Cycle Club was not the only secret Jacobite organisation to exist in Wales. In Montgomeryshire there was a group known as "the 27" while at Talgarth in 1727 a meeting of local Jacobite sympathisers actually ended up with members having to appear before a local magistrate to explain their actions.

In Pembrokeshire a Jacobite group known as The Sea Sergeants continued to meet until 1762. There were 24 sergeants in this group which may well have had connections with freemasonry and with smuggling – always a popular pastime in the far west of Wales. Their symbol was a dolphin set within a star but as they advertised their meetings in the local paper their commitment to the revolutionary cause has to be questioned.

When Charles Edward Stuart, the Young Pretender, landed in Scotland in 1745 – without the expected French army to back him up – Sir Watkin Williams Wynn and his friends were cautious not to commit themselves. They would rise, they decided, but only if there was a strong French army to ensure success. Bonnie Prince Charlie expected the Welsh Jacobites to come out in support but, in the end, Sir Watkin and his cronies did what they did best – they added another verse to their favourite drinking song.

One Welshman was made of sterner stuff. This was David Morgan from Penygraig outside Quakers Yard. Passionate about the Jacobite cause, he obtained a captain's commission in the army of the Young Pretender but was captured and executed for treason. It was a grisly death, hanging, drawing and quartering – and then his head displayed on Temple Bar in London.

Given the possibility of an end like that it's hardly surprising that most Welsh Jacobites covered their tracks most effectively. They never tired of ceremony and symbolism, as shown in their secret societies with their special rituals and toasting glasses. But solid deeds? They had only to think of the terrible end of David Morgan to put them off that. Much safer to keep their sympathies to themselves and enjoy a few glasses of wine with convivial companions.

27 – Iolo Morganwg – Scholar, Antiquarian and Forger

Iolo Morganwg remains one of the most intriguing characters of Welsh history. Many people remember him as the eccentric moving force behind the modern day Eisteddfod and, certainly, during the seventy-nine years of his life he was regarded as the leading expert on ancient and medieval Welsh culture. It was only after his death on 18th December 1826 that the truth was finally revealed – Iolo had forged many, if not most, of his manuscripts and ancient documents.

Born Edward Williams on 10th March 1847 at the village of Llancarfan, Iolo spent his childhood and early youth at Flemingston in the Vale of Glamorgan. His father was a stonemason, a trade Iolo also followed, but the ambitious young man soon developed a love of traditional Welsh poetry and actually began to compose it himself. This was firmly in the tradition of Welsh poetry writing where the practitioners were, largely, from the working classes.

He took the name Iolo Morganwg as his bardic name, thus commemorating his native county and spent the years between 1773 and 1777 in London where he became closely involved with the London-Welsh clique. Returning to Wales, Iolo married and, for a while, tried his hand at farming.

However, it was in the literary field that Iolo soon began to make his name. He began to produce manuscripts that proved the Welsh or Celtic druidic traditions had survived the trauma of the Roman conquest – and, indeed, the later barbarity of Edward I. Unfortunately, many of these documents had little or no relation to reality, having been conceived in the fertile mind and imagination of none other than Iolo Morgannwg himself.

He developed his own, rather mystical philosophy of life, helped perhaps by the fact that he was an inveterate and consistent user of laudanum. It was a strange creed, a coming together of Christianity and Arthurian legend, but it was a philosophy and a way of life that suited the lifestyle of this strange but compelling man.

Iolo even developed his own bardic alphabet, claiming that it was the system used by the ancient druids themselves. He regularly produced forged manuscripts and books, one of them being a book that he attributed to Saint Cadoc. He did find time to write some poetry of his own, a collection of his work (real and genuine) being published in 1794. After his death his son gathered together his various papers and produced them as The Iolo Manuscripts.

In 1789 Iolo published Barddoniaeth Dafydd ap Gwilym, supposedly a collection of poetry by the fourteenth-century poet Dafydd ap Gwilym. The collection was well received but it has since transpired that the book included several poems that had no connection to the old Welsh bard. They were actually written by Iolo himself.

In 1791 Iolo went back to London and on 21st June the following year, at Primrose Hill, he was instrumental in founding the Gorsedd, the community of Welsh bards. The ceremony and the proceedings, Iolo claimed, were based on ancient druidic rites. They were, of course, forgeries but at the time nobody seemed to notice and by the time the extent of his fabrication was discovered the traditions of the event were already accepted by most enthusiasts, far too well accepted to even consider a change.

Despite Iolo's efforts, it took time to establish – or re-establish – the Eisteddfod as a significant event in Welsh society. Not until 1819, when the Gorsedd of Bards held a special ceremony at the Ivy Bush Hotel in Carmarthen (the event is commemorated in a stained glass window in the hotel) and marched in full regalia through the town, was the imagination of the Welsh people truly caught by the idea of a celebration of art and culture. The first modern Eisteddfod, in its present form, was held at Aberdare in 1860 and by then Iolo was long dead. Despite his forgeries but due largely to his enthusiasm it has gone on from strength to strength.

The real significance of Iolo Morganwg is not that he forged so many of his supposedly ancient manuscripts but that, when it was most needed, he provided the Welsh people with a cultural and historical re-awakening.

Indeed, he is now viewed by many as one of the main architects of the Welsh nation. The Eisteddfod has survived his forgeries and so, too, has the concept of "Welshness", something that has been an essential commodity over the years.

In many respects Iolo Morganwg was a far-sighted and gifted individual. He was amongst the first to advocate a National Library for Wales – and, for that matter, a Folk Museum as well. He loved the Vale of Glamorgan and nearly all his activities were intended to assert the Welshness of South Wales, an area he considered had been unjustly anglicized over the years.

28 – The Last Invasion of Britain

Ask the average man or woman in the street when Britain was last invaded and the answer will probably be "1066". In fact the response would be wrong by about 700 years.

The last time any invaders foot ever stood upon the soil of mainland Britain was February 1797 when 1400 members of the French Legion Noire landed on the Pencaer Peninsula just outside Fishguard. They were a misbegotten and desperate band of villains, most of them convicts from the prisons of Brest and Le Havre, men kept in chains until the invasion fleet actually sailed. The rest were the worst and least disciplined soldiers from every assorted regiment in France.

French soldiers come ashore on Careg Wastad Point, an early and somewhat romanticized view of the last invasion, from 1797.

However, for a brief moment these vicious and terrifying warriors had the island of Britain at their mercy. Panic spread across the land, people really believing that the cream of French soldiery had come to slit their throats.

Led by a 70-year-old American soldier of fortune by the name of William Tate, the original aim of the Legion Noire was to attack Bristol, then the second city of Britain, and divert the attention of the Royal Navy from another assault, this one on the southern part of Ireland. The Irish plan failed but with the villains of the Legion Noire already assembled in Brest it was decided to launch the attack on Bristol and cause as much chaos as possible.

The intention was for the Legion Noire, once Bristol had been sacked, to wheel round and march into Wales. The Welsh nation, it was believed, would quickly flock to their standard, desperate to throw off the yoke of English tyranny. Even if the invaders had been well trained and highly disciplined soldiers it is doubtful if this element of the scheme would ever have worked. With men like the Legion Noire involved the plan was doomed to disaster from the very beginning.

Contrary winds prevented the French fleet from reaching Bristol and so Tate decided to land instead on the Welsh coast. When the fleet approached Fishguard on 22nd February 1797 they were met by a single shot from the town fort. The shot was a blank but it frightened Tate into landing over the rocks of Careg Wastad Point on the Pencaer Peninsula rather than in the town itself.

By late evening on 22nd most French troops were ashore, camped on the headland. To oppose them were Lt Colonel Thomas Knox and just 190 part-time soldiers, Fencibles as they were known. Throughout the long night Knox waited and watched. Then on the morning of 23rd February he decided there was no option but to withdraw towards Haverfordwest. The town of Fishguard now lay at the mercy of the French.

All that day the French soldiers, most of them half-starved and out of control, roamed the hills and fields above Fishguard. They were supposed to be searching for supplies and transport – in fact they were more intent on looting and finding whatever food and liquor they could in the farmhouses of the area. A coaster carrying port wine had recently gone aground in the area and, as a consequence, most of the farmhouses were more than liberally supplied with alcohol – of which the French were happy to relieve them.

A number of skirmishes took place between the French invaders and the Welsh people of the region. A party of sailors and men from nearby St David's encountered some of the enemy in a field below Carn Gelli. They quickly opened fire – when the smoke had cleared one Frenchman was dead, another injured, and the rest took to their heels.

Some of the encounters were simply ludicrous. At the farm of Brestgarn a drunken Frenchman, looking for more wine, heard what he took to be the click of a musket being cocked. He spun round and fired – straight through the face of a grandfather clock.

The undoubted hero of the hour was town cobbler Jemima

Nicholas. She marched out on to Pencaer and, single-handed, captured twelve French soldiers. They were probably drunk, ill and more than happy to find themselves in safe captivity but that should never detract from the courage of the brave woman.

General Tate soon found himself faced by a mutinous army that had little or no stomach for the coming fight. All day there were sightings and rumours of a relieving force under Lord Cawdor marching northwards towards Fishguard. And so, at 9.00 that evening, Tate asked for terms and surrendered. At midday on the 24th the Legion Noire marched on to Goodwick Sands, piled their arms and were marched away into captivity.

The invasion has always had more than a little of the farce about it, worthy of Gilbert and Sullivan at their best. It remains the classic "What if?" story. If the invading army had been quality soldiers, men who had the inclination and the training to fight, rather than the drunken rabble of the Legion Noire, then untold damage could and would have been caused. There were precious few defences and, once the protective screen thrown up by the Navy had been breached, almost no soldiers to fight a determined and resolute foe.

Even so the panic that spread all over Britain when news of the invasion broke was worrying. People demanded their money from the banks – given out in gold and silver coins in those days – and set about burying it in their gardens where, they felt, it would be safe from French hands. The Bank of England almost ran out of money and had no option but to issue promissory notes to the value of one and five pounds each, paper money that stayed with us for over a hundred years.

Legend and fact have blurred somewhat over the years and there remains a wonderful story of Lord Cawdor asking local Welsh women in their red shawls and tall stove pipe hats to masquerade as soldiers by marching around a large hill. The French, so the story goes, were totally taken in and promptly threw up their hands in horror.

Sadly, the story has little substance. There were Welsh women in Cawdor's relieving force and they were certainly there watching in great numbers when Tate surrendered but as for pretending to be British soldiers there was neither the time nor the inclination. It remains just a lovely story.

29 – General Picton, a Fast and Furious Life

Wales has had many heroes over the years but none more controversial than Thomas Picton, the most senior British officer to die at Waterloo. He was a brave and wholehearted man but a temperamental one, a general and administrator whose motto seems to have been "make them respect and hate you but most of all make them fear you".

Born at Poyston in Pembrokeshire in 1758, he decided on a military career early in his life and by 1773 had joined the 12th Regiment of Foot at Gibraltar as an ensign. Money talked in those days and Picton certainly had money – or, at least, his family did. By 1778 he had bought himself the rank of Captain in the 75th Regiment. Already he was acquiring for himself the reputation of a hard and even brutal taskmaster.

His courage was never in doubt and when, five years later, the 75th Regiment was disbanded he quelled an open mutiny by the soldiers, showing great bravery in the process, with little regard to his own safety. As a reward for that bravery he was promised the rank of Major but for some reason the promotion never came and Picton retired from the army in high dudgeon.

He spent the next ten years at home in Poyston. During this time his irascible temper quickly came to the fore and he even fought a duel because of some imagined insult. He might have been a good soldier but, clearly, he was no great shakes as a swordsman. He was seriously wounded in the affair and was lucky to survive.

By1794, however, Picton had been appointed aide-de-camp to Sir John Vaughan and was back in harness with the military. He fought with distinction in the various West Indian campaigns and by 1801, now with the rank of Brigadier General, he was made Governor of the Caribbean island of Trinidad.

Picton's regime on the island was hard and brutal, whipping, branding and arbitrary execution apparently being regular and common punishments. He was not a man to contemplate anything other than immediate acceptance of his views or desires. Disobey him at your peril, seems to have been the order of the day.

Eventually the brutality became too much. Picton was accused of torturing a young mulatto woman. He returned to Britain and stood trial, claiming that torture was not illegal under Spanish law and Trinidad was still, in the eyes of some, a Spanish possession. It was a flimsy defence and Picton was found guilty. Somebody – maybe even divine providence – seems to have been looking out for him, however. He appealed against the conviction and was released on bail. The original verdict was later overturned and friends of Picton covered the court costs.

None of this seemed to affect his military career. He was soon appointed Major General and, at the personal request of the Duke of Wellington, sailed for the Iberian Peninsula. He commanded a Division during the Peninsula War in Spain and covered himself in glory.

In 1812 Picton led his men in the storming of the breaches at Ciudad Rodrigo and, then, during the Battle of Badajoz was seriously wounded. He refused to leave his post and, afterwards, showed the contradictory side to his nature by personally giving each of his surviving soldiers a sovereign, out of his own pocket. Sick with his wounds and fever, Picton then returned to Britain.

When Napoleon escaped from Elba the wars, which everyone in Europe had hoped were ended for ever, began again. Thomas Picton soon found himself in Belgium. He fought with Wellington at Quatre Bras in the run up to the Waterloo battle and, never being one to keep out of the action, was again wounded.

He was well enough, however, to take his place at the head of the 5th Infantry Division at the momentous Battle of Waterloo. There, leading his men in a counter attack on d'Erlon's Corps, in the centre of the British line, Picton was shot through the temple by a musket ball and died.

Interestingly, Sir Thomas Picton was not in his uniform at the time of his death, something that would probably have caused him some distress. News of Napoleon's march into Belgium had come so quickly that he had left his luggage behind and at the time of his death it had still not caught up with him.

Despite his high-handed approach, Picton – although undoubtedly feared by his men – was admired by both Wellington and the government.

In the wake of his death a monument to him was erected in St Paul's and the impressive Picton Monument was built at the western end of Carmarthen town. That obelisk is still there today, a fitting tribute to the hard and sometimes contradictory man who helped keep Europe safe from the grasp of Napoleon Bonaparte.

30 – The Rebecca Riots

Mention the words Turnpike Trusts or the Rebecca Riots and most people immediately think of agrarian distress in the middle years of the nineteenth century.

It's hard to believe but the last turnpike toll gate in Britain, where money was charged to pass along the road, actually remained in use almost to the end of the 1800s and was not removed until November 1895. This last gate was situated on Ynys Mon and when you consider the furore that the Turnpike Trusts and their gates had caused fifty years before, its passing was remarkably smooth and low key.

The Rebecca Riots were a series of disturbances that broke out between May 1839 and the autumn of 1843. Beginning with an attack on the toll gate at Efail-Wen in Carmarthenshire, the Riots took place mainly in west Wales and were characterized by the rioters dressing themselves in women's clothes before attacking and destroying the gates of the hated Turnpike Trusts. In the months and years to come workhouses were also targeted, as was, on one occasion, the home of the tithe agent Rees Goring Thomas.

The causes of the Riots were many and varied. In the early- to mid-nineteenth century small farmers in west Wales were hit hard by wet harvests, by the levying of high rents by largely English-speaking landlords and by a sudden increase in the population. Taxes levied to pay for the building of new workhouses also helped build a sense of discontent and disgruntlement in rural Wales.

One of the main causes, however, was the web of toll gates that were to be found almost everywhere in Wales. Turnpike Trusts had been founded to repair and maintain road systems across the country, tolls being levied or charged in order to pay for the work. To begin with, at least, they were an effective and realistic way of improving the road network throughout the country.

However, by the middle of the nineteenth century toll gates had become far too common. There were, for example, no fewer than eleven different Turnpike Trusts operating around a town such as Carmarthen, each of them owning several gates. And each time people passed through the gates they had no choice but to pay.

The tolls charged by the Turnpike Companies were far too high for a distressed and struggling rural society. By the end of the 1830s the process of moving cattle or essential materials like lime and animal food to and from market had become prohibitively expensive. To some extent – and with hindsight – the Riots, or at least some form of protest, were inevitable as discontent simmered and began to turn into furious anger.

But why dress as women in order to carry out the raids? A traditional method of handing out social justice in Wales was to force the miscreant, whoever he might be, to ride through the streets on the ceffyl pren, a wooden horse. Blackened faces and cross dressing were part of the ritual, hiding the identity of those involved. Men dressing as women were seen to symbolize a world that had been turned upside down.

The name of the rioters possibly came from the book of Genesis where Rebecca and her daughters were supposed to possess the "gates of those which hate them". Legend, however, declares that one of the earliest rioters, Twm Carnabwth, borrowed clothes from a woman called Rebecca and the name just stuck.

For the four years after 1839 the riots raged. Toll gates were regularly smashed or burned and on June 19th 1843 a crowd of over 2000 people marched into Carmarthen to ransack the town workhouse. Dragoons charged at the mob but it did little to stop the Riots.

In August of the same year 3000 men and women marched on Mynydd Sylen in Pontyberem and such was the fear and concern of those in London that *The Times* newspaper even sent a reporter, one Thomas Foster, to find out the truth about the Rebecca Riots. His sympathetic reporting did much to air the grievances of the small farmers of west Wales.

No single "mastermind" for the Riots has ever been identified and, often, the attacks on gates and workhouses were totally uncoordinated. Hugh Williams, a Chartist and radical lawyer, has sometimes been credited for organising the destruction but nothing has ever been proved. As many of the outbreaks were the result of local disputes and arguments it is difficult to see one central figure controlling every outbreak or instance of gate smashing. It was far more likely to be a case of one group of rioters aping or imitating the actions of other groups as the need or desire took them – almost, it might be claimed, an early example of mob hysteria.

The Riots finally petered out in the autumn of 1843, following the death of Sarah Williams, the aged gatekeeper at Hendy, during a particularly violent demonstration. Popular support for the Riots began to fall away and when, in the coming months, several rioters were transported to Australia and others detained in prison it marked the end of a strange, not to say bizarre, period in Welsh history.

The Riots might have ended but not before they had achieved their aim. Partly due to the Riots themselves and partly due to the journalism of Thomas Foster, the government was forced to call a Commission of Enquiry to explore the grievances of the Welsh farmers.

As a result of the Enquiry, in 1844 all the Turnpike Trusts within each county of Wales were amalgamated and tolls on vital commodities like lime (used to help fertilise the land) were reduced by half. Rebecca and her daughters had won their victory – even though some of the gates lasted another fifty years.

And there are those who would say that the legacy of the Turnpike Trust system is still with us in the shape of the annual Road Tax and fees to cross the Severn Bridges.

31 – The Ladies of Llangollen

Most people have heard about the Ladies of Llangollen. Maybe some of us will own a print or even one of the early Victorian fairings (cheap porcelain figurines originally given out as prizes from fairground stalls) that depict the redoubtable pair. But not many of us will have any real understanding of the actual story of Lady Eleanor Charlotte Butler and the Honourable Sarah Ponsonby, the two ladies in question.

These two upper-class women lived together for many years outside Llangollen and despite their desire only for a peaceful and untroubled existence became, by the early years of the nineteenth century, something of a tourist attraction for the little North Wales town. They fascinated the public and intrigued the imagination of many who wondered, in public and in private, about their relationship – was it sexual? Nobody, either then or now, has been able to find out.

Eleanor Butler and Sarah Ponsonby were both born in Ireland, to aristocratic and well-off families, and met in 1868 when they immediately became great friends. In 1878, rather than be forced into arranged marriages that they did not want, Eleanor and Sarah scandalised polite society and ran away together.

They had tried to run away once before but their plans had been discovered and they had been prevented by their families. This second attempt was more successful. For many weeks their "elopement" was the talk of both Dublin and London coffee shops and salons. The two women did not care. They were happy in each other's company.

Together, they sailed from Ireland to Milford Haven and then journeyed north, eventually arriving in the Vale of Llangollen, an area they considered to be one of the most beautiful areas of countryside they had ever seen. Just outside Llangollen they found and, in 1780, bought a small house called Pen-y-Maes and settled down to life together.

The two women were, in the main, unsociable, took no notice of current fashions and wore basic, dark clothing at all times. The people of Llangollen accepted them and called them, simply, "The Ladies".

Despite the injunctions of their families, Eleanor and Sarah refused to return to Ireland. They began to redesign their cottage in the Gothic style and renamed it Plas Newydd. They spent the next fifty years studying literature, learning languages and gradually piecing together a huge collection of woodcarvings. Eleanor kept a diary of their life together – a life that was, really, quite mundane and often boring.

However, for some reason, their story and their lifestyle caught the public imagination. Soon visitors, unknown and famous, were besieging Plas Newydd.

People such as the poets Byron, Wordsworth and Shelley all came to talk and stare, as did the novelist Sir Walter Scott. Lady Caroline Lamb, friend of Byron and, by strange coincidence, a distant relative of Sarah Ponsonby, also found time to visit, as did the formidable Duke of Wellington. Visitors often brought with them pieces of wood carving which the ladies promptly added to their collection.

The exact relationship between the two women will never be known. At the end of the day it hardly matters. They were the greatest of friends and that friendship helped to sustain them through many years of what were, at times, quite gruelling problems.

Finances were never easy for them. Despite having an annual income of under three hundred pounds, their aristocratic backgrounds never quite disappeared and they insisted on maintaining a household that consisted of gardener, footman and several maids. One of the maids was Mary Caryll, a woman who had served them before, in Ireland. This insistence on servants and standards led to not inconsiderable debts, something with which they battled all their lives.

The Ladies of Llangollen were, eventually, reconciled with their families but continued to live in North Wales. And the public continued to come. Eleanor died on 2nd June 1829 while Sarah, sixteen years younger than her friend, lived on, alone at Plas Newydd, until December 1832.

The house at Llangollen is now a museum. It is run by Denbighshire County Council and is one of the main tourist locations in the town.

32 – Welsh Cowboys

When we think of America most of us will immediately conjure up a picture of the Wild West, of cowboys and gunfighters and the US 7th Cavalry. What most people don't realise is that Wales and the USA are more intimately connected than might be supposed, particularly where soldiers and gunfighters are concerned.

Over 250,000 people left Wales for the USA during the nineteenth century, a small enough figure when compared to the four million who emigrated from Ireland, but it was still a significant number. Many of these Welsh immigrants, about 20% of them, settled around the Pennsylvania area. Others spread along the eastern seaboard. The more adventurous ones headed west, joining the wagon trains across the plains in search of new territory to farm.

One of these, John Rees of Merthyr Tydfil, took part in the war against Mexico in the late 1830s, the same war that saw the death of Davy Crockett and the fall of the Alamo. Rees was one of only 28 survivors when the Mexicans massacred the Texicans – as they were known – at Goliad. He was taken prisoner but was released at the end of the war and returned, briefly, to Wales where he took part in the Chartist march on Newport in 1839. He managed to escape justice, however, sailing back to the USA and eventually settling in California.

Another Welsh soldier who served in the American army, albeit at a later date, was William Jones from Pencnwr Farm at Dinas. He emigrated to the United States in 1870, working as a coachman in Chicago before joining the 7th Cavalry in 1876. He was with George Armstrong Custer's unit at Little Big Horn in June that same year and was one of the 261 fatalities.

Someone who might also have been a victim of Custer's folly at the Battle of Little Big Horn was Lord Dunraven whose ancestral home was at Dunraven Castle in Southerndown. Travelling in America he hunted for elk with no less a person than Buffalo Bill Cody on the prairies of the mid-West and became friendly with General Phil Sheridan.

As the Earl later commented:

> "Colonel Custer invited me to join him on a punitive expedition against the Indians. Unluckily, as I thought,

> but fortunately as it turned out, I received the invitation too late. The whole outfit was wiped out."
> (Quoted in "Southerndown Golf Club: A Century of Memories".)

The history of the American West is littered with stories of fearless lawmen and one of these was Welshman John T Morris, Sheriff of Collins County in Texas during the 1870s.

In his most famous exploit he trailed an outlaw gang led by the notorious James Reed, a cattle rustler, bandit and husband of the infamous Belle Starr. He finally ran them to ground in Paris, Texas. While his posse surrounded the saloon where Reed and his gang were holed up, John Morris went inside and confronted the bandits.

Morris immediately challenged Reed and asked him to give himself up. Reed went for his gun but the Welsh Sheriff was faster on the draw. Within seconds Belle Starr's husband lay dead on the floor of the saloon.

Someone you might not automatically connect with the Wild West was the explorer Henry Morton Stanley. Originally from North Wales, Stanley (real name John Rowlands) was a journalist and in 1867 journeyed to the West to interview Wild Bill Hickok. That same year he also rode with the US Cavalry in their campaigns against the Indians and reported on his adventures for newspaper The Weekly Missouri Democrat.

The most famous cowboys of Welsh descent were, of course, the James gang. Jesse and Frank James were originally Confederate guerrilla fighters during the Civil War, men who found that they could not give up the violent way of life once the war was over.

Jesse and Frank James were decidedly not the "Robin Hood" figures usually depicted by American folk lore and, in fact, were vicious and violent killers who cut a swathe through the mid-west in the years after the war. Jesse was the worst of the lot.

Although Jesse was born in Clay County, Missouri on 5th September 1847, his family originated in Pembrokeshire. Several of his forebears were Baptist ministers and his father even helped to found the William Jewell College in Liberty, Missouri. Jesse's career went a different way, however, before he was finally shot down and killed by his cousin, Bob Ford, on 3rd April 1882.

There were undoubtedly thousands of Welsh farmers and industrial workers who emigrated to the USA and settled in various parts of the States. They might never have achieved the fame of those mentioned above but they all contributed towards the creation and the development of the United States of America.

33 – Take a Trip on the Train

Most of us, when travelling by train, rarely look outside the windows of our carriage. We bury our heads in our book or newspaper and only glance up to confirm our station has appeared. But a whole world of history is lurking out there and, if we only knew it, there is more than enough to keep us interested, whichever route we take.

The stretch of line from Llanelli to Carmarthen has to be one of the most beautiful lengths of railway line in the United Kingdom. It is also one that has so much history just lying alongside the train track, waiting to be discovered by the perceptive and interested train traveller.

Start with Llanelli Station itself. Opened in 1852, this is a Brunel-designed station building – the line was, of course, part of Brunel's wonderful railway – that has stone buildings with beautiful sandstone surrounds. In its heyday the station had connecting lines for London, Pontarddulais and for Shrewsbury. Even now this is the place to come if you are planning a trip on the Heart of Wales Line, another exquisite and enchanting railway journey.

The town of Llanelli, well visible from the train, was an industrial community – steel and the making of saucepans (hence Sospan Fach, the rugby song) – but these days it has re-branded itself as something of a tourist centre. Cycling, walking and top-quality golf are all available. And the Scarlets rugby team is now in possession of its new stadium at the eastern edge of the town.

Once Llanelli is left behind the train passes through 12 miles of the Millennium Coastal Path. The line follows the gentle curving arc of Carmarthen Bay, so close to the beach and estuary that it sometimes seems as if the train might topple easily into the sea. When the wind is up expect spray to mottle the windows – when it's calm the views out to Gower are spectacular.

Burry Port Harbour was once a centre for the export of coal; now it houses a marina. There were a couple of canals here, serving mines a little way inland and, in 1852, the Burry Port and Gwendraeth Valley Railway was opened – all long gone now, of course.

Next comes Pembrey Country Park. It now houses the National Motorsport Centre of Wales but this area was originally the site of RAF Pembrey, a fighter base in World War Two.

The aerodrome was the centre of an exciting episode in 1943 when a German Fokkewolf fighter landed and was captured intact. For some bizarre reason, the pilot apparently believed he was landing in France and the capture of his new aeroplane gave the Royal Air Force a valuable insight into the workings of this revolutionary German fighter.

The quay at Kidwelly was once a very busy port. In the sixteenth and seventeenth centuries ships of up to 400 tons berthed there on a regular basis but the growth of Burry Port, after the construction of its harbour in 1838, ended Kidwelly's importance.

The town's imposing Norman Castle sits adjacent to the river and is still a spectacular sight. Built around 1106, it dominates the town. This was one of the earliest Norman settlements in South Wales, English and Flemish farmers and wool merchants being brought in to transplant the native Welsh.

Ferryside Station sits alongside the estuary and the views across to Llansteffan are magnificent. Llansteffan Castle, on the hill above the estuary, is another Norman fortress but one that was later turned into a country house by the Tudors.

And so to Carmarthen town itself. This was reputedly the birthplace of the magician Merlin and there are those who say it was actually the site of Camelot. The run into the station is lovely, crossing the River Tywi and with the bridge where Dylan Thomas's story "A Visit to Grandpa's" comes to an end, waiting ahead of you.

The line from Llanelli to Carmarthen is a wonderful experience for anyone with the heart and soul to appreciate beauty and history. There are many other rail routes – the Heart of Wales Line, the trip down the west coast past Harlech – in Wales but I think you would be hard pressed to better this atmospheric and enchanting piece of railway architecture.

34 – Welsh Presidents of the USA

September and early October 2010 saw a sudden and huge influx of American visitors to our shores, most of whom arrived to support their team in the Ryder Cup series of golf matches against Europe. It was the first time the Cup had been contested on Welsh soil but links of an historical nature between the USA and Wales are lengthier and far more considerable than many people know.

For example, five of the first six Presidents of the USA were of Welsh descent and the country has had no fewer than ten Welsh-connected Presidents in all – plus, briefly, the President of the Confederate States of America.

The Welshmen at the helm of the most powerful country in the world were: John Adams, John Quincy Adams, Thomas Jefferson, James Morrison Jnr, James Monroe, William Harrison, Abraham Lincoln, Benjamin Harrison, James A Garfield and Calvin Coolidge. The Confederate President was, of course, Jefferson Davis.

John Adams, the second ever President and the first one to reside in the White House, was able to trace his ancestry to the town of Pembroke in Pembrokeshire and to Penybanc Farm at Llanboidy in Carmarthenshire. The earliest reference to his family comes in 1422 when a distant ancestor, John Adams of Pembroke, married the daughter of Penybanc Farm and duly took over the business.

David Adams, one of the later sons of Penybanc, was educated at Queen Elizabeth Grammar School in Carmarthen, took holy orders and in 1675 emigrated to America. Fifty years later his great grandson, the future President, was born.

John Adams's son, also called John, became the first and, for many years, the only son of a US President to also succeed to the Oval Office – a record that lasted until George W Bush succeeded his father a few years ago. John Quincy Adams became the sixth President in 1825.

Before that, however, there had been several other Presidents of Welsh descent. Amongst them was Thomas Jefferson who succeeded to the post in 1817. He was the main author and guiding light of the Declaration of Independence, a document that resonates with all the cadences and flowing poetry of the Welsh soul.

Jefferson's origins are a little unclear but he himself said that his father came from the foothills of Snowdon and in 1933 a US State Department official unveiled a plaque at Llanfair Ceiriog, the inscription reading "To the memory of a great Welshman, Thomas Jefferson."

The fifth President and yet another man of Welsh descent, James Monroe, was the official who conceived and implemented the Monroe Doctrine, a policy that declared that any attempt to colonise land on the continent of North America would be regarded as an act of war.

Yet another Welsh connection came in the person of the ninth President, William Harrison, who lasted just 32 days and became the first President to die in office. James Madison Jnr, the fourth President – who actually served two terms in office – was one of the Founding Fathers of the American nation and was the principal author of the US Constitution – another document that betrays its author's Welsh heritage in the style and quality of its composition.

Like Harrison, Abraham Lincoln, of course, also died in office, assassinated by John Wilkes Booth in April 1865. His Welsh lineage might be tentative and unclear but his surname comes from a fusion of Welsh and Latin, meaning "from the lake country".

Perhaps the most romantic of all the Welsh-connected Presidents – although maybe not the most politically correct – is Jefferson Davis who, after the secession of the southern states, was elected President of the Confederacy in February 1861.

Jefferson Davis had been Secretary of State for War and was a hero of the Indian Wars but had always viewed the southern states as a country within a country. The American Civil War was a violent and bloody conflict, like all civil wars, and the eventual defeat of the southern states was inevitable but the story of the war and its battles has long held a rather romanticized place in literature and films.

Davis was captured two days after the surrender of the southern states and was flung into prison where he was kept in irons for two years. His wife, a Welsh woman by the name of Varina Howell, campaigned tirelessly for his release and this was eventually granted. Jefferson Davis – named after Thomas Jefferson, one of the earliest Welsh Presidents – retired to New Orleans where he died, aged 82.

Interestingly, both John Adams and Thomas Jefferson – the only two Presidents to actually sign the Declaration of

Independence – died on exactly the same day. It was 4th July 1826, the 50th anniversary of the signing.

Connections between Wales and the USA certainly go far deeper than many people, Welsh or American, expect. American visitors received a great welcome when they came to Newport for the Ryder Cup in the autumn of 2010 – everywhere except on the golf course at Celtic Manor. In the months and years ahead they can happily look forward to hospitality of an equally warm nature. After all, Wales and America have many things in common.

35 – Robert Owen, Socialist and Visionary

Robert Owen is now something of a forgotten figure. Yet this far-sighted visionary, a man who was arguably born before his time, was one of the most original thinkers ever to come out of Wales. For this was a socialist long before the term "socialism" had ever been invented. He was also an educationalist par excellence and the man who laid the foundations for the later co-operative movement.

Owen was born in the mid Wales town of Newtown on 14th May 1771. He was the sixth of seven children, his father being an ironmonger and saddler, his mother coming from a long line of well-to-do farmers. A bright and capable child, Robert was schooled at Newtown and then, at the age of ten, was articled to a draper in the town. In due course he moved to London to continue his trade and establish himself in the world.

This he managed to do with some alacrity and with more than a little skill. A move to the sprawling, manufacturing metropolis of Manchester saw Robert Owen installed as manager of Drinkwater's cotton factory in the town. There were greater things still to come and on a visit to Scotland he met and fell in love with Caroline Dew, the daughter of David Dale, owner of the New Lanark cotton mill on the Falls of Clyde.

Owen married Caroline in 1799 and with four partners managed to raise enough capital to buy the New Lanark mills from Dale. He was not interested in simply making money, however. Owen wanted to run an enlightened regime at New Lanark.

He had over 2000 people working for him – and not just working; many of them lived in the tenement blocks set around the mill. Five hundred of these workers were young children, most of them small enough to crawl under the looms and spinning jennies to clean the machinery and gather in stray cotton or wool.

Although his father-in-law David Dale had run a reasonably humane ship, drunkenness, absenteeism and theft, amongst other social problems, were rife. Most of the workforce came from the poorer elements of society, from the squalid slums of Glasgow or Edinburgh, and managers expected little else from them. Owen believed he could change this. He was altruistic enough to want to help people less well off than himself but he also knew that better living conditions could only help to make better profits.

Soon his aims had become reality. Improved housing conditions – prizes were awarded for things like the best kept room on the block – and a unique system of quality control that let all employees know exactly how they were doing, led to a highly motivated work force. And that was only the start of what he had in mind.

Owen soon became a pioneer of nursery or early years education, setting up a schoolroom on the site where children would be educated before they began work in the mill – this, seventy years before formal and compulsory education for all was introduced in Britain. Such a system also provided an early form of child care while the mothers and fathers were working the looms.

Visitors to New Lanark today can visit this schoolroom and see for themselves the alphabet of animals that Robert Owen had painted on the walls of the building.

Most mills and mines had, for years, employed the truck system where workers were not paid in cash but in tokens that could only be redeemed at the company shop. Consequently, prices were exorbitant and many workers lived below the breadline. Not in Robert Owen's New Lanark.

Owen's shop sold goods at little more than their wholesale cost, thus ensuring that families had more than enough to live on. The goods on sale were top quality, unlike the poor pickings offered in many truck shops. By buying in bulk what Owen was able to do was pass on the savings to the customers, his work force. In effect, this was the basis and the beginning of the co-operative movement, something that still works and functions today.

Robert Owen wrote extensively about his ideas. He believed, for example, that an ideal community should consist of just over a thousand people, living in apartments grouped around an open square and with central kitchen and dining facilities. Children, he felt, were best brought up with their families until the age of three and then became the responsibility of the whole community.

This was an idea he tried to put into practice at his "ideal" community, New Harmony, in Indiana in the USA. Using much of his personal capital, he bought land and set out his plan. For two years Owen lived in America, trying desperately to make his dream reality. It didn't work, being a concept that was very much before its time. Eventually Owen was forced to return to Britain where other difficulties faced him.

After many disputes with his partners, who were always more interested in profits than in Owen's version of ideal living, he resigned from New Lanark in 1828. He moved to London but the glory days were gone and he was no longer the wealthy capitalist – albeit an enlightened one – that he had been when his work at the mills first began.

On a visit to his place of birth and childhood, he was suddenly taken ill and died on 17th November 1858. His dreams of a socialist nirvana never really came to anything – he was clearly before his time. But his legacy, his true legacy, lies in his system of child care and education. And, of course, the concept of a co-operative society where everyone would benefit, not just the men at the top of the tree.

36 – Welsh-American Place Names

A census taken in 2008 revealed that there were approximately 1.98 million Americans with a surname that had Welsh origins. Many of these, incidentally, were African Americans. Today there are hundreds of black Americans with names like Evans, Jones and Thomas. Such names are usually of Welsh origin. It all comes from the old slave tradition of workers taking the names of their slave masters and would therefore seem to indicate that many of the plantation owners – or, at least, the overseers – were Welsh. It is hardly something we, as a nation, should boast or be unduly happy about!

But quite apart from people's names there are also lots of American towns and cities that are named after original settlements in Wales. Some of them are well known.

So, we have Bangor in Maine, Newport on Rhode Island, even Swansea in Massachusetts. Some of these are quite well known yet not many Welshmen and women realise that there are no fewer than ten Cardiffs in the United States. These can be found in states such as Alabama, Colorado, Idaho, Maryland, Illinois, New Jersey, Pennsylvania, Tennessee, New York and Texas. That takes some imagining, doesn't it?

It's easy to see why immigrants to the USA should choose to name their new villages after places they knew and remembered in the old world. It meant a degree of security and familiarity in a strange and, in the early days at least, largely untamed land. When death and destruction could visit at any moment, in the shape of disease or famine, raiding war parties of Native Americans, even from attacks by Britain's traditional enemies like the French, it was important to keep some semblance of normality alive. It was something firm and tangible to hold on to.

In later years, once America had achieved independence from Britain and begun to develop as an industrial and economic power of major proportions, people from Wales continued to settle in the States. Many of these were coal and steel workers, eager to start a new and better life. And that is why many Welsh immigrants settled in areas of Pennsylvania.

Welsh settlement in Pennsylvania had been going on for many years, mind you. Thanks to the efforts of William Penn in the late seventeenth century, the Welsh Tract was created.

The Welsh Tract consisted of 40,000 acres of land in Pennsylvania, most of the settlers being Welsh Quakers. Welsh was the predominant language spoken in the region and this was reflected in the place names of many of the towns that soon grew up. Places like Bryn Mawr, Lower and Upper Meirion, Radnor and Haverford still exist and remain proud of their Welsh origins.

There are so many other towns and cities with names of Welsh origin in America. Some of them have fascinating histories.

Malad City in Idaho, for example, was created in the mid nineteenth century as a Welsh Mormon Settlement. And five towns in Maryland were built between 1850 and 1942 to house Welsh quarry workers who had made the dangerous trip across the Atlantic to work in the local quarries.

Dozens of Welsh-American Societies still meet on regular basis in all parts of the USA. Along with the surnames of thousands of Americans and the names of their cities they are part of a strong and undying link between the USA and the old country from which so many early settlers came.

37 – The Witch and the Warship

HMS *Caesar*, the battleship cursed by a witch, shown here just after her launch from the dockyard at Pembroke Dock.

Imagine the scene. The dockyard is full of workmen, women and children; bands are playing and eager spectators and townspeople mingle happily with dignitaries and naval officers. It is 21st July 1853 and the 90-gun wooden-hulled warship *Caesar* is about to be launched from the slipways of Pembroke Dockyard.

The appointed hour arrives, speeches are made and, to the accompaniment of loud cheers and encouraging shouts, the new ship begins to slide into the river – and then she sticks, fast. No matter what the dockyard officials and workmen try to do, the *Caesar* simply refuses to move. The crowd begins to mutter and murmur, workers run like helpless chickens around the hull of the new ship. A sense of despair begins to pervade the mighty dockyard.

When the matter is investigated it soon transpires that somebody – obviously with a keen eye to economy – has ordered fir wood to be used instead of oak for the launching ways, those stretches of planking along which any newly built ship is meant to slide until she reaches the water.

Unfortunately, fir wood is soft and, consequently, as the new hull took shape and as the ship grew heavier and heavier, the *Caesar* simply bedded herself into the launching ways. She couldn't have hit the water, even if she had wanted to! To make matters even worse, the tallow used to grease the launching ways was of very inferior quality – another unfortunate example of Admiralty cost-cutting.

For the people of Pembroke Dock, however, there was a much more sinister reason for the *Caesar*'s failure to enter the water. They knew that it had little to do with fir wood and inferior tallow. They knew the "real" reason for the failure.

Earlier that day a local woman called Betty Foggy, renowned in the area as a witch and spell caster, had tried to enter the dockyard to watch the launch.

It was customary at Pembroke Dock – and in most Royal dockyards – to throw open the gates and allow locals in to watch any launch. It was quite an occasion for the people of the town. In the middle years of Victorian Britain there was not much in the way of public entertainment, particularly in out-of-the-way places like Pembroke Dock, and the local people looked forward to such free treats.

However, when Betty Foggy tried to get in, an eagle-eyed policeman recognised her and quickly turned her away. "You can't come in," he said. "It would be unlucky." No matter how much she protested the policeman was adamant. There was to be no admission for Betty Foggy.

Dozens of people saw Betty held at the gate and then turned away as they passed easily and happily into the yards. And, more importantly, many of them heard her words. "Very well," she mumbled. "If I can't come in, then there'll be no launch today." Most of those who heard her laughed or took the words with a pinch of salt. After all, how could one old woman halt such a thing as a ship launch? It was not possible.

However, Betty's curse seemed to work and before evening the story of the failed launch and Betty's supposed part in the affair was all around Pembroke Dock and nearby Pembroke. Betty Foggy had put a curse on the launch. There was no doubting now. Everyone knew the power of the Pembroke witch; Betty Foggy and her name was bandied about with fear and trepidation in the pubs and drinking dens of the dockyard town.

The dockyard officials, embarrassed and unhappy over the matter of the fir and tallow, were happy to agree. It was, they agreed, all the fault of the local witch.

It was Sunday 7th August, when most people of the town were

conveniently engaged in morning service, before the *Caesar* finally slid into the waters of the Cleddau River. For 17 days workmen had been quietly building huge wooden structures, known as camels, under the hull of the ship. Slowly but surely the *Caesar*'s keel was raised up out of the fir wood into which it had sunk.

Never being the people to admit a mistake, the dockyard officials were quite sanguine in their explanations – "Betty has lifted her curse!" they declared. The people of the town believed them and the story has gone down in Pembroke Dock folklore, the witch who cursed the launch of HMS *Caesar*.

38 – Sarah Jacobs, the Fasting Girl

At the end of the nineteenth century she was known as the Welsh Fasting Girl and regarded as a miracle, the little twelve-year-old who had not eaten for over two years. In an age where spirituality clashed with the new teachings of science, she was an undoubted phenomenon but whether or not her "miracle" was of her own making or something that was forced on her by manipulative parents remains unclear.

However you view it, the story of Sarah Jacobs is one of fascinating and tragic proportions. In the end she was killed by her own fame, a fame that, to begin with at least, she seemed more than eager to grasp.

Sarah Jacobs was born on 12th May 1857 on a farm just outside the village of Llanfihangel-ar-Arth in Carmarthenshire. Her parents, Evan and Hannah Jacobs, held respectable positions in this rural community, Evan having been a deacon in the local chapel. Then, at the age of nine Sarah fell ill with convulsions of some type.

As she recovered she was allowed to sleep in her parents' bedroom, a warm and comfortable environment compared to the loft where she would otherwise have spent her days. There was no denying that lying in bed all day, composing poems and reading the Bible, was far preferable to looking after the animals on the farm.

Spoiled and cosseted, she began to refuse food. She was genuinely religious but whether her refusal to eat had spiritual undertones or was simply the machinations of a manipulative anorexic has never been clear.

Sarah was a self-possessed and bright child and, whatever the cause, she soon began to see the value in what she was doing. Perhaps her parents encouraged her in what was clearly a deception that fooled virtually everybody. Evan and Hannah later claimed that their daughter had had no food whatsoever from 10th October 1867 until her death two years later in December 1869.

As the fasting went on Sarah became something of a local celebrity, people from the village wondering at her refusal to either eat or drink. And so it might have remained if the local vicar had not written to the newspapers about this amazing miracle that was occurring in his parish.

Almost overnight Sarah's fame was assured. Soon people were coming from far afield, from the English cities as well as Wales, catching the train to Pencader and walking over two miles to the farm to stand gazing in wonder at this young girl who was defying the laws of nature. They brought gifts and money for her, dropping their sovereigns onto the bedspread as she lay, surrounded by flowers, reading and quoting the Bible. Everyone marvelled at her appearance, one visitor remarking:

> "Her eyes shone like pearls, as alert as my own – she had rosy cheeks and looked like a lily amongst thorns."

To live for over two years without food or water is, clearly, impossible but in the Victorian Age people really believed they were witnessing a miracle.

How Sarah got her food is not known. Some believe her sister was feeding her, passing titbits from her mouth whenever they kissed. Others are inclined to the view that Sarah fed herself, climbing out of bed when the rest of the house was asleep. Her body would have become used to reduced amounts of food but, then, she had often refused to eat her lunch in the past, when at school, asking her class mates not to tell anyone, her parents in particular.

With her case attracting more and more interest it was decided, by the vicar and the medical profession, to mount a watch over Sarah. This was to last for a fortnight. Evan Jacob agreed but the watch did not last both day and night and the findings were unclear.

As Sarah grew fatter and plumper, reaching full maturity despite her lack of food, people began to suspect fraud. Dr Phillips of Guy's Hospital decided to organise another vigil. Six nurses were brought in to mount a twenty-four hour watch on the girl.

And now Sarah's position became really untenable. If she had previously been able to slip out of bed to find food in the night, now it was impossible. She could not admit to fraud or lying, pride or religious conviction, or even her undiagnosed medical condition, would not let her. And so she simply lay there, waiting to die, as the nurses watched and made notes in their diaries.

The experiment was cruel as the nurses were instructed not to treat or help, simply to mount a watch. If Sarah asked for food they were to give it but otherwise they were to do nothing. And, of course, she did not; the tragedy was to be played out until the bitter end. Even *The Lancet*, the main journal of the medical profession, later commented that practitioners everywhere should be "filled with feelings of shame and indignation".

After four or five days Sarah lapsed into semi-consciousness and on 12th December 1869 she died. The miracle was over.

An autopsy was held at the Eagle Inn in the village and a sticky substance and the bones of a small bird or fish were found in Sarah's stomach. Clearly, she had eaten something. More tragic, however, were the grooves found on her toes – as if she had been trying to open the cap of the stone water bottle that had been placed in her bed, a desperate attempt to get water.

Evan and Hannah Jacob were subsequently convicted of manslaughter and spent twelve and six months, respectively, in Swansea prison. No one could prove that they had deliberately starved and, eventually, killed their daughter but they – like the medical profession, although the doctors and nurses were never prosecuted – were certainly guilty of doing nothing to protect her. Perhaps they really believed they were witnessing a miracle?

So, Sarah Jacobs? A genuine miracle or a cynical exercise in fraud? Many people call her Wales's first anorexic – and there are certainly elements of that awful condition in her history. But above all, this is the tragic story of a young girl on the threshold of life, a young life that was, because of her own personality or because of pressure from outside, cut brutally short.

39 – James James, Composer of Hen Wlad Fy Nhadau

Every year thousands of Welsh rugby fans will stand with tears in their eyes as the band plays and the national team prepares to take on the might of England, Ireland, the All Blacks or whoever. They will bawl out the words – most of them only half-remembered – and happily sing or hum to the tune of Hen Wlad Fy Nhadau. And they will never give a thought to the man who composed the music for what is, possibly, the most atmospheric and memorable of all national anthems.

James James was born in 1833 and died on 11th January 1902 – very nearly a hundred years ago. These days he remains something of a forgotten man but this was the musician who composed our national anthem. And as if that wasn't enough it was his father, Evan James, who wrote the words.

James James was a musician of note. He competed in many eisteddfodau around the Pontypridd area and held the bardic name Iago ap Ieuan.

James lived in Pontypridd at the bottom of the Rhondda valley and was heavily influenced by his surroundings. In fact, to begin with, his magical piece of music was actually known as Glan Rhondda. Under that title it was performed many times, in chapels or at eisteddfodau. Only when the tune and its lyrics were included in a collection of manuscript music, "Gems of Welsh Melody", was the title changed to the one we know today.

James James was a harpist who was well known in the Pontypridd area. He ran a pub in the town and was a regular performer at other taverns where his music was always in demand for dancing. Indeed, Hen Wlad Fy Nhadau was originally intended to be played at a much faster pace – to allow for dancing – but had to be slowed down when it was sung or performed by choirs.

Legend declares that James composed the piece in his head as he was walking alongside the river in his native town in late 1855 or early 1856. He then supposedly went home and hummed the tune to his father – a noted bardic poet – and asked him to put some lyrics to the tune. It took, so the story goes, just one night and by the following day all three verses and chorus were written.

The second and third verses of the anthem are rarely used these days. But they are clearly an attempt to invoke the patriotic spirit in all Welshmen:

"If the enemy violated my country underfoot
The old language of the Welsh is alive as ever,
The spirit isn't hindered by the awful, treacherous deed
Nor the sweet harp of my country."

The words are undoubtedly more powerful in Welsh rather than the English translation but they certainly make their point – in either language.

Hen Wlad Fy Nhadau was first performed (as Glan Rhondda) at Tabor Chapel in Maesteg in January 1856, the soloist being Elizabeth John of Pontypridd. It went on to be sung at many subsequent eisteddfodau and in March 1899 was one of the first Welsh-language songs to be recorded on vinyl when a singer by the name of Madge Breese included it in a collection of songs she was recording.

In the years following its composition the song had become increasingly used at patriotic gatherings and gradually found itself metamorphosing into a national anthem.

In 1905, as a riposte to the New Zealand All Blacks and the psychological use of their traditional pre-match haka, it was decided to encourage the crowd to sing Hen Wlad Fy Nhadau before the kick off. Up to that moment there had been no history of singing national anthems before a game but there was such an impressive response (and, of course, Wales won in one of the most famous of all games) that it soon became traditional for all international sides to stand and sing their anthem before kick off.

James James died on 11th January 1902 in his sixty-ninth year. He was buried in the churchyard at Aberdare along with his wife Cecilia and daughter Louise.

There is a memorial to James – and to his father Evan – in Ynysangharad Park in their native Pontypridd. It takes the form of two figures, one representing music, the other poetry, and is a fitting tribute to the two men who gave Wales her national anthem.

40 – Solomon Andrews, Cardiff Entrepreneur

One of the great Victorian entrepreneurs, the name of Solomon Andrews has now largely disappeared from public knowledge and view. Yet this amazing man, someone who literally rose from rags to riches, epitomizes the Victorian ideal of "self help". He was a man who carved out for himself and his family one of the great financial success stories of the nineteenth century.

Born in Trowbridge, Wiltshire, in 1835, Solomon Andrews came to Cardiff equipped with just a wooden tray to sling around his neck and a stock of trinkets and sweets to sell in the street. This was in the year 1851 and Cardiff was just beginning to grow and develop. It was the ideal place for a young, ambitious individual and within ten years Solomon Andrews was virtually a millionaire with interests in transport, draperies, coal mines and property.

The energy and drive of this dynamic man can only be imagined. Despite starting with almost nothing, by 1856 he had amassed enough capital (and nerve) to lease a shop and set himself up in the bakery and confectionery business. Eight years later he had expanded his interests and branched out into running cabs and horse brakes. By 1873 he was running 35 buses and coaches through the streets of Cardiff.

In 1872 Andrews bought a coach-building works and began constructing his own vehicles. Within a few years he was operating buses – usually horse-drawn – in places as diverse as Portsmouth, Plymouth, Belfast and London.

Something of a "transport war" between Andrews and the other owners of buses and trams in Cardiff soon erupted and there are stories of Andrews' buses deliberately driving along the lines of the tram cars in order to slow down the competition. There are also darker tales of wooden railway sleepers being laid across the tram lines in order to derail or damage vehicles. Quite what the passengers thought of these tactics is not known but the tales seem to sum up the vibrant and competitive – or even combative – nature of Victorian society.

Eventually the "war" came to an amicable conclusion and Solomon Andrews sold his transport interests, retaining only the routes between Cardiff, Penarth and Llandaff.

Solomon Andrews did not confine his business interests just to

Cardiff and south Wales. He built houses and business premises all over the country. What he did create in the Cardiff area, however, was quite spectacular.

The Market Buildings in St Mary's Street, Cardiff, opened in 1884, was just one of his major concerns – the swirling contours and towering ceiling, along with Andrews' name above the St Mary's Street entrance, can still be seen today. And perhaps more importantly, the market with its jumble of stalls and shops is still in use.

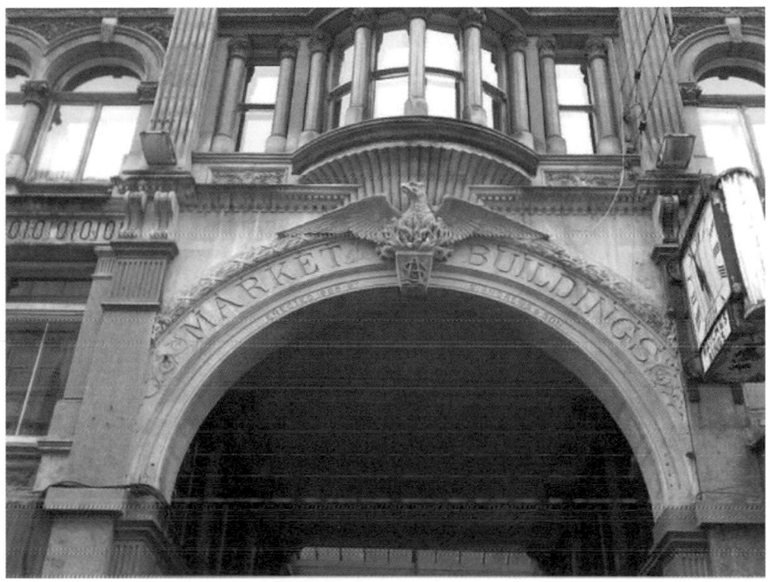

The entrance to Cardiff Market in St Mary's Street, one of many buildings created by Solomon Andrews in the nineteenth century.

Other major enterprises for Solomon Andrews were the shopping arcade in Penarth and many of the grander buildings along Penarth's main thoroughfare, Windsor Road. He opened the David Evans Department Stores in Cardiff and Swansea and even had business concerns in Australia.

In the early years of the twentieth century Solomon Andrews was instrumental in developing the north Wales town of Pwllheli. On holiday in Llandudno, Andrews heard of land available in the town on the south coast of the Llyn Peninsula, and immediately laid plans to create a holiday resort. His enterprises within the town included the Promenade, a public bandstand, a golf course and the West End Hotel.

He bought Glyn-y-Weddw house to the west of Pwllheli and then built a tramway along the sand dunes to run out to the place. The house was converted into an Art Gallery – in which guise it still runs – and a ballroom was created out of the old stable yard. Evening dances at Glyn-y-Weddw remained popular for many years.

Solomon Andrews remains the archetypal Victorian self-made man. His fingers reached into many different spheres and areas and he created a dynasty which remains to this day, perhaps not as obvious as old Solomon himself but one that is, in its own way, equally as successful.

41 – David Davies, Wales's First Millionaire

The story of David Davies, the man who can justifiably claim to be Wales's first millionaire, is a classic. There is no other way to describe it; his life can only be regarded as a fairy tale and he has to be seen as the epitome of the Victorian dream.

Born in 1818 at Llandinam in Montgomeryshire, David was the eldest of nine children and yet rose from being a humble sawyer to a position of power and prestige at the very top of Welsh society. When he died in 1890 his personal estate was valued at over four hundred thousand pounds. And yet for the first thirty years of his life he could barely read or write.

When he left school at the age of eleven, David Davies began to work on the farm and in the sawpits of his father, also called David Davies. The young man's nickname, "Top Sawyer", dates from this time – he was proud to record and tell the story of how he had always had the good sense to work at the top of the sawpit and thus avoid being covered by shavings and sawdust.

For several years Davies worked as a sawyer, farmer and local contractor but then, after the early death of his father from TB, he was given the opportunity to create the foundations and the approaches to a new bridge across the Severn at Llandinam. The County Surveyor, one Thomas Penson, was so impressed with the work that he began to put other projects Davies' way. He was on the road to success.

Commenting on the death of his father and brother at this time, Herbert Williams, Davies' biographer, has written:

> "The cause of death of David Davies, farmer, is given as 'Decline,' and the next column, reserved for the signature, description and residence of the informant, bears the words 'The Mark X of David Davies, Present at the Death.' Eight weeks later he made his mark a second time as witness to the death of his brother."
> (Quoted in *Davies the Ocean* by Herbert Williams)

Within a few years, however, there exist letters and documents written by David Davies, particularly with regard to his forthcoming marriage. He had clearly taught himself to read in the years between the death of his brother and his marriage to

Margaret Jones of Llanfair Caereinion. And from then on it was all upwards for the young entrepreneur.

As well as roads and bridges, Davies built several railways across mid Wales, his most notable achievement being the crossing of the mighty Tregaron Bog to finish the line between Lampeter and Aberystwyth. Building railways soon became second nature to him and he even headed to the southwest to construct the Pembroke to Tenby line.

By the 1850s he might have become an important and wealthy man but Davies never lost touch with his roots. In his book *Davies the Ocean*, Herbert Williams has written:

> "He was still the old Davy, ready to roll up his sleeves and turn to with the lads. One morning he saw them struggling to roll heavy stones into trucks in a quarry and with a cry of 'Sweet boys, up with them!' helped them shoulder the stones into place. His effort was all the more impressive in that he was on his way to London on business and wearing a dark suit which was so covered in dust that he had to go home to change before making the journey."

Then, in 1864 David Davies bought land in the Upper Rhondda Valley and sank the Parc and Maerdy coal pits. Further mines followed, including the Garw and the Lady Windsor. So successful was the enterprise that in 1887 the Ocean Coal Company Ltd was established, one of the most enterprising coal companies in Wales.

As the Taff Vale Railway Company and Cardiff Docks were unable to cope with the traffic from Ocean Collieries, Davies promptly built himself a new dock at Barry – not without considerable opposition from Parliament and the powerful lobby of Lord Bute, who owned the land around Cardiff Docks.

David Davies was a Liberal MP for many years, representing the town and then the county of Cardiganshire. But as an opponent of Irish Home Rule, he quarrelled with Gladstone and lost the 1886 election by a margin of just nine votes. It was devastating blow, one from which he never really recovered, and Davies died just four years later.

He had made an incredible journey, from humble labourer to the richest man in Wales. David Davies symbolises the energetic, hard-working and imaginative Victorian entrepreneur, a self-made man who knew exactly where he was going and, more importantly, precisely how he was going to get there.

42 – Newport Transporter Bridge

The transporter bridge in Newport is an iconic symbol, the one structure that any visitor to the town has to see. It is one of only three such bridges in Britain, one of only eight in the whole world.

The bridge was opened on 12th September 1906. Designed by French engineer Ferdinand Arnodin and built by the contractor Alfred Thorne of Westminster, it was the culmination of many years' discussion and consideration. There had been numerous proposals for bridges and subways under the River Usk at this eastern end of the town but none of them had come to fruition, mainly due to the nature of the work required and the high cost.

The banks of the river were – and still are – very low at this point and it would have required long steep approach ramps to build a bridge with sufficient height to allow ships to pass underneath. A subway or tunnel would have been prohibitively expensive. A ferry would not do the job as the rise and fall of the river has always been great and at low tide boats would simply not be able to dock.

And so nothing was done until 1896 when John Lysaght proposed building a new steelworks to the south west of the town. In order to attract and encourage him the Borough Council decided that they would have to "bite the bullet" – a crossing of some sort would have to be built.

Borough engineer R H Hayes had heard of transporter bridges and travelled to Rouen to see an example that had been built by Ferdinand Arnodin. The idea of a transporter bridge – in effect an aerial ferry – would eliminate the problem of the low banks and it would be considerably cheaper than excavating a tunnel below the waters of the Usk. Hayes returned, convinced, and by 1900 Parliamentary approval had been granted. Work began.

The transporter bridge was to have tall twin towers on either side of the river, reaching up for nearly 250 feet into the air, while the horizontal beam from which the transporter platform or gondola was to hang was some seventy feet lower. This gondola would travel the 600 feet above the water at a rate of ten feet per second.

The transporter bridge cost nearly one hundred thousand pounds to construct – hardly a vast sum of money, even in those days – and was intended to take both vehicles and passengers across the river. At the opening ceremony on 12th September 1906 – the official opening being conducted by Viscount Tredegar – the new bridge was described as:

> "A giant with the grace of Apollo and the strength of Hercules."

The bridge has featured in numerous television programmes and films over the years – notably the 1959 film "Tiger Bay" which gave Hayley Mills her screen debut. The film was supposedly set in Cardiff but was shot in Newport, causing many later visitors to Cardiff to ask where their transporter bridge was located.

The bridge has had a chequered history, having been closed for a three million pound refurbishment in 1985. Despite being reopened in 1995 it closed again in 2007. It is now due to reopen once again and, hopefully, this time it will remain open.

When it is fully operational the transporter bridge can cater for up to six light vehicles and 120 pedestrians. This Grade 1 listed building remains the largest of the world's eight transporter bridges and is an important part of Newport's history.

43 – The Welsh Florence Nightingale

Everybody has heard about Florence Nightingale, the Lady with the Lamp. A woman of undoubted power and drive, she certainly deserves to be remembered as the founder of modern nursing. Many will have heard about Mary Seacole, the black nurse who was turned down for inclusion in Nightingale's party because of issues like race, class and education – it didn't stop her, she went to the Crimea where she worked as tirelessly as Florence Nightingale to help Britain's wounded soldiers.

But only very few will have heard of Betsi Cadwaladr, the remarkable Welsh woman who also worked with Nightingale in the Crimea.

Her story is a remarkable one, in its way every bit as memorable as those of Nightingale and Mary Seacole. Born at Bala on 24th May 1789, she was one of sixteen children, taking charge of the family and effectively bringing up the other children after her mother died when Betsi was just five years old.

When she grew up, Betsi (real name Elizabeth) was a traveller of note, working as a servant and as a companion for various people, ships' captains and titled ladies amongst them. Her work took her around the world several times – and this in an age when most working-class men, let alone working-class women, never travelled more than a dozen miles from their front doors!

Not, officially, a nurse, Betsi's various jobs in all parts of the world inevitably involved her in nursing duties and, in particular, convinced her of the need for cleanliness as an aid to recovery from disease and illness.

The Crimean War broke out in 1854 and, thanks to the regular despatches of journalists like William Russell, it quickly became apparent that the campaign was appallingly organised. One of the worst injustices was the total lack of care for wounded and dying soldiers. Learning that Florence Nightingale had been commissioned to provide a cadre or squad of suitable nurses, Betsi Cadwaladr applied to join the group.

However, Nightingale had already left for Scutari and Betsi was forced to join one of the subsequent parties organised and led by Mrs Herbert.

When Betsi did eventually reach Scutari she met Nightingale and from the beginning it was clear that there was a major clash of personalities. Apart from anything else Betsi was working-class, through and through – Florence Nightingale came from a much more privileged background. Kept waiting for several weeks, Betsi fumed and demanded to be sent to the front:

"I did not like the name Nightingale," she later commented in a book on her life. "When I first learn a name I know by my feelings whether I shall like the person who bears it."

Clearly, then, Betsi and Florence Nightingale disliked each other from the first and Nightingale eventually washed her hands of this argumentative and truculent Welsh woman who, despite all advice, made her way to the front lines where she cared for the wounded and injured soldiers.

Living and working just behind the front lines, she cooked, cleaned and nursed, working twenty hours a day and only sleeping when she found the time. Usually she slept on the floor with seven other nurses. Inevitably such conditions took their toll on a woman who was already over seventy years of age.

When Nightingale visited the battlefront and saw the amazing work that Betsi had done, she changed her mind about a woman who she had previously considered only to be an irritant. She begged Betsi to stay on – after she had taken time away for a little rest – but Betsi refused. She knew her limitations, as well as her dislike of Florence Nightingale, and despite the repeated requests of the "Lady with the Lamp", she duly returned home

The author Jane Williams wrote a book about Betsi's life and adventures but Betsi did not live to enjoy the fruits of fame.

Worn out by her exertions in the Crimea, she died on 17th July 1870 and was, for many years, something of a forgotten heroine – even though she was one of a mere handful of men or women who ever dared challenge the redoubtable Florence Nightingale.

Some belated degree of recognition came in 2009 when the Betsi Cadwaladr Health Board was created to include the six local health boards along the North Wales coast. This is the largest health board in Wales, employing over 18,000 staff. Somehow, you feel, Betsi would be proud.

44 – The Welsh Whisky Galore!

As the rain fell and waves thundered and crashed onto the beach, women pushed bottles of whisky down the legs of their bloomers and hurried back to their houses. Children raced between the beach and the village pushing wheelbarrows full of alcohol while men battled with the waves to pull cases of liquor out of the water before the inevitable arrival of the Customs Officers put a stop to the jubilation.

It was a cold winter's night and a heavy sea was running, the waves driving in from the Atlantic with a ferocity that the people of the area knew only too well. It was pitch black, apart from a faint light at the western edge of Thorn Island, and all across South Pembrokeshire most honest folk were happily tucked up in bed. But not all of them. Just off shore from the village of Angle a strange and bizarre drama was unfolding.

Thorn Island at the mouth of Milford Haven, scene of the Welsh Whisky Galore in 1894. The waterway and the island look peaceful enough here but when the wind howls off the Atlantic Ocean they can be a death trap.

The fort on Thorn Island at the mouth of Milford Haven had been built to protect nearby Pembroke Dockyard. It was one of several similar forts around the coast, Palmerston Follies as they were known. They had been given the nickname in honour, dubious as it might be, of the Prime Minister who had commissioned them and carried on building them after the war with the French, which demanded their building in the first place, had long since ended.

But whatever its original purpose, on the night of 30th January 1894 this tiny island was the scene of a maritime disaster when the schooner *Loch Shiel,* bound for Adelaide with what now seems to be the lethal cargo of 100% proof whisky and gunpowder, was wrecked on its rocky fringes.

Unable to make headway against the wind and tide, the *Loch Shiel* found herself being pushed towards land. With a grinding roar, she struck the rocks below Thorn Island just before midnight and it soon became clear that, no matter how hard the sailors worked, the ship's pumps could not keep out the water.

A mattress soaked in paraffin was lit on deck as a distress signal and the Angle lifeboat was launched. She quickly arrived on the scene and passengers and crew were taken off in an effective, almost exemplary rescue.

The real story of the *Loch Shiel*, however, was only just beginning. As the ship began to break up under the brutal battering of the waves, her cargo started to float inland. Never being averse to a little judicious looting, the Angle people arrived at the beach to see what they could find and soon realised what was contained in the wooden cases that were being steadily washed steadily towards them.

Long before the Customs Officers arrived on the scene, dozens of cases and bottles of whisky were "spirited" away by the locals. With the powers of officialdom now beginning to scour the village for the contraband, many of the bottles were stacked into alcoves in the cottage walls and simply boarded up and then papered over, ready for drinking once "the heat had died down". It didn't always happen – some lay hidden for so long they were forgotten and only came to light fifty years later when houses were being renovated!

There was a tragic side to the story, however. Three men died, two of them drowned while trying to recover whisky from the sea, the other from alcohol poisoning after drinking the 100% proof whisky.

It could so easily have been many more – several locals were apprehended by the Customs as they carried home what they believed to be whisky but were, in fact, cases of gunpowder. The thought of what heat from the fire might have done to the gunpowder, sitting hidden in a fireside alcove, hardly bears thinking about.

History does not record the party that the villagers of Angle enjoyed in the wake of their Whisky Galore but scuba divers still sometimes pull up bottles from the site of the wreck. And they say it's still drinkable!

45 – The Life and Death of John Hughes, Ironmaster of Yuzovka

Imagine the scene. It is 1870 and a hundred burly iron workers from Merthyr Tydfil, Dowlais and Rhymney suddenly find themselves in the wilds of Czarist Russia, in the area we now know as the Ukraine. The culture is strange, the climate is brutal, the people are distant and cold. Everything is vastly different from anything they have ever encountered in the Welsh valleys and along the coastal industrial belt of their now very distant homeland.

Those intrepid and, probably, rather tentative iron workers were accompanying a fifty-five year old Welsh industrialist and entrepreneur who had just won a contract from Imperial Russia to provide armour for a new naval fortress at Kronstadt. His name was John Hughes and within the space of ten years the township he established around his new ironworks would be christened Yusovka (or Hughesovka as it is sometimes called) in his honour.

John Hughes was born in Merthyr in 1815, his father being an engineer in the Cyfarthfa Ironworks. John followed in his father's trade at Cyfarthfa before taking up senior positions in Ebbw Vale and at the Uskside Foundry in Newport.

Such was the success of Hughes at Uskside that he was given a seat on the board of the company and when, in due course, he moved on to become Director of Millwall Engineering and Shipbuilding in London, his company quickly earned a massive reputation for the making of composite ships – vessels that had wooden framework overlaid with iron armoured plating.

In 1870, thanks to the worldwide reputation of his company, the Russians decided that this was the man they needed to build their new fortress. It was too good a chance to miss and Hughes obviously loved a challenge. A challenge this would certainly be as there was, quite literally, nothing waiting for him in Russia, just an empty wilderness and a burning desire to succeed.

Undaunted, excited even, Hughes sailed to the Ukraine with eight shiploads of equipment and a team of specialist iron workers and miners from his native land. As well as the fortress they were to build and run a new metallurgical plant and rail factory. It was the beginning of a dynasty.

The town that was created alongside the ironworks – originally intended just for the Welsh iron workers – quickly grew as Russians and other nationalities flocked to what was soon seen to be a thriving community.

From bare and basic beginnings it soon boasted hospitals, schools, churches, bathhouses and tearooms. Soon there was even a town fire brigade, something that was sorely needed as, to begin with, the new town was made solely from wood. And the driving force behind the new community was John Hughes who planned, designed and oversaw much of the development.

The Imperial Russian government was delighted with the work of John Hughes and his team, a team that was soon augmented by Russian workers from various parts of the Czar's Empire, all keen to learn the iron trade from the Welsh specialists.

However, Hughes was nothing if not a driven man and it is quite possible that he pushed himself too far and too fast. On 29th June 1889, while on a visit to the Imperial city of St Petersburg, he died suddenly and unexpectedly. He was 74 years old but no one considered him as anything but a young man of great vigour and energy.

The company was taken over by Hughes's four sons and the work continued, the ironworks expanding several times in the years before the First World War. Then, in 1917, came the Bolshevik revolution. Although the works continued to prosper, most of the Welsh workers – or the descendents of the Welsh workers – soon left the country.

Despite this, the company and the ironworks prospered under Communist control and although, since 1969, the town has been known as Donetsk, it was, for many years, one of the largest metallurgical centres in the USSR. And it all came from the efforts of one amazing Welsh industrialist – John Hughes of Yusovka.

46 – To Be a Sailor Boy

The Press Gang, giant East Indiamen battling up the Channel, sailors with girls in every port – we all have vastly different visions of our naval heritage. In the bustling ports of the country and at the seaside resorts that they loved, Victorians would have been reminded of this heritage every second of the day. In one way in particular.

A hundred years ago old wooden battleships lay moored and wallowing in many of the rivers and estuaries of Wales. These were the training ships of Victorian Britain, places where boys whose dreams of a life at sea could actually become reality – if they survived the harsh regimes, the crippling cold, poor food and diseases like enteric fever and rickets.

A whole range of training ships was available, from ships for the poor to those provided for the sons of the wealthy and privileged.

Reformatory Ships were designed to cater for hardened delinquent boys, some as young as ten. Such boys could expect brutal treatment on board these vessels, often being doused with cold water, beaten with birch rods that left permanent scarring and enduring solitary confinement for the slightest misdemeanour.

The Royal Navy refused to take boys from Reformatory Ships, believing them to be beyond redemption, whatever treatment the ships had given. But there were other aspects of sea-faring open to them and if they survived five years of such brutal treatment, employment in the Merchant Navy or in the fishing fleets of Britain must have seemed like paradise.

There were no Reformatory Ships in Wales but there were two on the Mersey, at Liverpool and Birkenhead, and these regularly took boys from places like Cardiff and Newport.

However, Industrial School Ships, for boys who might easily become delinquent if they were not helped, did exist in Wales.

Firstly there was the *Havannah*, an old and famous ship that had escorted Napoleon into exile on St Helena in 1815. She lay beached on the mud close to Penarth Road in Cardiff, having been established as an Industrial School and Training Ship in 1861. Cardiff, then, was a bustling and vibrant seaport, full of sailors from around the world. Life was cheap. As the reformer Mary Carpenter wrote in the *Cardiff and Merthyr Guardian*:

> "If such a school is needed in any part of the world it certainly is at Cardiff."

The second Welsh Industrial School Ship was the *Clio*, moored off Bangor Pier in 1877. A small Racoon Class corvette, conditions on board were always cramped and her history is full of recorded instances of bullying – even, on one occasion, an untimely death, when one of the boys was bullied, beaten and eventually killed by bigger, tougher lads.

The Training Ship *Clio*, seen here moored off Bangor Pier

Wales also saw two training ships of slightly higher calibre. The *Indefatigable* had started life as an Industrial School Ship on the River Mersey at Liverpool but soon went "up market," taking children of needy but honest parents.

In 1941 the *Indefatigable* was moved to the Menai Straits to avoid German bombing and in 1944 became shore based at Plas Menai where the establishment ran as a Public School until the end of the twentieth century.

The other, perhaps more famous, training ship in Wales was the *Conway*, designed to train boys for positions as officers in the Merchant Navy.

Moored in the Menai Straits, she may well have been intended for officers but conditions on board were no better or easier than on the Reformatory and Industrial Ships. After operating for nearly a hundred years, *Conway* was wrecked while being towed to Birkenhead for repair in April 1953, lying for many weeks on the foreshore with her back broken and all hope of repair long gone.

Training Ships have now disappeared from our coasts. But the *Foudroyant* – a privately owned training ship that was once moored in Milford Haven – is still afloat. Based at Hartlepool, she is open to the public as one of the oldest sailing ships in the world. A visit must surely give some indication of the conditions boy trainees had to endure a hundred years ago.

47 – Evan Roberts and the 1904 Revival

In these days of easy commercialism and clear scepticism in all matters theological, it is hard to conjure a picture of Wales in 1904 and 1905 when, for many months, the whole country was gripped by a religious revival that swept like a tidal wave across the land. The man at the head of that revival was a young trainee minister called Evan Roberts.

In the autumn of 1904 Evan Roberts was 26 years old. He came from Loughor, some six or seven miles west of Swansea, having been born in 1878. He left school at the age of eleven to work down the coal pit with his father. It was a job he kept for 12 years before becoming an apprentice to his uncle, a blacksmith, in Pontarddulais.

Evan Roberts might have been, in the eyes of the public, an ordinary labouring man but he had been a committed Christian for many years. He regularly attended Moriah Calvinistic Methodist Church in Loughor where he was a renowned Sunday School teacher. Indeed, his whole life consisted of work, studying the Bible and contemplation and consideration of the words of God.

For many years Roberts had felt a "calling". Always a spiritual man, someone who would sometimes stay up all night engaged in deep communion with God, he knew that his life was not meant to be lived down the pits or at the blacksmith's forge. And so, in 1904, he enrolled at a Grammar School in Newcastle Emlyn to help improve his educational standards, prior to taking up a place at theological college.

Just two weeks after arriving at the school Evan Roberts took part in a Convention at Blaenanerch and there underwent what he called "a fresh baptism of the spirit". Instantly the young man from Loughor was transformed into a Revivalist who felt instructed by God to share his vision and his views with others.

On 29th September 1904, at Moriah Church in Loughor, he rose to his feet to make four pronouncements. He wanted people to confess their known sins, to get rid of any doubts they might have about the significance of God in their lives, to obey the Holy Spirit and to confess publicly that they would follow Christ. He continued to preach and urge people to join him.

By the end of the first week 60 people had repented their sins and Roberts promptly undertook a whirlwind tour of the Welsh valleys. At Revivalist meetings in each of the mining towns, Evan Roberts and his brother Dan preached and a small choir of five girl singers accompanied them. The movement began to gather real force and impetus and within a year over 100,000 converts had joined the church – thanks to Roberts and his party.

Quite simply, a firestorm had hit the churches. Roberts appealed to young and old alike – but particularly to the young who were in desperate need of direction in their lives. He gave them fire in their bellies and hope in their hearts. As Evan Roberts and his followers journeyed all over Wales the effects of his "missionary journeys" were astounding.

Quite apart from the converts who had suddenly found purpose in their lives, there were also clear social benefits. Crime rates dropped wherever he came to preach and huge numbers of people gave up alcohol. Pubs, hotels and inns all over the country reported major losses in trade.

And the movement spread. Soon cities in England were holding Revivalist meetings and religious fervour even spread across the Atlantic to the United States of America.

Of course, it could not last. A movement like the 1904 Revival depended on one man, one individual, for its success. A charismatic leader was essential but by 1906 Roberts was ill. He had, almost literally, worked himself into the ground and duly suffered a physical and emotional breakdown. He went to Leicester to recuperate and in his absence the Revivalist Movement lost its way and its momentum.

Evan Roberts accepted it as God's way. As he said:

> "The movement is not of me, it is of God. I would not dare to try to direct it."

Nevertheless, the Revival had been an amazing experience for everyone who had seen it or taken part. Evan Roberts lived on for another forty-five years, dying on 29th September 1951. His 1904 -Revival had been, probably, the last great outpouring of Christian values and belief. Who knows when there might be another.

48 – The Zulu Wars

There has always been something of a debate about the Anglo-Zulu Wars of 1879, particularly with regard to the numbers of Welsh soldiers involved in the Battle of Isandlwana and at the defence of Rorke's Drift. Often legend and romance have taken over from reality. If you have ever watched the film *Zulu,* for example, you could be excused for thinking that the action at Rorke's Drift was carried out by a Welsh male voice choir led by Stanley Baker, Michael Caine and Ivor Emmanuel!

Arguments have ranged widely across the spectrum – there were few Welsh soldiers present; the British regiments were predominantly Welsh-based. And so on.

From looking at the regimental rolls it is clear that a Welsh-based regiment bore the brunt of the fighting, particularly at Rorke's Drift, and from the letters and statements of many of the soldiers themselves it is equally apparent that the events on the African veldt in 1879 would come back to haunt the men for many years to come.

It was a war that should never have been fought. The British government had little stomach for a fight with the Zulu tribes. Britain was already engaged in costly campaigns in Afghanistan and the thought of further expense in South Africa was not one to be taken lightly.

However, administrators out in South Africa, particularly the new British High Commissioner Sir Henry Bartle Frere, saw the Zulus as a threat to British control and determined on war in order to create a federation of states rather like the one in Canada. For their part, the Zulus had no reason to allow their traditional homelands – areas rich in coal and other minerals – to be taken from them.

The Zulu king, Cetshwayo, was presented with a deliberately harsh ultimatum – lay down your arms by 12th January 1879 or face invasion. The concept of "the warrior" was central to Zulu culture and Bartle Frere knew that the ultimatum could only be ignored.

On 12th January, the very day the ultimatum expired, Lord Chelmsford, military commander in the region, took his column across the Buffalo River into Zululand. Prominent in the column of marching men was the 24th Regiment of Foot.

At the time of the Anglo-Zulu War, the 24th Regiment was known as the Warwickshires, the area from which they had originated, but by 1879 their home base was at Brecon and within a few years the regiment would change its name to The South Wales Borderers.

About 30% of the regiment was Welsh, the 24th regularly recruiting in Breconshire, Radnorshire and Monmouthshire. Soldiers were even recruited from places like Caernarfon. Using his native Welsh tongue, Private Owen Ellis wrote to his parents in North Wales on the eve of the campaign:

> "The 2nd Battalion of the 24th arrived here about 4 o'clock on Sunday afternoon and the 1st Battalion welcomed them by treating them to bread, tea and meat – if Cetshwayo does not come to terms we will demand his lands, kill his people as they cross our path and burn all his kraals or villages."

A few weeks later Owen was to write his last ever letter, on 19th January 1879:

> "It is now Sunday afternoon, just after dinner, and I am sitting on a small box to write you these few lines. We are moving off at 6am tomorrow. I only wishes (sic) they would finish this row so that I might go to some town and see something else besides grassland. Dear father, perhaps I shall have to go a long time after this without writing, so don't be worried if you don't hear from me."

Owen Ellis was one of over 1300 soldiers massacred by the Zulu impi at the Battle of Isandlwana on 22nd January. There were many reasons for the defeat – Chelmsford had split his force, taking half of them away to search for the Zulu army; nobody knew where the Zulus actually were; no effective defensive line had been created; the front line of soldiers was too extended and too far away from ammunition. Whatever the reasons it was one of the worst defeats ever suffered by British colonial troops and many of the dead were young Welshmen. And we should never forget, of course, that close on 4000 Zulus also died in the battle.

The rugged and unmistakable outline of Isandlwana, scene of the greatest Colonial defeat for British troops – many of them were Welshmen.

When Lord Chelmsford and his half of the invasion force returned to Isandlwana they were met by an horrific sight, as Private William Meredith of Pontypool noted in a letter to his brother:

> "I could describe the battlefield to you – the sooner I get it off my mind the better. Over a thousand white men lying on the field, cut to pieces and stripped naked. Even the little boys that we had in the band, they were hung up and opened like sheep. These are the Pontypool boys that got killed in battle: Alf Farr, Dick Treverton and Charley Long."

For some of the men the sight was just too horrible. Some, like Henry Moses, also of Pontypool, began to reflect on their future and on what had brought them to this:

> "I know what soldiering is now. We are in fear every night and have had to fight the Zulus. Dear father and sisters and brothers, goodbye. We may never meet again. I repent the day that I took the shilling."

The Zulus next target was the hospital base at Rorke's Drift. The story of the heroic defence is too well known to require re-telling here. The action took place over the night of 22nd/23rd January, approximately 4000 Zulu warriors attacking the hospital and mission station that was defended by just over 100 men. And it is clear that a large number of these defenders were Welshmen. It was a desperate struggle that saw nearly 500 Zulu casualties (for the loss of just 17 soldiers of the 24th Foot). As Private Henry Hook, decidedly not the drunken reprobate portrayed in the film *Zulu*, was to later write to his mother in Monmouth:

> "Every man fought dearly for his life. We were all determined to sell our lives like soldiers and to keep up the credit of our regiment."

The result of the battle was a victory for the 24th and several of the Welsh soldiers, men who survived the action, now lie buried in their native soil. John Fielding, who won the Victoria Cross for his bravery that night (one of 11 won during the battle), is buried at Llantarnam. He had enlisted under the name John Williams as he was technically under age and his parents did not approve of him taking the Queen's shilling.

John Fielding lived to a ripe old age, dying in 1932, but others, like Robert Jones, another VC winner, suffered from headaches and nightmares for the rest of his life:

> "I found a crowd (of Zulus) in front of the hospital and coming into our doorway. We crossed our bayonets and as fast as they came up to the doorway we bayoneted them until the doorway was nearly filled with dead and wounded Zulus. I had three assegi wounds."

Unable to cope with the stresses and strains of life after Rorke's Drift, at the age of 41 Robert Jones gave up the struggle and killed himself.

49 – Ernest Willows, Welsh Pioneer Airman

There is a pub named after him at the bottom end of City Road and even a High School in the Splott area of the capital but how many of us know anything else about Ernest Thompson Willows? He was an amazing man but these days is someone who has been rather overlooked in the pantheon of early aviation heroes.

Ernest Willows was born on 11th July 1886 in Cardiff. Educated at Clifton College he left school at the age of fifteen in order to train as a dentist. But he had a fascination with aviation – in particular with ballooning – and this was the area where he proposed to make his name.

It was not just Willows. In the early years of the twentieth century it seemed as if the whole world was obsessed with flight. It was an age of experimentation and invention, almost every red-blooded young man with a yen for science and adventure wanting to get into the air and fly.

Ernest Willows built his first rigid balloon – Willows 1 as he soon named it – in 1905. He was just 19 years old at the time and flew the machine from East Moors to the east of Cardiff. The balloon , its envelope or gas bag made out of silk, was powered by a motorbike engine and, on its first flight, was in the air for over eighty minutes. Willows piloted the machine from a gondola suspended below the bag and, in all, made six dramatic flights, the longest of them lasting for over two hours.

Willows quickly designed and built a new, improved version of his balloon called, appropriately enough, Willows 2. In this craft he made flights to places like Cheltenham and London and even became the first man to make a powered flight across the Bristol Channel. On 4th June 1910 he landed Willows 2 on the open field in front of Cardiff's City Hall where he received an enthusiastic welcome from the people of his home town.

When Willows came up with another new airship (Willows 3) he decided to fly it to France. This was a hazardous undertaking and although he duly became the first man to make an airship crossing of the English Channel at night, the flight was not without adventure.

Firstly Willows lost his maps over the side of the gondola and then there were problems with the craft's envelope. He was forced to land at Douai in order to make repairs to the silk bag before taking once more to the air and arriving in Paris on 28th December 1910.

After this experience Willows decided to stay on in Paris for a few weeks. He celebrated New Year by making several circuits around the Eiffel Tower in his miraculous machine, much to the delight of the spectators on the ground.

When, in 1912, the intrepid Welsh aviator sold his next balloon, Willows 4, to the Royal Navy it brought him the huge sum of one thousand pounds. Willows used this to build a spherical gas balloon and, then, Willows 5, in which he was soon offering joy rides to the public over the city of London.

However, with the outbreak of the First World War, the age of the air balloon as a commercial and military machine was rapidly coming to an end. Rigid wing aeroplanes began to assume a position of dominance in the minds of military planners.

After some initial success, the eventual failure of the giant German Zeppelin airships – billed, initially, by the German High Command and by the British press as the new "terror weapons" – seemed to underline this fact and Ernest Willows spent a relatively quiet war, designing and building early versions of the barrage balloon – something that only really came into its own during the Second World War – in his home town of Cardiff.

None of this diminished the enthusiasm of Willows for ballooning and for airships. However, on 23rd August 1926 he was tragically killed when his new balloon crashed at Hoo Park in Bedford. Two passengers who were with him in the gondola died at the same time.

Willows was a man of great enterprise and skill. He was, perhaps, a man out of his time. Had he been born twenty years before he could have enjoyed far more fame and success in the field of ballooning.

If he had been born twenty years later he might have become one of the great aircraft designers of all time. As it is he remains a largely forgotten figure, his name living on in the shape of a public house and a large High School in the city that he called home.

50 – Welsh Seaside Piers

Penarth Pier, shown here in the grip of a high tide and an autumn storm.

Seaside piers – ice cream cones and candyfloss, pleasure steamers and elegant Victorian ladies in crinolines and parasols parading down the decking. The picture is an attractive one. And Wales, like so many coastal regions of Britain had – and still has – more than its fair share of piers.

The last fifty years of the nineteenth century saw over 50 piers built around the British coast – pier mania, if ever it was. The 1871 Bank Holiday Act gave workers the right to certain "Bank" holidays and seaside towns quickly realised that, with more and more people pouring into the resorts, a pier was an essential centre of entertainment.

Minstrel troupes, dancers, boats and paddle steamers – the piers had it all. And of course, one of their greatest attractions was that ladies and gentlemen could stroll along the decking or sit in deck chairs at the end, just contemplating the sun, sea and sky. To all intents and purposes they could have been at sea but with one vital ingredient missing – no sea sickness!

When, in 1893, there was a delay in building the pier at Penarth the suggestion was made that the town should buy a second-hand pier from Douglas on the Isle of Man. There was much support for the idea. As the editor of *The Penarth Observer* wrote:

"Any pier would be better than none – we do trust that

another season will not be allowed to pass without one of some sort being erected, but we understand that the one proposed will be altogether superior to the condemned one at Douglas."
(Quoted in *Penarth Pier* by Phil Carradice)

The editor needn't have worried. A year later Penarth got its new pier and the second-hand one went, instead, to Rhos-on-Sea where it was set up to rival the new brand pier at Colwyn Bay.

The owners of pleasure steamers, in particular the Campbell family who ran The White Funnel Fleet in the Bristol Channel, also quickly realised the possibilities that piers offered their businesses. The Bristol Channel, with the second highest rise and fall of tide in the world, often left miles of mud and shingle when the tide receded. Piers that stretched out into the Channel would make landing and embarking so much easier.

Even at high tide, in the early days of the steamers passengers who wanted to go ashore often had to be carried on the backs of brawny sailors. With the advent of the pleasure pier this was a practice that was quickly ended.

Piers, of course, were commercial enterprises. Pleasure steamers were charged to dock – the charge being conveniently passed on to the customers – and anyone who visited to stroll along the planks above the waves was also charged for the privilege.

The longest pier in Wales was built at Llandudno but the most famous of them all was probably the one at Aberystwyth. This pier was designed by Eugenius Birch, the doyen of pier builders, as renowned in his own field as Capability Brown and Josiah Wedgwood. Opened on Good Friday 1865, just a few months later over a hundred feet of this, the finest pier in Wales, was washed away in a storm. Its truncated inland half remains in the town to this day.

As the Aberystwyth disaster shows, the piers were not always as sturdy as they seemed. The risk of fire was an ever-present concern. Colwyn Bay Pier was destroyed twice by fire, once in 1922 and again in 1933. Penarth Pier was partially burned out in 1931 and then suffered the ignominy of being rammed by a cargo ship, the *Port Royal Park*, in 1947.

Sometimes it was simple neglect that caused the problem. Tenby's pier, the Royal Victoria Pier, was a regular port of call for the pleasure steamers of the Bristol Channel but little was done to maintain it and it was eventually demolished in the late 1940s.

These days people can still walk out along piers like Penarth, Mumbles, Aberystwyth and Llandudno. They are an essential part of our social heritage, as enjoyable now as they were at the end of the nineteenth century.

51 – The Treason of the Blue Books

In the year 1847 the British government commissioned a report into the state of education in Wales. Not, in itself, such a momentous event but when the remit of the report was widened to include a study of the morals of the Welsh people it resulted in a furore that still rumbles on to this very day. Never can a civil service document have excited such passion as the 1847 Report of the Commissioners of Enquiry into the State of Education in Wales.

The Report, known throughout Wales as The Treason of the Blue Books (all government reports being bound in blue covers), was the result of a motion put forward a year earlier by William Williams, the Welsh MP for Coventry. He was particularly concerned about the lack of opportunity for poor children in his homeland to gain knowledge of the English language.

Kay Shuttleworth, secretary to the Council on Education, wrote the terms of reference for the Enquiry in October 1846 and it is clear, right from the beginning, that education was only one of the government's concerns. From the 1820s to the late 1840s Wales had appeared to be the centre of major discontentment.

In the 1820s there had been serious disturbances in Tredegar and Merthyr while in Ceridigion there had been a virtual war over the issue of land enclosures. From 1839 to the mid 1840s the Rebecca Riots caused mayhem across mid and south Wales while in 1939 the Chartist march on Newport provoked huge worry and concerns in government circles. Clearly Wales needed to be looked at in some detail and to English officials and civil servants it seemed highly likely that, in the far west, sedition was being planned – in the Welsh language.

There is no doubt that education for poor children in Wales was inadequate – it was also inadequate in England! There was a desperate requirement for quality education for all, education that would, the government felt – long before the Commissioners reported back – be predominantly in the English language. And central to this was the need to provide trained teachers.

The trouble came when the extra clause was slipped into the terms of reference, to look at the morals and behaviour of the Welsh people. Quite why this was inserted is not clear – certainly it could have little impact on the educational element of the Report who could and would educate their charges efficiently.

Since the predominance of Welsh was one of the main reasons for the report it would have been reasonable to expect the Commissioners appointed to oversee the inspections to have a knowledge of the Welsh tongue. Not so. Commissioners Lingen, Simons and Vaughan Johnson spoke no Welsh, were not even educationalists and, importantly, had no experience of the type of fervent non-conformity to be found in Wales.

A number of assistant commissioners were appointed and, by and large, these were the men who toured the schools, towns and villages. The questions they asked, the passages of literature (usually the Bible) they required children to read and the problems that were meant to be worked out in the head of each child were framed in English – many of the school teachers had difficulty understanding them, let alone their pupils.

The non-conformist Sunday Schools (where teaching and such education as was offered were in Welsh) were, in the main, praised in the Report – the ordinary day schools were certainly not. It was hardly surprising when pupils were expected to work out subtraction problems such as "Take 1799 from 2471," in their heads, answer expected within a few seconds. And the condition of the schools themselves was under equal scrutiny :

> "The school is held in the mistress's house. I shall never forget the hot sickening smell which struck me on opening the door of that low, dark room in which 30 girls and 20 boys were huddled together."
> (From "The Blue Books," 1847)

But there were other issues, other matters of concern for the Commissioners. They had also been charged with making a study of the moral state of the country and it was a task they were happy to carry out. When looking at the morals of the nation the Anglican vicars, many of whom felt isolated and apart from the parish in which they lived, were quite content to help out with comments that were little more than a little condemnatory:

> "It is difficult – to describe in proper terms the state of the common people of Wales in the intercourse of the sexes. I believe the proportion of illegitimate children to the population in Anglesey, with only one exception,

> and that is also in Wales, exceeds that in any other county in the kingdom."
> (From "The Blue Books," 1847)

When the Report was published it was scathing and sweeping in its findings. Welsh children were poorly educated, poorly taught and had little or no understanding of the English language. They were ignorant, dirty and poorly motivated. Welsh women were not just lax in their morals – many of them being late home from chapel meetings! – they were also non-conformist lax! So to reinforce the power of the established church and to make English the required mode of teaching and expression in schools is the main thrust of the Report.

Howls of protest were to be expected – and they duly came. Yet the sobriquet "Treason of the Blue Books" did not come into popular usage until seven years later when Robert Jones, Derfel, wrote a play called, in Welsh, *Brad y Llyfrau Gleision* – in English *The Treason of the Blue Books*. Derfel's play opens in Hell where the Devil decides that the Welsh people are too good and too godly and are becoming more godly by the hour thanks to the influence of non-conformity. He promptly hatches a plan to bring down this pure and godly people.

The play has shaped the opinions of many, even at this late stage. Many people believe the findings of the Enquiry had been more or less decided before the Commissioners even began their work. One thing is clear, however. The Report gives us a fascinating snapshot of life in the 1840s and for a brief while, at least, it did manage to put education high on the political agenda.

Ultimately, however, the Treason of the Blue Books helped to create a view, a rather smirking and disrespectful view, of Welsh morals that has lasted until the twenty-first century.

And it is questionable whether or not the Welsh language has yet managed to break free from the disapproval of the Commissioners. Publication of The Report of the Commissioners of Enquiry remains one of the most important moments in Welsh history.

52 – Vivian Hewitt, First Man to Fly the Irish Sea

Everybody knows the names Louis Bleriot and Charles Lindbergh, early aviators who were, respectively, the first men to fly the English Channel and the Atlantic Ocean.

But how many people have ever heard of Vivian Hewitt? He is now a forgotten hero, his fame lost in the glory of later aviation feats. And that is a shame because the year 2010 marked the 45th anniversary of the death of this incredibly brave man, who in 1912 became the first person to fly across the Irish Sea.

Vivian Hewitt was not Welsh by birth but when he was still a young boy his family moved to North Wales to live. It was a seminal moment in his life and Vivian spent his formative years wandering happily along the Welsh coastline.

In 1909, inspired by Bleriot's crossing of the Channel, he rented a shed on a field – hardly an airfield – in Surrey and taught himself to fly. He returned to Wales and bought a strip of land near Rhyl. It was just a strip of grassy land but, very grandly Hewitt called it Voryd Aerodrome and, after 1911, it became his base for flights around the North Wales coast.

Hewitt had always harboured the ambition to be the first man to fly across the Irish Sea. He thought that he had lost his chance when, early in 1912, it was reported that another pioneer aviator, Leslie Allen, was in Holyhead on Anglesey, preparing to make the flight.

Then came the news that Allen had crashed into the sea and drowned. Tragic as that might be, Hewitt knew that he still had a chance to fulfill his dream.

He took off from Voryd Aerodrome and flew to Holyhead, ready to make his attempt. Despite terrible weather conditions, Hewitt finally set off on 26th April 1912. Halfway across the Irish Sea he ran into a thick bank of fog. Almost immediately he became disorientated, not knowing if he was climbing or diving in his flimsy Bleriot monoplane.

It was a terrifying situation, one that could have caused a lesser man to panic. He had no compass, no navigational aids of any sort, and only managed to survive because he had previously noticed the shadow of the sun on his wings. Remembering the angle, he adjusted his flight path so that he was able to continue flying on the same path as before.

Vivian Hewitt battled on and eventually he sighted land, the Wicklow Mountains – he was ten miles off course. He flew north, following, first, Dublin Bay and then the River Liffey and crossed Dublin at a height of just 2000 feet.

To the dismay of spectators on the ground below, a pocket of what we would now call turbulence nearly flipped over his plane, its speed having been drastically reduced by the wind, and he was more than pleased to land in what he later learned was the famous Phoenix Park.

Hewitt's flight had lasted an hour and a half, rather longer than he had originally estimated, mainly due to the fact that his encounter with the fog bank had pulled him several miles off course.

Hewitt was lionised in Dublin, hundreds of eager spectators coming to see his aeroplane as it stood on the grass in Phoenix Park. For a modest man he coped with the adulation very well. He made no comment on the fame and adulation he was given but did, briefly, write in his logbook the simple statement, "Passage very rough and the wind strong and the machine took some handling."

Vivian Hewitt was undoubtedly one of the great early pioneers of flight. He returned to Wales and lived on Anglesey until the ripe old age of 77, dying in 1965 when travel across the Irish Sea had become commonplace. Yet his remarkable achievement should never be forgotten, the first man to fly across the Irish Sea.

53 – Postcard Mania in Wales

Most people who are interested in history like to get in touch with the past – by reading about people and events, by visiting historical sites, by looking at and holding artefacts.

Artefacts don't just exist in museums and these days it is easier than you ever thought possible to find a piece of the past, by collecting bits of paper that were worth only a few coppers when they were first made – the humble postcard.

No matter what aspect of Welsh history interests you, there is a postcard that relates to it. Topographical cards showing places like Llandrindod Wells, Aberystwyth or Cardiff in the early years of the twentieth century; cards about poets and musicians such as Hedd Wyn and Joseph Parry; cards showing great sporting events like Wales playing the All Blacks; they are all out there, waiting to be collected, waiting to provide a fascinating glimpse of the past.

The "Golden Age of Postcards" was between 1900 and 1914 when thousands – probably millions of the things – were bought and posted by virtually everybody in the country. For those fourteen years there was something of a "postcard mania" when everyone collected cards of some description and kept them in albums or boxes.

What this has meant is that those cards are now readily available for today's historians to study and even buy. They tell us what it was like in Llandudno on August Bank Holiday. They give us a vivid and compelling picture of life in the coal mines, toiling in the steel works or working night and day on the railways. They show us the humour of the ordinary, average Welsh man or woman. They show us our forefathers and are an invaluable aid to the social history of our country.

And, of course, they tell us what life was really like in those days before television and radio, before the iPod and the mobile phone.

"One of the main reasons for postcards coming into fashion in the 'Golden Age,'" says Peter Godding in an article in *Cardtalk*, the magazine of the South Wales Postcard Club, "was the efficiency of the postal service. The collections were regular and sorting of the mail continued at all times. Cards bearing Christmas Day postings are not uncommon and there were several deliveries per day. Mail addressed locally would often be delivered within a few hours."

Over the last thirty or forty years postcard collecting has become a hobby to rival stamp collecting. Postcard Fairs are regularly held, all over the country, offering enthusiasts the chance to buy cards about their chosen areas.

Most decent museums and even many libraries now hold collections. But there is nothing to quite rival assembling your own collection. Whether your interest is in Welsh piers, Norman castles or village churches, you can put together a fascinating archive – how much you choose to spend is up to you. Some cards cost a phenomenal amount, *Titanic*-related cards regularly fetching hundreds of pounds. But your local church or town hall is hardly likely to be in that league.

The postcard was, indeed, once 'humble.' Not any longer. Now it is a valuable social and historical artefact.

54 – Disaster on the Snowdon Mountain Railway

A trip up Mount Snowdon, the highest mountain in England and Wales, is an experience not to be missed. For those who are fit enough, and have the energy, there are several possible routes and the sense of achievement when the summit is finally reached should never be underestimated.

However, for those who would prefer it, there is another way – a trip on the Snowdon Mountain Railway. The highest railway in Britain, this rack and pinion narrow gauge line stretches 4.7 miles from the terminus in Llanberis to the summit of the mountain, 3560 feet above sea level. It has always been, and remains, an engineering masterpiece but the running of the railway has not always been without incident.

The idea of constructing a railway up the mountain was first proposed back in 1869 but there were objections from people living in the area as many believed such a railway would only serve to spoil the scenery of Snowdon and the surrounding countryside. The plan was therefore dropped for several years.

Only when a rival proposal to build a line from Rhyd Ddu to the summit was put forward did the original idea re-surface. The Snowdon Mountain Railway and Hotel Company was quickly formed and the possibility of a summit railway now became a genuine option.

As the railway was to be built on private land no Act of Parliament was required in order to give permission for the railway – as was the case with all other railway projects. And, at the same time, the line would not come under Board of Trade regulations and control.

Once the plan was hatched and the Company formed , building began. It was a quick project, the line being constructed between December 1894 and February 1896, a period of just over twelve months. This meant working through two winters when conditions on Snowdon were nothing less than horrific. Nevertheless progress was excellent, the first locomotives being delivered in the summer of 1895 and, with the lines being laid from Llanberis upwards, they were used to transport raw materials up the mountain.

As the railway was planned or designed, there were a number of stations on the route where passengers could join or leave the train but, inevitably, most people were aiming for the summit. The work did not come cheaply. The final cost of the project was in the region of sixty-three thousand pounds. These days that figure would translate to somewhere in the region of eight million pounds.

A few days before the official opening of the line, contractors ran a locomotive up to the summit. A boulder that had fallen from the rock face actually derailed several of the engine's wheels but workmen quickly manoeuvred these back onto the track and everything was put in place for opening day.

This occurred on 6th April 1896 and two trains were duly dispatched for the summit. The ascent was fine but on the way down disaster struck.

The first engine, "LADAS," driven by William Pickles from Yorkshire, ran into difficulties a few hundred yards above Clogwyn Station. The load was simply too great and Pickles had great difficulty keeping the engine under control. The wheels jumped the rail, the train thereby losing its ability to brake, and it simply ran away.

Pickles applied the handbrake but it did not work. With the train now gathering speed downhill Pickles and the fireman decided that discretion was the better part of valour and leapt off the footplate. The engine continued its descent, going faster every second until, failing to negotiate a left-hand curve, it toppled and fell gracefully over the side of the mountain.

Climbers coming up the mountain towards Clogwyn later commented that they thought they saw a huge boulder falling towards them. In fact it was the runaway engine that was now tumbling down the mountainside.

Back on the track things did not get any easier. The two carriages, now minus their engine, also gathered speed until, at last, the automatic brakes slammed on and they came to a graceful halt. Unfortunately, one passenger, a Mr Ellis Roberts of Llanberis, had witnessed the driver and fireman leap off the engine and, with the carriages in which he sat also out of control, he thought he would do the same. Unfortunately, he was not so lucky as William Pickles. He smashed his head on the rocks and debris alongside the line, being so badly injured that he died a few days later.

As if all that was not enough, the second train now appeared on the scene. Weather conditions were poor with mist over the top half of the mountain and there was no way news of the disaster could be sent to the second train. It ploughed into the rear of the carriages at Clogwyn, de-railing the engine and passenger accommodation. Luckily, there were no serious injuries.

At the subsequent inquiry the cause of the disaster was stated to be settlement of the track and excess speed due to the weight of the engine and its carriages. Weight for all future trains would have to be reduced. It meant ordering lighter carriages and the introduction of a "gripper" rail system to improve safety. The line up Snowdon was closed for just over twelve months, no more trains running until 9th April 1897.

Since then the Snowdon Mountain Railway has run continuously, even though passengers were not allowed to travel to the summit during the Second World War. Full service was reintroduced in 1946 when, interestingly, due to fuel shortages old army boots were burned in the boilers of the engines. Ex-servicemen on the trains would probably have thought it an appropriate end to those hated pieces of footwear.

The famous Summit Cafe – for some a boon, for others an eyesore – was demolished in 2006 and a new building, called Hafod Eryri (roughly translated as The High House of Snowdon) opened in the summer of 2009.

Passengers still regularly travel up the line, enjoying the engine and the trip as much as the scenery. It remains one of the great Welsh experiences for any visitor but most of them will never have heard about the disaster that befell the line on opening day.

55 – Ivor Novello, the Welsh Nightingale

Most people have, at some stage in their lives, listened to the song "Keep the Home Fires Burning". It was one of the most popular tunes in the trenches during the First World War and still has the ability to bring a pang to the throat or a tear to the eye. Yet how many people realise that this sentimental ditty was just one of dozens produced by a remarkable young Welshman who, at the time, was serving in the Royal Naval Air Service?

Ivor Novello was born in Cowbridge Road East in Cardiff on 15th January 1893. The house, just to the west of the River Taf, was called Llwyn Yr Eos (Grove of the Nightingales) and can be identified by a plaque on the front wall.

Ivor Novello's real name was David Ivor Davies. He was the son of Clara Novello Davies, a noted and renowned singer and teacher who had also founded the Welsh Ladies Choir. His father, David Davies, was by comparison a fairly staid and ordinary man – he was a tax collector. Under his mother's influence the young Ivor Novello was performing at eisteddfodau across the country from an early age and, in due course, went on to Magdalene College, Oxford, to study for a degree.

However, the outbreak of war brought a sudden and dramatic change to his lifestyle. In 1916 Ivor joined the RNAS and began training as a pilot. It has to be admitted that he was not a very good airman. He completed his training on dual control aircraft but proceeded to crash during his very first solo flight. Given a second chance he did exactly the same again and, as a result, the RNAS grounded him for the duration of the war.

Ivor Novello's real contribution to the war effort, however, was not as a pilot but as a song writer. He was producing songs like "Keep the Home Fires Burning" and "We'll Gather Lilacs" on a regular basis and in 1917, while still serving with the RNAS, his show "Theodore and Co" was produced on the West End. It was the hit of the year. He went on to write, produce and act in many more stage shows over the coming decades.

Ivor Novello wrote all of the music for his shows and, as an accomplished dramatist in his own right, some of the librettos as well. By and large, however, the lyrics for his touching and catchy songs were written by his collaborator Christopher Hassall – a man who later went on to write the standard biography of the poet

Rupert Brooke.

When the war ended in 1918 Novello was discharged and immediately took up a career on the stage and in the emerging film industry.

This was the age of the silent movie and for a while he specialised in films with an underworld theme. The first of them was called *The Rat* and was a huge success. He also made two silent films for Alfred Hitchcock, the most famous being *The Lodger*. It was a film that Novello was to remake, this time as a talkie, in 1933.

Interestingly, Ivor Novello also wrote the dialogue and screen play for the first *Tarzan of the Apes* talkie – although quite how much talking was involved is not really clear!

Despite his film work, despite several stints in Hollywood, Ivor continued to write and produce stage hits in Britain. The most notable of these is probably "The Dancing Years" which was produced in the West End in 1939.

Despite his well known homosexuality – something to which the police seemed to have turned a blind eye – Novello was one of the early stage and screen idols. He was loved and idolised by people from all over the world and the depiction of him, and the way people felt about him, in the recent film *Gosford Park* seems to be a fairly accurate or realistic portrayal

One of his gay relationships was with the war poet Siegfried Sassoon. It was not an easy or comfortable liaison and did not bring happiness to either man. For a brief period, however, Sassoon was fascinated by Novello – even though, while serving in the trenches on the Western Front, he had once vowed to find and shoot the man who had written "Keep the Home Fires Burning".

Another of Novello's relationships was with the actor Bobbie Andrews. Novello may not have suffered from the repressive and draconian homosexuality laws of the time but he did serve an eight-week prison term during the Second World War – for misuse of petrol coupons.

In 1951 Ivor Novello died suddenly, from a heart attack, at the relatively early age of just fifty-eight. He had continued to write songs and musicals almost to the moment of his death. Cremated at Golders Green Crematorium, his ashes were, appropriately enough, scattered under a lilac bush.

Nowadays he is commemorated in the annual Ivor Novello Awards when the British Academy honours outstanding contributions to the performing arts. There is also a recently unveiled statue to him outside the Millennium Centre in Cardiff, a fitting tribute from his home town to a man of great skill and talent.

56 – The Oldest Golf Clubs in Wales

In October 2010 many visitors from "over the pond" came to the Wales, most of them for the first time, in order to watch the Ryder Cup. But as well as watching golf they also took time to play on what are now regarded as some of the finest golf courses to be found anywhere in Britain.

There are some wonderful golf courses in Wales, the like of which most Americans, with their manufactured and manicured courses, had never seen.

There are mountain top courses where the wind and rain batter at the fairways all year long. There are glorious stretches of links where deep heather and gorse are augmented by sand traps that sometimes feel a mile deep. And there are parkland layouts, beautifully manicured and a delight to the eye. There are nine hole courses, eighteen hole courses – even an eleven hole course. There are courses that are flat, courses that often seem best suited for mountain goats. There is, quite literally, something for everyone.

The oldest golf club in Wales? Tenby links, seen here in the 1950s, has held dozens of important championship events and is still regarded as one of the best courses in the country.

But which is actually the oldest course in Wales? Golf in the Principality is a relatively new sport, even though the game itself has been around for centuries.

Tenby is usually reckoned to be the oldest Welsh golf course, the club being founded in 1888. However, it is on record that the

Mayor of Tenby once actually adjourned a court in order to play a round of golf on the sand hills to the west of the town. That was in 1875 so it is clear that golf was being played in the area long before the club was actually founded.

Tenby, now, is one of the best and most atmospheric courses in the country. It borders the Bristol Channel and has magnificent views out towards Caldey Island – and, on a fine day, to far off Lundy as well. You won't find many trees here but you will find plenty of gorse and sand traps and you only have to play it once to realise why Tenby has hosted so many major championship events.

Borth and Ynyslas, on the shores of Cardigan Bay just north of Aberystwyth, also lays claims to be the oldest club in Wales. Although that accolade has been given to Tenby, members at Borth claim that their club was in existence by 1885, some three years earlier.

The course at Borth and Ynyslas sits on the margins of a fine sandy beach, being set amongst the deep and rolling sand dunes of Ynyslas. It is one of the most picturesque of all Welsh courses but when the wind blows in off the Irish Sea – a wind that sometimes seems to blow vertically and horizontally at the same time – it is undoubtedly one of the hardest.

The other course with claims of longevity is Pontnewydd, just five or six miles away from the Ryder Cup venue of the Celtic Manor, on the fringes of Cwmbran.

Club members and local historians insist that the club was up and running by 1875, well before either Tenby or Borth and Ynyslas. It is, however, unfortunate that there is no documentary evidence to prove this claim, one way or another. Members will tell of players coming by train, then walking or driving in horse pulled brakes that were lined up in ranks outside the station, waiting expectantly for the journey up to the course.

Pontnewydd is now an eleven-hole mountainside course. Players tackle the existing holes and then play seven of them again, albeit from different tee positions. It is a quirky and unusual golf course, one you will either immediately fall in love with or hate on sight.

Wherever you choose to play in Wales, history sits waiting to greet you. All of the clubs have wonderful old photographs on their walls, showing past members and events – and they all have staff and players who are more than happy to sit and talk about past glories and the state of the game today.

The modern courses of Wales, places like Celtic Manor and the Vale of Glamorgan, are fine tests of golf and are well worth a visit. But if you want to experience the history of Welsh golf then take time to visit places like Tenby, Borth and Ynyslas and Pontnewydd. You will not be disappointed.

57 – The Blackening of Wales – Wales and Industrialisation

Modern visitors to Wales, people from places like the USA and the Far East, men and women who know little or nothing about Welsh history, heritage and culture might be excused for thinking that many, if not most, of our valleys were never industrialised at all. They might have heard stories about hymn-singing Welsh miners on their way to and from the pit but where, they might ask, is the evidence?

Such is the extent of modern day de-industrialisation that in many places visitors invariably see only green hills and rugged mountains – the coal mines and iron works, the copper mills and the steel works, that once littered the valley floors might never have existed at all. And yet, as those of us who live in Wales know only too well, nothing could be further from the truth.

And yet it did not begin that way. Until the middle years of the eighteenth century it is fair to say that industry, where it existed in Wales, was decidedly small-scale with a mixed and part-time work force. Throughout the seventeenth and eighteenth centuries, men, women and children would labour in the fields, on the farms, during the summer months and at harvest time. But when agrarian needs were not so pressing they would move across to the coal mines and iron foundries to earn their daily bread.

The first reference to coal in the country came in 1248 but it was not until many years later, in 1695, that Humphrey Mackworth began to use the fuel to smelt copper in the area around Neath. It was a slow beginning of a process that took years to reach fulfilment.

Two of the driving forces behind the industrialisation of the country were war and a desire for improved social environments. Conflicts such as the costly Napoleonic War demanded new weapons – guns and cannon – while better wages and living conditions in cities like London meant that there was an urgent need for more luxury goods.

From the 1850s onwards, as the Industrial Revolution began to throw up an unprecedented demand for iron, copper and tinplate, people began to realise that Wales might be the answer to difficulties such as supply and demand.

By the middle years of the 1860s the Mona and Parys copper

mines on Anglesey had been created and were employing no fewer than a thousand men – and women. The slate mines and quarries of Blaenau Ffestiniog and Llanberis gave employment to thousands more. When a copper smelting plant was established at Swansea it created a community that soon became known as "Copper Kingdom", its sailing ships travelling across the world with cargoes of the precious metal.

When, at the end of the nineteenth century, investors like John Guest and Richard Crawshay saw that all the materials needed to produce iron – iron ore, limestone, coal and wood – were readily available in Wales, there was a rush to the valleys of South Wales. By 1820, just five years after the end of the Napoleonic War, under the leadership of men like Crawshay and Francis and Samuel Homfray, the ironworks of Wales were producing nearly half of all Britain's iron exports.

And coal? Until the 1830s Welsh coal had been used principally as household fuel. Then came the steam ships of the Royal Navy and the burgeoning of the new railway system. And coal, its production and delivery, became an industry in its own right rather than being simply an extra, an adjunct to the smelting of iron and copper.

In 1850 the Rhondda Valleys, both Fach and Fawr, boasted fewer than 1000 inhabitants. By 1910 the coal rush – for such it was – had increased the population of the two valleys to over 150,000. People worked long hours in difficult and dangerous conditions. Wages, although no doubt better than would have been earned on the farms of the rural homelands, were low and many workers were paid in tokens that were only redeemable in the company truck shop – where prices were, of course, very high.

Almost overnight the valleys turned black from smoke and soot and grime. The angular arches of pit winding gear and huge mountains of slag littered the hills. Houses lined the valley sides and the delicate infrastructure of the communities was simply not able to cope.

Poor housing, awful sanitary arrangements, dreadful living conditions – they brought diseases such as cholera, typhoid and typhus. And, of course, it was inevitable that, sooner or later, discontent would be sure to raise its head.

The Merthyr Riots of 1831, which saw the death of more than a dozen rioters and the arrest and subsequent execution of Dic Penderyn, were just the tip of the iceberg. Bands of men, known as

Scotch Cattle, were soon roaming the valleys and hillsides, supposedly punishing those who sided with the mine and foundry owners but, in reality, stealing, looting and bullying anyone with whom they did not agree.

The Chartist movement had begun in the 1830s. It was a movement dedicated to social and political reform and its members were committed to achieving fair representation for all working men. Their six point charter of 1838 demanded, amongst other things, the vote for all men over the age of twenty-one, a secret ballot and payment for all MPs. In Wales, with the appalling conditions of the industrial areas clear for all to see, the Chartists were well supported.

On 2nd November 1839 Welsh Chartists planned a march to Newport. Men came from all the industrial areas of south-east Wales and at the town's Westgate Hotel, with feelings running high on both sides, there was a full-scale clash between the marchers and soldiers. Twenty men were killed and the Chartist leaders – John Frost, Zephaniah Williams and William Jones – were arrested and later transported.

Welsh opposition to the mine owners and the drive to improve conditions in the mines, factories, steel and iron works of the country did not end with the failure of Chartism. Men and women continued to fight for their rights but, despite terrible conditions, it was not until the nationalisation of most of Britain's industries in the years directly after the Second World War that working conditions really improved.

As the twentieth century drew to a close it was clear that the industrial valleys of Wales were also nearing the end of their working life. Coal seams were petering out, cheaper fuel was available from abroad and the iron and steel industries were but a shadow of their former selves. Visitors to the now green-again valleys might applaud the process but it is difficult to know if those who spent their lives underground or working in the blast furnaces would agree or not.

58 – Whitchurch Hospital

Most people in Cardiff know of Whitchurch Hospital. The huge and elegant buildings lie alongside one of the main roads into the city and while many of those who come to Cardiff to work or shop may never have entered the place they will certainly have seen the buildings from the upper deck of their bus or from their cars.

The idea for Whitchurch Hospital, formerly the Cardiff City Mental Hospital – or Cardiff City Asylum as it was sometimes known – was first mooted at the end of the nineteenth century. Even though it did not formally open until 1908, Whitchurch was undoubtedly a product of Victorian Age thinking and medical practice. Arguably this is something from which it has suffered ever since.

There was very little provision for people who were mentally ill during the early part of the nineteenth century, mental illness being closely associated – in the minds of the general public – with poverty and crime. The wealthy could afford to hire doctors or nurses for members of their family who had mental health problems, could even place them, if necessary, in private hospitals or asylums.

For the poor, however, there was little provision – just a small scattering of public hospitals or, inevitably, the workhouse. As the Industrial Revolution changed the make-up of society the problem of vagrancy and of paupers with significant mental health problems became significant. As a result county asylums were created, places where "pauper lunatics," as they were known, could be conveniently herded – and forgotten.

Cardiff saw an enormous rise in its population as the nineteenth century unfolded. In 1851 it was 18,351 – twenty years later that figure had risen to nearly 40,000. Inevitably there was a growing need for mental health provision. By the closing years of the century there were 476 Cardiff residents "boarded out" in the Glamorgan Asylum, a further 500 to 600 being held in hospitals in places as far away as Chester and Carmarthen. The need for a specific provision, for the town of Cardiff alone, was clearly apparent.

Whitchurch Hospital took ten years to build and cost nearly three hundred and fifty thousand pounds, an amazing sum of money for those days. The main hospital building covered nearly five acres and was designed to accommodate 750 patients. Banded brickwork and the 150 foot water tower dominated the site which consisted of ten hospital blocks, five for men and five for women. A self-contained farm was to be an important feature of the hospital, providing food and therapeutic work for patients.

There was much controversy over this farm which was originally intended to cost some four thousand pounds. The plan was castigated in the Welsh press, cartoonists in particular having a field day. The proposed plans were soon altered and the cost reduced to just two thousand.

The first medical superintendent was Dr Edwin Goodall and the first patients arrived at the doors of the hospital on 1st May 1908. By the end of June over 600 patients, mostly male but a large contingent of women as well, had been admitted.

Within a few years Whitchurch Hospital had acquired a remarkable reputation at the forefront of mental health care. This was down to the quality and commitment of the nurses and medical staff and, in particular, Dr Goodall. Concern for the welfare of patients went beyond simple custodial care and there was a very real desire to help people with their problems and, if possible, to assist them in taking a place in society, however limited that involvement might be.

During the First World War the hospital was run by the military as a general medical and surgical institution, its patients having been disbanded to other mental hospitals around the area. In 1919 things returned to normal, patients returning from their enforced stays elsewhere.

During the 1930s the hospital constantly received good reports, a high proportion of the nurses being qualified in both general and mental health nursing. Until the late 1930s, however, those nurses worked a sixty-hour week, living in the hospital where their private and social lives were stringently governed and controlled.

Research into the causes and treatment of mental illness was always a part of Dr Goodall's programmes and Whitchurch was well equipped with laboratories and research equipment. The number of patients discharged from Whitchurch was better than almost every other similar institution in Britain – and after-care was equally as important to Goodall and his team.

During the Second World War part of the hospital was again in use by the military. Eight hundred beds were handed over to the military, making Whitchurch the largest emergency services hospital in Wales. Unlike the First World War, 200 beds were retained for civilian mental health patients. Over the six years of conflict British, American and, occasionally, even German soldiers were treated there for wounds and for the psychological trauma of modern warfare.

On 5th July 1948, however, the hospital was taken over by the Ministry of Health as the National Health Service came into existence. The hospital continued to be well-used throughout the 1960s and 70s, even though many were now questioning the viability of large, outmoded institutions such as this.

Care in the community was considered preferable in many cases and, as a consequence, Whitchurch came to be seen by many as little more than a last ditch resort where containment was more important than care and treatment. It was an emotive point and the hospital retained many ardent supporters. Even so, it was clear that the physical environment – perfect, perhaps, in the nineteenth century – was somewhat limited for modern medical needs.

In the early years of the twenty-first century plans were made to close the old hospital with its echoing corridors and looming shadows. A combination of day care, specialised provision at nearby Llandough Hospital and a small, purpose-built set of wards on the site of the old Harvey Jones Adolescent Unit would be in the best interests of patients and staff.

However, financial restrictions prevented the plans from going ahead and, for the moment at least, Whitchurch Hospital survives. It has a wonderful history – the task now is to make sure the future is equally as impressive.

59 – The Great Storm of 1908

The Bristol Channel is used to storms. Winter or summer, they come sweeping in from the west, hammering at the coastline and playing havoc with shipping in the western approaches. But no storm was more severe or more dangerous than the great storm of September 1908.

The storm began on the afternoon and evening of Monday 31st August when the wind strengthened, the barometer fell and torrential rain squalls began to hit the coast.

By morning of 1st September the gale had increased to hurricane proportions, winds reaching upwards of 80 and even 90 miles an hour. All day the storm raged, winds only finally dying away on the Wednesday morning. What they left in their wake was a trail of destruction and disaster that stretched right along the coast of south Wales, from Pembrokeshire in the west to Newport and Gwent in the east.

At places like the steelworks in Port Talbot huge cranes had been toppled as if they were made from a child's building blocks while trees were uprooted and roofs ripped off the tops of buildings all across the country. Roads were flooded or blocked by fallen debris while the main railway between Cardiff and Swansea closed because of trees across the line.

Huge hailstones battered at the windows of houses along the coast and enormous flashes of lightning lit up the sky. Terrified farm animals ran for shelter and nobody moved outside their homes unless it was an essential journey.

As might be expected, however, it was at sea that the most dangerous problems occurred. With waves of nearly 60 feet many captains wisely decided to remain in port but for those on voyage when the storm broke there was little option but to brave the elements and trust to fortune.

The Helwick lightship, moored out in the entrance to the Channel, was so badly damaged by the waves that her crew was forced to radio for help. The Tenby lifeboat carried out a courageous rescue, the lifeboat men rowing for over six hours to bring the stranded sailors to shore.

The barque *Verajean*, running up the Channel before the storm, was caught and driven ashore on to the rocks of Rhoose Point. Luckily the crew all managed to escape and the unlucky sailing ship lay on the sand and shingle for many weeks, dismasted and abandoned, a sudden and unusual tourist attraction for the Vale of Glamorgan people.

A more serious disaster took place on the sands near Margam when the *Amazon* was also driven ashore. Captain Garrick had tried to ride out the gale, anchored off the Mumbles headland, but at 6.00 a.m. on 1st September the *Amazon*'s cables parted and the ship was driven eastwards. At 8.00 that morning she was thrown up, bow first, onto Margam Sands. Pounded by the waves, the stricken vessel swung sideways on to the storm.

Several men tried to swim ashore but most of them were immediately lost in the huge seas. When the Port Talbot Lifesaving Company arrived on the scene only two men were left alive on the ship. Twenty-one of the crew were drowned, including Captain Garrick and five young apprentices. There were just eight survivors.

When the storm finally died on the morning of Wednesday 2nd September, it was time to count the cost. Luckily there had been no fatalities on land but damage to houses and industrial plants amounted to a sum well in excess of two hundred thousand pounds. These days that figure would be in the millions. Dozens of small boats had been tossed up on to shore by the waves and many people had been cut and injured by falling slates and trees.

The Great Storm of 1908 was one of the worst natural disasters to hit the South Wales coast. Small wonder people, when witnessing such fury, would thank their stars they were safe on land and whisper to themselves "God help sailors on a night like this."

60 – The Tonypandy Riots of 1910

November 2010 saw the 100th anniversary of the Tonypandy riots. These short-lived but violent events have always held a special place in the memories of most Welshmen, attracting legends and stories, truths and half-truths in equal number – Churchill sent in the troops, Churchill held back the troops, Willie Llewellyn's chemist shop was deliberately spared by the rioters, the shop was off the main street and so the rioters missed it and so on. As with most folklore, the truth probably lies somewhere in between all the various stories and reports.

The riots took place on the evenings of 7th and 8th November 1910 and involved violent clashes between striking miners and members of the Glamorganshire Constabulary – backed up by both the Bristol and the Metropolitan police. Despite what many believe, involvement of the military was, at most, rather limited.

In 1910 the Cambrian Collective opened a new seam at their Naval Colliery in Penygraig. It was decided that a test period to determine the rate of production or extraction should take place, an investigation involving a small corps of just 70 miners.

When they saw the results the company promptly declared that the men had worked far too slowly – a strange allegation considering that miners at that time were paid by the tonnage of coal they produced rather than an hourly rate. They had, quite simply, no reason to work slowly.

Whatever their motives, the mine owners now instituted a lock out and closed the mine, not just to the 70 "test men" but to all 950 workers at the colliery. The miners responded by calling a strike and when the Cambrian Collective duly brought in strike-breakers from outside the area it was clear that serious trouble lay ahead.

The South Wales Miners Federation (the Fed as it was universally known) balloted workers on 1st November and within days 12,000 men from all the Cambrian pits were out on strike.

Lionel Lindsay, Chief Constable of Glamorganshire, knew that his resources were stretched as there was already a month-old strike at pits in the nearby Cynon Valley and as soon as the Fed announced the strike he was appealing to the War Office for troops to help with the crisis. None were sent but by Sunday 6th November extra policemen from forces like Bristol had been brought to the Rhondda Valley.

By now the only pit left working was Llwynypia Colliery where strike-breakers were maintaining the pumps and other machinery.

On the evening of 7th November striking miners surrounded the colliery and, as tempers began to boil, stones were thrown. Fierce hand to hand fighting with the police took place and after several baton charges the miners were pushed back into the square at Tonypandy. There they were charged by mounted police from Cardiff and there were several injuries on both sides. Lionel Lindsay again asked for military backup.

Winston Churchill, as Home Secretary, was not desperately keen to send in troops, feeling that people on the spot were perhaps over reacting. He ordered that soldiers, despatched by the War Office from barracks at Tidworth, should be held back, kept in readiness at Cardiff and Swindon.

Churchill did agree, however, to send in an extra 270 mounted and foot officers from the Metropolitan police force. These men, along with those already in the Rhondda, were exceptionally hostile to the miners, acting, apparently, more like an army of occupation than regular detachments of police. Their attitude served only to infuriate the striking miners.

Further rioting occurred on the evening of 8th November and this time the windows of many shops in the town were smashed. A large number of the shops were then looted by men already at the end of their tether. It was reported that miners (and their wives and children) were parading around Tonypandy in clothes taken from the shops but that a general air of festivity seemed to abound.

Detachments of the Metropolitan Police arrived in the town square just before 11.00 p.m., several hours after the rioting began – they had been busy protecting the homes and property of the mine owners – and by then the disturbances had, in the main, already subsided. Whether or not their presence in the town centre could have prevented the rioting is something that remains unknown.

It was not until the following morning, on 9th November, that soldiers eventually arrived on the scene, patrolling without serious incident in the Tonypandy and Llwynypia areas. There were clashes in Porth and Pontypridd but, generally speaking, the soldiers were – at the time, at least – more welcome than the policemen from outside the valley.

The strike ground on for several months although the violence of the initial riots in Tonypandy was rarely repeated – even though one miner died, it was said, from injuries inflicted by a police baton during an altercation. The strike finally ended in August 1911, twelve months after the lock-out that had begun it. It left bitter scars on the community of the Rhondda, particularly as the miners were forced to return to work after agreeing to a paltry figure of just two shillings and three pence per ton of coal extracted.

Churchill was, until his dying day, reviled by many as the man who sent in the troops – even though he had, initially, held them back. The fact that he and other members of the government were even prepared to consider their use was, in the eyes of many, his worst failing.

And Willie Llewellyn's shop? Unlike so many of the businesses in Tonypandy it was left untouched by the rioters. One theory was that Willie, as a Welsh rugby international and a member of the famous 1905 side that had beaten the All Blacks, was a much-loved son of the town – and nobody was going to damage his business. It remains a matter of conjecture.

61 – The Welsh Super Tramp

Many people – in Wales, England, all over the world – are familiar with the lines:

> "What is this life, if full of care
> We have no time to stand and stare."

Some may even be able to quote the whole poem. Yet probably very few realise that the man who wrote the poem ("Leisure" to give the proper title) was someone who spent several years as a tramp or hobo, riding the freight trains of America. Often he would be forced to beg for a crust, just to survive, and sometimes he would deliberately get himself caught for minor crimes, knowing that a warm prison cell was far preferable to freezing to death on the barren prairies of the American mid-West. He was also a Welshman.

W H (William Henry) Davies was born in Newport on 3rd July 1871, being brought up by his grandparents in the Church House Inn in the Pill area of the town.

He was a wild, ungovernable adolescent whose school life came to a rather abrupt end when he was fifteen years old. Caught shoplifting, he was sentenced to twelve strokes of the birch. Thereafter his grandmother decided it was high time William left school and the young tearaway was apprenticed to a frame maker in Newport.

Davies found the job boring and had a hankering to try life in America. He quit his job and worked his passage across the Atlantic on a cattle boat. This was in 1893 and for the next six years he wandered across America, jumping the freight cars on the American railroads and scratching a living how and when he could. His descriptions of these adventures, later published as *The Autobiography of a Super Tramp*, make fascinating reading and , even if they are only a quarter true, give an insiders view of life on the road in the final years of the nineteenth century.

Needing to earn a little money, W H Davies crossed and re-crossed the Atlantic several times, working on cattle boats – and once with a cargo of sheep. It was an experience he vowed never to repeat and commemorated the trip in a poem called simply "Sheep". He wrote:

"They sniffed, poor things, for their green fields,
They cried so loud I could not sleep:
For fifty thousand shillings down
I would not sail again with sheep."

In 1899 disaster struck. Heading for the gold fields of the Klondike, Davies slipped while trying to jump a train at Penfrew, Ontario. His leg was crushed by the carriage wheels and later had to be amputated below the knee. For the rest of his life he wore a wooden leg. It was a useful begging tool but sometimes it caused more than a little confusion.

Soon after he achieved fame as a writer he somehow managed to break the leg. Fellow poet (and fellow Welshman) Edward Thomas drew a sketch or diagram and asked the local carpenter to make a new one. Decorum prohibited him saying what the contraption actually was and when Thomas received the bill it was made out for "a curiosity cricket bat".

After his accident W H Davies returned to Britain where he "lived rough" in doss houses and hostels for several years. He had always been an avid reader and now took to composing poems in his head, only putting them down on paper later, when his fellow inmates had gone to bed. They had to be simple in style and format, otherwise he would never have remembered them, and it is by this simplicity or straightforward style that he is now remembered.

He borrowed money and typed up his poems, hawking them from door to door in the style of old ballad makers. When the enterprise failed he burned the sheets in a fit of temper. Within a short period of time, however, Davies had managed to borrow a lump sum from his allowance – a pension given to him by his grandmother, something he kept well hidden from the other tramps – and paid for a book to be published.

This book, *The Soul's Destroyer*, was well received, Davies taking the unusual step of sending copies to well-known people and asking them, if they liked it, to send him half a crown in return. Among those who sent money were the journalist Arthur Adcock and the famous playwright George Bernard Shaw.

Within months W H Davies was being lionized by the literary elite of Britain, his poems praised for their simplicity and refreshing beauty. A tramp-poet was certainly unusual but people were also quick to see that there was real talent and skill in

Davies' deceptively simple creations. Soon his poems were appearing in the influential anthologies of the Georgian Poets, most of them, like "Leisure," praising the wonders of nature.

Among his friends were people such as Rupert Brooke, Edward Thomas and Joseph Conrad. Thomas even rented a cottage for Davies, close to his own home in Sevenoaks, Kent – no more doss houses for W H Davies.

The First World War destroyed the pastoral idyll of the Georgian Poets and cut away many of Davies' friends, men like Brooke and Thomas. By 1918 he was rather a lonely and forlorn figure but in 1923, to the amazement of everyone, he met and married Helen Payne. Davies wrote a book about their relationship, *Young Emma*, revealing – amongst other things – that she was actually pregnant when they met. The book was not published until after the deaths of both Davies and his wife.

W H Davies never returned to Wales to live. But he did move close. He and Helen rented a number of houses in various parts of the country before finally settling at Nailsworth on the English-Welsh border.

In 1938 he went back to Newport for the unveiling of a plaque on the wall of Church House Inn but by then he was already ill. It was virtually his last public appearance and in September 1940 he died, aged just 69 years. He would undoubtedly have said that it was a life well spent.

62 – Christopher Williams – Local Boy Makes Good

Take a trip to the Town Hall in Maesteg. Quite apart from the wonders of the building and the intricate clock mechanism high above the Hall, here you will find six startling paintings by one of Wales's greatest artists, the Maesteg-born Christopher Williams. They are on public view and they give a brief insight into the talent of a truly magnificent but now sadly neglected painter.

Christopher Williams was born in Commercial Street, Maesteg on 7th January 1873. His mother died when he was young and his father, Evan, dearly wanted Christopher to become a doctor. Christopher wanted none of it. An innate talent and visits to art galleries had convinced him that his future lay in art. There was considerable conflict between the two men, Christopher later claiming that he had deliberately failed exams in order to forestall his father's ambitions for him.

And so an artist he became. He studied at the Royal College of Art and at the Royal Academy School and, to begin with at least, it was a severe financial strain for the young man. Despite Evan's thwarted aims, he was obliged to support his son for several years. He was rewarded with success when, in 1902, Christopher's painting "Paolo and Francesca" was hung in the Royal Academy. A portrait of Evan himself followed the year after. Despite his opposition to his son's chosen career, Evan must have been proud.

In 1910 Christopher was invited to become a member of the Royal Society of British Artists. Over the next ten years he exhibited nearly forty paintings in their gallery.

Real success, however, came in 1911 when he was commissioned to paint the investiture of the Prince of Wales at Caernarfon Castle. Following up this breakthrough he went on to paint many members of the Royal family. Lloyd George, MP for Caernarfon Boroughs and later Prime Minister of Great Britain, loved his work, calling him, "one of the most gifted of all Welsh artists".

It was Lloyd George who was responsible for what is arguably Williams's greatest painting. At the end of 1916 he was commissioned for a painting to commemorate the Welsh Division's attack on Mametz Wood during the Battle of the Somme. The Welsh Division (the 38th Division, to give it its proper title) had spent five days in the woods, engaged in fierce hand to hand fighting with the defending Prussian Guards before finally emerging victorious.

Christopher Williams visited the site of the battle and actually used soldiers who had taken part in the action to pose for him. The result is a startling and gripping depiction of war in all its horrors. Never had a bayonet charge been so realistically portrayed.

Indeed, so brutal and terrifying was the finished painting that, when it went on display in Cardiff, there was something of an outcry from people who had had their sensitivities jolted out of their stupor. The painting was withdrawn and did not see the light of day again until after the war. Now owned by the National Museum of Wales, it hangs in the museum of the Royal Welch Fusiliers in Caernarfon Castle, a suitable location for a magnificent and humbling piece of art.

Williams had become fascinated by Celtic and, in particular, Welsh traditions after a visit to Bangor to paint the portrait of one of the University professors in the years before the Great War. He was particularly fascinated by the Charlotte Guest translation of The Mabinogion. As he wrote to his wife Emily:

> "It is a goldmine untouched and full of Welsh fire and imagination."

The result was three outstanding depictions of female characters from the legend – Ceridwen (1910), Branwen (1915) and Bodewedd (1930). These, along with his painting of the Welsh attack on Mametz Wood, remain some of his strongest and most riveting works.

The painting of Branwen was presented to the Glyn Vivian Art Gallery in Swansea shortly before Williams's death in 1934. Three years later there was an exhibition for the centenary of his birth, paintings being shown at the Glyn Vivian, the National Museum in Cardiff and at Maesteg Town Hall. A plaque, commemorating his birth, was duly erected in Commercial Street, Maesteg.

Christopher Williams was an artist of consummate skill and ability. Visit the Town Hall in Maesteg – or even the Museum of the Royal Welch Fusiliers in Caernarfon – and see for yourself the range and talent of this sadly neglected artist..

63 – Captain Scott and the Cardiff Connection

Nearly everybody knows the name of Captain Robert Falcon Scott and the story of his doomed attempt to reach the South Pole. Scott may not have been the best of organisers – or always the most understanding of leaders – but there is no denying the heroism of the man and of his team of explorers and adventurers. And when he and his ship *Terra Nova* left Britain for Antarctica they did so from the port of Cardiff. It was 15th June 1910.

The Cardiff connection with the expedition owes much to the efforts of Scott's deputy or second in command, Lieutenant Teddy Evans. He had been to Antarctica with Scott and Shackleton on a previously unsuccessful attempt on the Pole and, like the other two, was determined to try again. Evans had distant and somewhat tentative connections with Wales, his grandfather probably having been born in Cardiff, and decided that Wales could play a valuable fund-raising role for a proposed expedition.

Evans was nothing if not energetic and managed to convince the editor of the *Western Mail* to give him publicity and back him in a bid to raise the huge sum of money that would be needed. Scott, meanwhile, was also attempting to gather together resources and money for his own second attempt.

Despite some initial scepticism on the part of Robert Scott, the President of the Royal Geographical Society managed to persuade the two men to join forces and unite in the forthcoming expedition. It was estimated that about sixty thousand pounds would be needed to make the attempt viable and as there was no central or government funding the money would all have to be raised by public donation. To work together was, therefore, the logical solution.

Teddy Evans spent much of 1909 in a never-ending round of lectures and speaking engagements in Cardiff and the surrounding area and by December of that year Cardiff ship owners and industrialists had pledged nearly £1500. Just as important was the offer of free towage and docking facilities for the Terra Nova, the ship that had been bought to transport the expedition members to Antarctica.

The *Terra Nova* left London on 1st June 1910, Teddy Evans in command, and managed to arrive in Cardiff twelve hours early. Despite this embarrassment for Cardiff's civil dignitaries, she tied up in Roath Dock on 10th June and immediately attracted thousands of eager well-wishers and sightseers.

On the evening of 13th June Scott and his officers were given a spectacular farewell dinner at the Royal Hotel in St Mary's Street, the rest of the crew having to make do with dinner in the less ostentatious Barry Hotel. Further fund-raising that night brought the total raised by the city of Cardiff to a staggering two and a half thousand pounds, more than any other city in Britain.

At 1 o'clock the next day, 15th June 1910, the *Terra Nova* was towed out of Roath Dock by the tugs *Bantam Cock* and *Falcon*. A huge crowd gathered on the dock and on nearby Penarth Head to watch her go while the paddle steamers *Ravenswood* and *Devonia* and a flotilla of small vessels accompanied her part of the way down the Bristol Channel. At her mast head the *Terra Nova* flew the flag and coat of arms of Cardiff and the Welsh dragon.

Very few of the excited spectators knew that the *Terra Nova* was already leaking like a sieve and serious flaws, even at this early stage, were beginning to emerge in Scott's organisation. They were faults that, two years later, were to lead Scott, Oates, Wilson Bowers and Petty Officer Evans to disaster on the Polar icecap.

Interestingly, considering the pomp and ceremony of the departure, Scott left the *Terra Nova* almost immediately after she sailed from Cardiff, disembarking with the Lord Mayor and other dignitaries who were on board, at the Breaksea Light. Scott returned to London for more fund-raising and expedition business and did not rejoin the ship until it reached New Zealand.

Captain Scott had promised that the *Terra Nova* would return to Cardiff. She did, on 14th June 1913 – virtually three years to the day after she had sailed – under the command of Teddy Evans. Lady Scott, the explorer's widow, and her son Peter were there to greet her.

A memorial lighthouse, erected by public subscription in 1915, still exists on Roath Park Lake, as does another memorial, a tablet or plaque in City Hall, unveiled a year later.

The Welsh connections with the expedition of Captain Scott were significant. Not only did Cardiff play a major part in raising the necessary funds, Petty Officer Evans – who died alongside Scott in Antarctica – was a Welshman. Considering the fact that Cardiff was then one of the most important ports in Britain, it seems an appropriate honour.

64 – Haggar's Cinema in Pembroke

Time was, every community in Wales had its own "fleapit" cinema, showing two features a week – and a special show on Sundays. They were the social centres of the town, people dressing in their best clothes and queuing round the block to get a seat.

Cinemas had their origins in the travelling picture shows, the bioscopes, which were part of the fairs that visited towns across the country in the late nineteenth century. The fairground traders and showmen, in particular those who ran the entertainments, were clearly early entrepreneurs of amazing ability and courage. As far as the bioscope owners were concerned, people like Harry Scard, Mitchell and Kenyon and, in particular, William Haggar, they not only showed films, they also made them.

William Haggar was a renowned musician and a showman, someone who had spent years working on the fairgrounds as a barker, running various entertainments and live shows. He had always been interested in photography and soon, as technology developed, moved on from "still" photography to moving pictures.

Beginning with short features such as *A Ride on the Mumbles Railway* and a film about the Boer War – actually shot in the Rhymney Valley – William Haggar saw a niche in the market and was soon producing early classics such as *The Life and Death of Charles Peace* and *The Maid of Cefn Ydfa*.

The Charles Peace film, incidentally, was about the notorious Victorian burglar and murderer and was shot in Pembroke Dock. It is the oldest extant British story film. Some of the scenes are exceptionally graphic, particularly the execution of Charlie Peace – there was clearly little censorship in those days. The films were shown on the fairgrounds where Haggar and his family continued to run their shows.

By the end of the First World War most bioscopes had stopped touring with the fairgrounds and found themselves permanent homes. The Haggar family created cinemas in places such as Llanelli, Pontardulais, and, in particular, the west Wales town of Pembroke.

William Haggar retired to Aberdare but the cinemas he had established continued to be owned and run by his sons. The Pembroke cinema was built and run by William Haggar Jnr, being taken over, in turn, by his son Len – always a family concern.

The author and members of the Haggar family inside the old cinema in Pembroke, now being used as a Night Club.

"We were always being brought in to sell tickets or ice cream," says Sarah Haggar, granddaughter of Len, "it was just something you did. Years later I became an actress and I think my love of the stage and acting came from my involvement with Haggar's Cinema when I was young."

Of course, it was not just a matter of showing films. The old tradition of the fairgrounds did not die easily and a night at a cinema such as Haggar's meant all kinds of delight for the people of Pembroke town. Ice cream, fruit and chocolate were just some of the items sold in the cinema shop – and in the aisles themselves. Selling ice cream in the cinema was not a job for the faint hearted as Len's daughter Dinah recalls:

> "One evening I was told to sell ice cream and the picture that night was a desert one, 'Lawrence of Arabia' or something like that. I didn't really know what to do so I just went up to people and said 'Do you want an ice cream?' Of course, on the screen there were miles of sand and nothing but blazing heat. I think we broke the record on ice cream sales that night."

Haggar's Cinema ran for many years, only finally closing in 1982, the last privately owned cinema in Wales and the building – once Pembroke's Assembly Rooms – now operates as a Night Club. William Haggar, always conscious of providing entertainment for the people, would probably have been pleased that although the cinema might have gone, the premises are still in use for entertainment of the public.

"I'm proud that my family were amongst the pioneers of British cinema," says Susan Haggar, great-granddaughter of William Haggar. "And also to think that they provided so much entertainment for so long to the people of Pembroke."

65 – Soldiers' Poetry of the First World War

Strange as it may seem, there was little attempt at censorship during the First World War, the monitoring of mail from the trenches invariably being left to the officers in charge of the various units. Thanks to things like the Pals Battalions many officers and other ranks came from the same towns, even the same villages, and Welsh soldiers often wrote home with stories of dreadful conditions and terrible battles.

Because of universal education, the First World War was a "literate" war. For the first time in history virtually all the soldiers who took part were able to read and write. And many of them, perhaps feeling sentimental, perhaps being shaken and appalled by what they had experienced, wrote poetry.

Welsh newspapers – national ones like *The Western Mail*, regional ones like *The Western Telegraph* and local ones like *The Penarth Times* – happily printed these poems in their pages.

The soldiers' poetry provided a vivid insight for readers back home. It was often little more than doggerel, not every Private being a latent Wilfred Owen, but it was invariably heart-felt. Take this example about the qualities of the British Tommy :

"He's the pepper and the mustard and the salt, you see,
And the Germans they will rue it.
He isn't only one of them but all the blessed three.
He's a perfect breakfast cruet."
(Anon)

Even when cynicism tinged the writing the Welsh papers were still happy to print the soldiers' efforts, like this one from a soldier complaining about the attitudes of those men who had steadfastly refused to enlist and who had remained at home, safe from bombs and bullets. The poem is ironic and heartfelt:

"Now out here things are different
And life is fancy free;
We have no butter on our bread
Or cow's milk in our tea.
And all we have to bother us
Are bullets, bombs and shells,

Bully beef and biscuits
And awful nasty smells."
(Private C Maunder – *The Penarth Times*)

The local papers in Wales had circulations in the tens of thousands, so the men who sent in their poems could be sure of a huge audience for their work – poets like Siegfried Sassoon or Robert Graves, who published in the "literary journals", were read by a mere handful, if they were lucky. And sometimes the efforts of these ordinary soldier poets – people's poets as they should be known – resulted in work of real quality:

"Above your graves no wattle blooms
Nor flowers from English dells,
You men who sleep uneasily
Beside the Dardanelles."

Thanks to the lack of censorship, the Welsh newspapers of the First World War provide a fascinating insight into the lives and experiences of front line soldiers. They are essential reading for anyone with an interest in either the war itself or in poetry.

"In Flanders Fields the poppies blow" – the eternal symbol of loss and suffering in the First World War.

66 – The Battle of Mametz Wood

The only real purpose of studying history is to ensure that we never repeat the mistakes of the past. So, rather than push them away, it is important to consider the effects and consequences of tragic conflicts like the First World War.

Over eight million men were killed in the conflict, 37 million wounded, and nowhere was the slaughter greater than on the Somme battlefield. In a battle that began on 1st July 1916 and went on to last for several months, the opening day of the offensive saw no fewer than 20,000 British dead, the worst casualty figures ever endured by the British Army in a single day.

As part of the battle the 38th or Welsh Division – Lloyd George's Division as it was sometimes known – was detailed to attack and capture Mametz Wood, the largest wood on the whole Somme battlefront. Nearly a mile wide and over a mile deep, Mametz was made up of thick trees and dense undergrowth. The wood was heavily fortified with machine guns, trenches and mortars and was defended by the well-trained and elite Lehr Regiment of Prussian Guards.

The 38th Division was comprised of soldiers from several Welsh Regiments, including the Royal Welch Fusiliers and the Welsh Regiment, young men who had been urged to enlist by the rhetoric of David Lloyd George and by the thought of exciting adventures. They were amateur soldiers, full of enthusiasm and courage but, like many of Kitchener's New Army who fought on the Somme, they were poorly trained, ill-equipped and badly hampered by the tactics of their commanders.

The Battle of Mametz Wood began on 7th July 1916. The wood was supposed – by the generals, at least – to be taken in a matter of hours. In the event the battle lasted for five days as the Germans fiercely resisted the assaults of the Welsh Division.

On the first day alone over 400 casualties were sustained. Among these were the Tregaskis brothers who came, originally, from Penarth. They had emigrated to Canada before the war began but, answering the call for volunteers, had returned to join up and fight for Britain. One of the brothers was shot in the head during the first assault; the other brother went to help him and was also killed. The two men now lie buried in one of the quiet but haunting cemeteries that mark the Somme battlefield.

Over the five days that the battle raged Mametz Wood was devastated as artillery shells fell continuously on the area. The wood was occupied by German troops and every yard of ground had to be fought for, neither side wanting to give up.

Fighting was furious – hand to hand combat in many instances, as men battled for every inch and yard of ground. The poet Robert Graves fought in the battle and, having gone back into the wood once the battle was finally over, wrote:

> "It was full of dead Prussian Guards, big men, and dead Royal Welch Fusiliers and South Wales Borderers, little men. Not a single tree in the wood remained unbroken."

When the battle was over and the wood finally captured, casualty figures for the Welsh Division amounted to 46 officers and 556 other ranks killed. When the wounded and those listed as "missing" – men blown to pieces or buried alive by shell blasts – were counted the total number of casualties was 3993. And that is not counting the numbers of German dead which must have been somewhat similar.

Yet despite achieving their objectives and driving the Germans back to their second line of defences the Welsh Division was never given real recognition for its achievement.

There was even an accusation that the Division had failed to advance with enough spirit – in other words the men of the Welsh Division were accused of cowardice. It was an accusation that was later withdrawn but it left a sour taste in the throats of many of the men who had seen comrades killed and mutilated in one of the most bloody battles of the whole war.

The First World War was a war of such horror and ferociousness that it has never quite left the consciousness of historians and writers. When men, like those of the Welsh Division, flocked to join up in the days and weeks after the declaration of war they had no concept of what was waiting for them on the killing fields of Flanders and the Somme. They confidently expected a quick victory – "Home by Christmas", they quipped.

Now there is no one left alive who actually fought in the war and it will not be long before the whole terrible conflict is consigned just to history books. The horror of the trenches and surviving the carnage of a battle like Mametz Wood will become simply dry facts, studied in schools and colleges. The essential message of the war – that such slaughter must never be allowed to happen again – will be forgotten. That is why Remembrance Sunday remains such an important moment in the calendar.

On that day, if on no other, take a few moments to remember the men – on both sides – who died at Mametz Wood.

The impressive memorial for the Welsh Division. Designed by Welsh sculptor Dave Peterson, it stands on the ridge overlooking Mametz Wood.

67 – Welsh Air Aces of the First World War

Most people know the name of the Red Baron, Manfred von Richtofen. He was the greatest "ace" of the First World War, a conflict where young men took to the air in flimsy, canvas machines and where a pilot's life expectancy could be measured in weeks rather than months. Richtofen destroyed eighty Allied aircraft before he, too, was eventually shot down and killed.

Wales also had many fliers in the war, people whose names are now long forgotten. They may not have enjoyed the celebrity of Richtofen but, like him, they were brave and fearless. And like him they all have stories needing to be told.

One of them, Lieutenant T Rees, who came from Cardiff, had a more than passing involvement with von Richtofen – he was actually the Red Baron's first victim. Rees was acting as observer for his friend L B F Morris on 17th September 1916 when their old and out-dated reconnaissance plane was spotted by Richtofen.

Despite the best efforts of the Red Baron, Rees kept him at bay for quite some time, loosing off bursts of machine gun fire whenever he came in range. It was an uneven contest, however, as superior speed and manoeuvrability eventually gave Richtofen a chance.

Richtofen finally attacked from below the British aircraft, – a tactic that would soon become his trademark. Rees was wounded and slumped to the floor of his cockpit. The British plane was now helpless and, after several more bursts of machine gun fire from the Red Baron, crashed behind German lines.

Richtofen landed to find some souvenirs amongst the wreckage. He himself wrote that Lt Rees was still alive in the wreck. However, as he lifted Rees from the smashed aircraft the young Welshman opened his eyes and, with a smile, died. Richtofen never forgot the courage of his first victim.

Arthur Rhys Davids was the son of a Welshman, even though he had been born in South London. A dashing and brave pilot, he joined the Royal Flying Corps in August 1916 and won the DFC (and Bar) and the MC before he and his aeroplane just disappeared on 27th October 1917.

Before that, however, Rhys Davids had managed to score many victories in aerial combat, one of them being over the great German ace Werner Voss – a man many considered to be braver and a better pilot than the great Manfred von Richtofen.

Wales's highest scoring ace of the First World War was Ira "Taffy" Jones. He was born just outside St Clears in west Wales in April 1896 and joined the RFC in June 1915, first as an observer/gunner and then as a pilot. After training he was posted to No 74 Squadron where he fought alongside the legendary Mick Mannock.

"Taffy" Jones scored 37 victories, six of them coming in an eleven-day period in 1918, a feat that earned him the DFC. And yet, Jones was not a great pilot. He often crashed on landing, a problem caused by poor depth perception – he had been lucky even to pass the medical to get into the RFC.

Ira "Taffy" Jones stayed on in what had now become the RAF once the war finished, retiring in 1936 after a career that had lasted twenty-one years – not bad when most of the men he had fought with had been killed long before. In 1939 Jones rejoined the RAF and flew again in the Second World War, a truly indomitable and remarkable figure.

He was not just a fighter pilot. He wrote one of the great books about First World War flying, *King of Airfighters*, the life of Mick Mannock. He unveiled the war memorial in the main street of St Clears and there is a tablet about this remarkable man alongside the memorial on that site. He died, after falling down the stairs at his home, on 20th August 1966, the last of the Welsh aces.

68 – The Black Chair and the Death of Hedd Wyn

Every August the National Eisteddfod of Wales takes place, alternating between the northern and southern parts of the country. In 1917, with the First World War still raging, it took place in Birkenhead. The month of the Eisteddfod has changed, the days for the awarding of certain prizes may be different, but the importance of the Eisteddfod remains exactly the same. And the year 1917, in particular, retains a significance that is unique in Welsh culture.

By midday on Thursday 6th September 1917 the crowds around the Eisteddfod pavilion were standing three or four deep. There was no room to move and it seemed as if the whole of Wales had come to Birkenhead to find out who had won that year's Bardic Chair.

Thursday at the Eisteddfod was known as Lloyd George's Day and, as always, the famous politician – the only Welshman ever to become Prime Minister of Britain – had made his speech. Now it was time for the judgement.

But when the trumpets sounded and T Gwyn Jones stood up to announce the decision nobody moved. In bald, understated prose, the *Western Mail* later said:

> "The name of the successful competitor was called and no response was forthcoming – the Archdruid, after consulting the records, announced that the successful competitor was Ellis Evans, Trawsfynydd, who had sent his composition in July last. Since then he had been sent with his draft to France and there, like so many others, had laid down his life for his country."

Ellis Evans, writing under his bardic name of Hedd Wyn, had been killed on the opening day of the Third Battle of Ypres, Passchendaele as it is better known. Ellis had already made a name for himself in Welsh poetry, having come second in the previous year's Eisteddfod and won several local eisteddfodau at various places across the country. His death in battle shocked, not just those present at the Eisteddfod but the whole of Wales.

A stunned silence fell over the Eisteddfod field as the news finally began to sink in. The Archdruid summed up the feelings of the gathering when he said, simply "Yr wyl yn ei dagrau a'r Bardd yn ei fedd – the festival in tears and the poet in his grave."

There could be no question of any form of investiture and amidst a funereal silence the Bardic Chair, the Chair that now belonged to the dead poet, was solemnly draped in black cloth. Afterwards the Chair, still covered in its black cloth, was taken in solemn procession to Ellis Evans's home, the farm of Yr Ysgwrn where he had lived with his parents, brothers and sisters and where, until his enlistment in the army, he had worked as a hill shepherd.

The Birkenhead Eisteddfod of 1917 has gone down in Welsh history and folklore as "The Eisteddfod of the Black Chair". The empty Chair, draped in its symbolic black pall, was then – and is now – seen by many as representing the thousands of other empty chairs in houses across Wales. A grieving nation took the story of Hedd Wyn and his tragic death to its heart.

The death of Ellis Evans, or Hedd Wyn to give him his bardic name, undoubtedly robbed Wales of a significant talent but it is as a symbol – of loss, of untimely death, of the futility and barbarity of war – that his story really hits home. It is a story that still has the power to move, to cause emotion to well up in any sensitive reader. He was not a "war poet" as such but the war and its consequences were significant factors in the writing he produced just prior to his death.

The final words of this short article should, really, be Hedd Wyn's, albeit in translation. Written in 1916 they remain a poignant reminder of what had been lost and were almost a foreshadowing of his own demise barely a year later:

> "The lads' wild anguish fills the breeze.
> Their blood is mingled with the rain."

69 – War Memorials

War memorials now stand in most towns and many villages in Wales but before 1918 there were only a handful of such monuments – such was the extent of the carnage caused by the First World War.

Virtually every town in the country has one – and many villages, too. There are nearly 40,000 of them across Britain.

Amazingly, given the military and maritime history of Britain, there were very few war memorials – in the sense that we know them today – before 1918. In Georgian and Victorian Britain most soldiers joined the army to escape poverty and retribution from the law, so when they died nobody considered commemorating them.

Officers might be remembered on a tablet in their local church but for the ordinary soldier there was little or no form of remembrance. When they were remembered it was as a mass, as a member of a Regiment or, as in the case of the Culloden battlefield, as a member of a specific clan.

The First World War changed all that. It was a war fought, not by what Wellington and his generals considered to be "scum" but by volunteer armies – clerks and steel workers, miners and shopkeepers. These were men who would be remembered.

War memorials had their origins in the shrines that bereaved people set up on the village green or simply on the street corner during the war years, the modern equivalent being the flowers left by friends and relatives at the roadside after a fatal car accident. When peace came in 1918 there was a demand for permanent memorials to the fallen.

"The memorials were community affairs," says Marcus Payne, Senior Librarian at Penarth Library. "Perhaps for the first time people were demanding something off the government or their councils. They got it. And the process continued after the Second World War. Nowadays, of course, the lists of the dead contained on the memorials are used by family historians and by schoolchildren looking at the history of their town."

The memorials from the First and Second World Wars are hugely moving, be they imposing structures like the one on the sea front at Swansea or the smaller Abergavenny memorial that has the figure of a British Tommy, arms resting on his rifle.

One of the most impressive is Charles Jagger's tribute to men of the Great Western Railway, men who volunteered despite being in a job which could have made them exempt from military service. It takes the form of a soldier reading a letter from home, which can be seen on Paddington station.

Eric Gill's magnificent obelisk at Chirk with the carved figure of a soldier crouching under his greatcoat is a wonderful piece of artwork, taking the humble war memorial to a new level of artistic endeavour.

The memorial at Aberystwyth, designed by Mario Rutelli in 1923, is unusual in that it does not feature soldiers but, rather, Winged Victory on the top and the nude female figure of

Humanity on the bottom.

Some memorials are marked by their location, such as the isolated cross at Freshwater West in Pembrokeshire which stands high above the dunes, gazing out in solitary splendour over the Atlantic. It commemorates the death of over a hundred marines, drowned off the beach when their landing craft sank in 1943.

"War Memorials are invaluable to historians," comments Marcus Payne, "but they are also an important part of society. I look at the recent tributes to the dead of Iraq and Afghanistan in Wootton Bassett – a great tribute – and then I wonder how those men are going to be permanently remembered."

70 – Frongoch Prison Camp

In the wake of the Irish Rising of 1916, when the so-called rebels or dissidents, mainly members of the Irish Volunteer Army, seized the General Post Office in the centre of Dublin and held it for five days, the British government was frightened into the worst type of "knee-jerk reaction".

Hasty courts-martial saw the immediate execution of the rebellion's leaders, James Connelly even being taken to the firing squad strapped into a chair because he had been so badly wounded.

And then the government realised that they had a more significant problem – what were they to do with all the rest of the rebels? Many of the more senior surviving officers were sent to high security British prisons but 1863 of the rank and file Republicans, along with men like Michael Collins and Arthur Griffith who had managed to play down their roles and hide from the British their involvement in the Rising, found themselves incarcerated in an old whisky distillery in north Wales.

This was Frongoch Prison Camp. Situated two miles to the west of Bala in Gwynedd, the Frongoch Distillery had been founded by R Lloyd Price in 1897, allegedly because of the purity of the water from the nearby river. However, by 1910 the enterprise had gone bankrupt and when war was declared against Germany in 1914 the old buildings were taken over as a Prisoner of War camp.

Several German prisoners died there and were buried in the village churchyard – their bodies were later disinterred and moved to other sites.

Following the Irish Rising it was decided that this remote location would be the ideal place to incarcerate the rebels.

There were two parts to the camp. South Camp was located in the old distillery buildings, North Camp being based in wooden huts a little higher up the hillside close to Capel Celyn. The two camps were connected by a road that passed a large field – here the first ever game of hurley to be played in Wales took place when two teams of prisoners battled it out in the autumn of 1916.

Conditions at Frongoch were never easy. The old whisky distillery buildings were bitterly cold at night, very hot during the day, and the prisoners – soon reduced to about five hundred in number – were plagued by an infestation of rats.

The prisoners themselves kept order within the camp with the result that, to the later chagrin of the British government, what was created was, literally, a "University of Revolution" where the ideals of independence and the discipline with which to create it were truly forged.

Interestingly, not one escape attempt was ever recorded at Frongoch, even though prisoners sometimes carried the rifles of their guards (usually men too old to serve on the Western Front) when walking across the hills or between the two camps.

Although the camp was guarded by soldiers, many locals worked there, in the kitchens and barrack blocks, and came into regular contact with the Irishmen. They had much in common. As one prisoner later commented:

> "We marvelled at the fine national spirit of these men and their love for their native tongue."

Indeed, the General Council of prisoners soon added study of the Welsh language to the subjects that were taught, unofficially of course, to the inmates – things like guerrilla warfare and military tactics. Other activities included open-air concerts, fancy-dress parades, cross-country walks or route marches and sporting events. It is recorded that Michael Collins won the 100-yard sprint in an athletics event held in August 1916. His time, it seems, was just under 11 seconds.

While obviously hating the conditions in which they were held, many of the Irish prisoners soon grew to love the wild Welsh countryside around Frongoch. It was very similar to the hills of southern Ireland and must have caused more than a few degrees of homesickness in the minds and hearts of many.

The camp at Frongoch was closed and the Irish prisoners discharged in December 1916. It had been a short-lived and misguided experiment where the ideals of Irish Republicanism were forged and hardened rather than broken down.

Yet the creation of the camp remains a fascinating and little-known moment in Welsh history. Nothing now remains of the old distillery or the prison camp. A school sits on the site and perhaps that is as it should be – looking towards the future, not the past.

71 – Gareth Jones – Investigative Journalist

These days we live in a world of investigative journalism – much of it not very palatable. But back in the 1930s, when the term hadn't even been invented, one Welshman used his pen to expose what was, in effect, a holocaust of major proportions.

The man in question was Gareth Jones, a young journalist from Barry, and the man-made disaster he wrote about was the famine in the Ukraine.

"He was a brilliant student," says historian Patrick Wright. "He got a 1st in French at Cambridge and taught himself Russian. When he left University he worked as a journalist and as Secretary to Lloyd George. He visited Germany regularly but Russia, where his mother had once lived, was where he really wanted to go."

In the late 1920s this was not possible – it was barely ten years since the Communists had killed the Czar and set up the USSR. Britain had backed, supplied and taken part in an invasion of Russia by a White Russian force – as opposed to the Reds – and relations between western powers and the Soviet Union were for several years, to say the least, frosty.

However, in 1930 a diplomatic thaw gave Gareth his chance and over the next four years he made three visits to the Soviet Union. What he saw horrified him.

With his knowledge of Russian, Gareth Jones was able to get off the beaten path and look at people and places that no other westerner possibly could. He roamed the country, met the people and saw for himself that Stalin's wonderful "new world," particularly in the Ukraine, was very far from ideal.

Murder, mass deportation, burning of farms, deprivation of essential food and medical aid, Gareth Jones witnessed it all. On his return he wrote about the conditions of the Ukraine, where the persecution of the people eventually resulted in ten million deaths – state directed genocide on a massive scale. Stalin and his government were not best pleased, to put it mildly, and banned him from the country.

For some reason, even many western journalists howled him down. To his eternal disgrace, men like Pulitzer Prize winner Walter Duranty, desperate to maintain his good relations with the Soviet Union, wrote:

"There is no death from starvation in the Ukraine – but there is widespread mortality from diseases due to malnutrition."

Gareth Jones did not back down in the face of such idiocy or such criticism. He was determined that the world should hear about the famine that had destroyed, and would continue to destroy, so many lives. He did not care what Stalin and his government thought. He wanted just to tell the truth, like the good investigative journalist he had undoubtedly become.

Photo courtesy of Margaret Colley

Gareth Jones, one of the earliest investigative journalists, seen here in a quiet moment.

And his journalistic career continued unabated. He went to America and was a spectator to the great Depression. His reports on the tragedy were harrowing and realistic.

As if all this was not enough, Gareth Jones then travelled to report on events in Germany. Again, it was a time of huge national turmoil, Germany worrying itself into a position where the Nazi Party had recently taken control, promising all kinds of salvation in the years ahead. On one occasion Gareth actually flew in the same plane as Adolf Hitler. And even spoke to the dictator:

"If this aeroplane should crash," he wrote, "the whole history of Europe would be changed. For a few feet away sits Adolf Hitler, Chancellor of Germany and leader of the most volcanic nationalist awakening the world has ever seen – he does not look impressive. His handshake was firm, but his large outstanding eyes seemed emotionless as he greeted me."

Sadly, Gareth himself did not have long left to live. His curiosity in world events next took him to China. He travelled to Inner Mongolia. And here, on the eve of his thirtieth birthday, he was captured by bandits and killed. The report of his death is confusing and leaves an unpleasant taste in the mouth.

It was a troubled time in this part of the world and there is no doubt that Chinese leaders knew what Gareth had uncovered in Russia. Whether or not his death was politically motivated will probably never be known – and if it was, who or what was the moving force behind the murder?

72 – Ralph Hancock, the Welsh Capability Brown

Ralph Hancock, Wales's own Capability Brown.

Ralph Hancock, born in Cardiff in the year 1893, was undoubtedly the Capability Brown of the domestic and city garden – and yet, these days, virtually nobody has heard of this Welsh gardening genius.

Hancock had an adventurous and dynamic life, one that saw him serve in the army during the First World War and, over a period of six short years, change career from Marine and Insurance Broker to garden designer. He had no formal training as a gardener but, clearly, it was an interest that he developed and extended into a new career.

During the dark days of the Second World War Hancock even dabbled in the building of air-raid and gas shelters. Yet it was as a garden designer that he found fame and fortune, creating a rock and water garden for Princess Victoria, the daughter of the late King Edward VII, in 1927. Hancock was proud of that design, thereafter promoting himself as "Landscape Gardener to HRH the Princess Victoria of England".

When he moved to America to further his career Ralph Hancock designed an exhibition garden at Erie Station in New York and, in 1933, won several awards at the Massachusetts Horticultural Show.

His crowning achievement in America, however, has to be the "Gardens of Nations", a series of roof gardens on the eleventh floor of the Rockefeller Centre in New York. Built between 1933 and 1935, this hugely ambitious project was designed to reflect the cultural style of gardens from places as diverse as Holland, Japan and Britain. It was a monumental undertaking, over 3,000 tons of earth, 500 tons of brick, 100 tons of natural stone and 2,000 trees and shrubs being hauled up the side of the skyscrapers by block and tackle.

Hancock's next project saw him return to Britain, to create a roof garden at Derry and Toms Department Store in Kensington. When the gardens opened in 1938 they contained over five hundred varieties of trees, set in just two foot of earth, and several water features.

Even though Derry and Toms has now closed, the gardens are still open to the public while ducks and pink flamingos continue to make their homes on this rooftop garden in the middle of London.

"Ralph was a very creative man," says Angela Buck, Hancock's granddaughter. "He was never very good at keeping records or plans, the creation of his gardens was all that mattered to him. I suppose he must have been difficult to live with at times. His wife called him 'Dear tempestuous genius'. But that's what you get when you live with a creative mind like that."

Despite losing a son during the war, Hancock continued to work and design gardens after 1945. At the end of the 1940s he was commissioned to build the gardens at Twyn yr Hydd at Margam in south Wales. They were probably the last gardens he worked on before his death in 1950 and are now part of Neath Port

Talbot College.

“It is perhaps fitting that this last garden is in Wales,” says Bob Priddle, Lecturer in Horticulture at the College, “the land of his birth. They are now used by horticultural students at the College – something I’m sure Hancock would have approved of.”

73 – Gwyneth Morgan and Tredegar House

Tredegar House in Newport was, for years, the family seat of the Lords Tredegar, one of the richest families in Wales. And for a while, in December 1924, the disappearance of Gwyneth, daughter of Courtenay Morgan, then holder of the Tredegar title, caused a furore in the country.

Gwyneth, always something of a wild child, had been staying at a house in Wimbledon, possibly "drying out" after drug or alcohol abuse. She just walked out one foggy morning, with seventy pounds in her pocket, and five months later her lifeless body, weighted down with stones, was discovered in the Thames at Limehouse.

For the media of the day it was too good a chance to miss. Newspapers, in Britain and America, leapt on the story. Wicked oriental opium dealers, they claimed, had lured this beautiful heiress into the Limehouse drug dens where she had been used, abused and then discarded.

We will never really know what happened to Gwyneth Morgan. Quite probably she overdosed on drugs and whoever was running the opium den in the East End of London simply dumped her comatose body in the Thames. Newport historians Will Cross and Monty Dart have spent years investigating the disappearance.

"One of the saddest things about Gwyneth's death," says Will, "was the turquoise amulet found on her body. It had been given to her by her brother Evan and was held together by a piece of wire from a ginger beer bottle – this on one of the richest women in Britain. It must have meant a lot to her."

Drugs were not illegal in Britain until they were outlawed by the Defence of the Realm Act in 1917. Almost immediately an underground drugs network was created and Gwyneth, who came from a strange and dysfunctional family – her mother believed she was a bird and her brother Evan was a friend of the black magician Aleister Crowley – was almost a natural victim of that drugs scene.

Gwyneth now lies buried in Bassaleg churchyard, on the outskirts of Newport, all but forgotten by the world.

"Lord Tredegar used his influence to get an open verdict at the inquest," says Paul Busby, biographer of Gwyneth's brother Evan. "Anything to avoid a verdict of suicide – that was unthinkable.

And then he had her buried, quietly and anonymously, in London. It was only when Evan succeeded to the title – and to Tredegar House – that her body was disinterred and moved back to Wales."

Gwyneth Morgan was one of Wales's first victims – certainly the most high-profile victim – of the drug culture. There were soon to be many more.

The memorial to Gwyneth Morgan that stands in the churchyard at Bassaleg. Recently repaired after damage to its nose, the memorial is one of the few acknowledgments to a tragic and forgotten woman.

We will never know what dèmons forced Gwyneth into the arms of the opium dealers but next time you drive past Tredegar House remember the tragedy of the young heiress who had so much to live for and died so needlessly.

74 – World Records on the Sands at Pendine

The rock hard sands at Pendine stretch for over seven miles along the shore of Carmarthen Bay, running between Laugharne Sands in the east and the village of Pendine itself in the west.

These days they are an ideal tourist location where sand castles and walks along the beach are the order of the day. But it was not so many years ago that young would-be drivers of Pembrokeshire and Carmarthenshire sat behind the wheels of their parents' cars and, inexpertly and perhaps a little reluctantly, took their first stab at manoeuvring their vehicles along the sands.

Safe from the problems of traffic and other road users, it was the ideal place to learn to drive. Yet these tyro drivers were simply following in the footsteps of more famous men before them. For Pendine Sands were once the home to roaring motorbikes and daring attempts to break the world land-speed record.

The sands at Pendine are rock hard, particularly the eastern stretch, and in the early days of motoring were often safer and more uniform than roads and racing tracks. From 1922, for several years, the annual Welsh TT Races were held on the sands. They offered a smooth surface on which to race and, importantly, a long straight track where the motorcyclists could put their throttles down and achieve the maximum possible speed on their early machines.

Due to the success of the TT Races it soon became obvious that Pendine Sands might be the ideal location for world land-speed record attempts. Such attempts needed not just the measured mile but also a build-up and run-out area. It was estimated that any attempt at a speed record would require at least five miles of open track – and Pendine had seven.

The famous Malcolm Campbell was the first man to use the area for a record attempt. And it was a successful one. Driving his car, the first Blue Bird, on 25th September 1925 he established a new world land-speed record of 146.16 miles per hour.

Four other record-breaking attempts were made on Pendine Sands between 1925 and 1927. Two of these were by Campbell and two by his arch-rival, the Welsh driver J G Parry-Thomas in his car which he named Babs.

In February 1927, driving the second Blue Bird, Malcolm Campbell managed to hit 174.22 miles per hour, an incredible time for the 1920s. Parry-Thomas was adamant that the record could be broken and on 3rd March the same year made his attempt.

Driving at 170 miles per hour, on his final run, tragedy struck. The drive chain on Babs – which was exposed rather than hidden under the bonnet – snapped, whipping up and back towards the driver. It struck Parry-Thomas in the neck, partially decapitating him and killing him instantly. Babs slewed out of control, crashed and rolled over onto the sand.

J G Parry-Thomas was the first driver ever to be killed while attempting to break the world land-speed record and his death marked the end of Pendine Sands as a location for such attempts. His car, Babs, was buried in the sand dunes as a mark of respect and the sleepy little Welsh village returned to insignificance. It did, however, have its memories.

For years many parents, during a summer day out on the beach – and all eager for a little respite from their demanding offspring – would tell their children to go and see if they could dig up the car of Parry-Thomas. The children dug for hours but never managed to find the car. However, in 1969 Owen Wyn Owen from Bangor was given permission to excavate Babs from her sandy grave. He then spent fifteen years renovating the car which now goes on display at the Pendine Museum of Speed every summer..

The sands at Pendine have, over the years, also been used as a landing field for aircraft – early, propeller-driven aircraft, not modern jets – and postcard views of aeroplanes on the sands are now eagerly sought.

During the Second World War Amy Johnson and Jim Mollison took off from Pendine Sands in their De Haviland Rapide on a non-stop flight to America. The Ministry of Defence also acquired a large portion of the Sands during the war, using it as a firing range and putting much of the area out of public use.

Pendine Sands do still, occasionally, hit the headlines. In June 2002 the grandson of Malcolm Campbell set the UK electric land-speed record at Pendine, clocking up an amazing speed of 137 miles per hour. It may not rank alongside the modern jet-propelled records but Malcolm Campbell would be proud of his grandson's achievement on the same stretch of sand where he once risked life and limb back in the 1920s.

75 – Augustus John, Bohemian and Painter

One of the most eccentric and fascinating characters ever to come out of Wales, the painter Augustus John was a Pembrokeshire man through and through. Even after he grew up and achieved international fame he often returned to the county of his birth, affording it a warm and fond place in his heart.

The third of four children, both Augustus and his older sister Gwen became celebrated and distinguished artists. Indeed, there are many who say that for all his posing and bohemian ways, Gwen was actually the better painter of the two. The jury, as they say, is out on that one.

Augustus John came from the county town of Haverfordwest where his father was a solicitor. However, he was actually born in the nearby seaside town of Tenby on 4th January 1878. Late in 1877 there had been a serious outbreak of scarlet fever in Haverfordwest and with the new baby due any day Augustus's mother and her young family left their house in Victoria Place and decamped to Tenby where Augustus was duly born a few weeks later.

Much of the future painter's childhood was spent in Tenby, the open sands and fine sea bathing making it an ideal place to grow up. Even though his mother died when he was just six years old, it seems to have been a happy childhood. To begin with, at least, he was a mild and quiet child.

However an accident while bathing – diving into water that was too shallow – resulted in an injury that became life-changing. The simplistic view is that he dived into the sea, smashed his head on a rock or the sea bed and suffered a character change – the rampaging bohemian was born.

The truth of the matter is probably that the accident gave him a long period of enforced convalescence. During this time Augustus John sat and thought about life and art – and his role in it. The period certainly filled him with ideas and stimulated a passion for what can only be described as "adventure".

John's ability as an artist was soon noticed and he studied first at Tenby School of Art. Quickly outgrowing this, he went to the Slade School of Art in London where he became renowned as an exceptionally able pupil of artist and teacher Henry Tonks. Soon he was accepted as the most brilliant draughtsman the college had produced and, almost inevitably, won the Slade Prize in 1898. Leaving the Slade he went to Paris and then journeyed through France until he found the most perfect spot to live and paint in the Provence region of the country.

Early in 1900 Augustus John married his first wife, Ida. Always passionately interested in the Romany way of life, for many years he travelled, together with a pack of dogs, his wife Ida, his mistress Dorelia McNeill and children from both women, around the countryside in a gypsy caravan. It was a bohemian lifestyle that caught the public imagination and made his looming, bearded figure famous throughout the land.

When Ida died in 1907 Augustus continued to travel and live with Dorelia – all the while managing to keep a mistress or two in close company. He did later marry Dorelia. The bohemian lifestyle did not seem to affect the children too much. One of the sons from John's first marriage, Casper, decided on a career in the Navy and rose to become First Sea Lord at the Admiralty..

During the First World War John was appointed official War Artist with the Canadian forces. Together with the King he was one of the few soldiers (his position as War Artist meant that he was officially a serving soldier) allowed to keep his beard and other facial hair!

He did little painting, however, and after two short months in France he got himself involved in a brawl. Shipped home in disgrace, he managed to avoid a court-martial – thanks to the intervention of Lord Beaverbrook – and he returned to France where he did actually manage to produce one or two paintings. The most famous of these is Fraternity, a depiction of three soldiers standing close together in front of a bombed-out building.

In his early days Augustus John had been known as an exponent of Post-Impressionism and for his abilities as an etcher and sketcher in oil. After the war, however, he turned more and more to portrait painting and was soon regarded as Britain's finest artist in this field. Amongst others he painted people like Lawrence of Arabia, George Bernard Shaw and Dylan Thomas.

It was Augustus John who actually introduced Dylan Thomas to his future wife, Caitlin Macnamara. Caitlin was at that time John's mistress and in a famous episode during the return from a drunken excursion to west Wales, the jealous Augustus John actually knocked Dylan down. It did not stop Caitlin transferring her allegiance to the Welsh poet.

Augustus John continued to paint and write (he produced two autobiographies) until his death at Fordingbridge in Hampshire on 31st October 1961. He left behind a huge body of work, some quite brilliant, some possibly not so good. His real legacy, however, lies in the tales of rampaging hedonism that seemed to follow him wherever he went – truly one of Wales's great eccentric characters.

76 – Ernest Jones, the Biographer of Sigmund Freud

The name Alfred Ernest Jones might mean very little to most people but, for some time, this enigmatic and fascinating man was the leader of the psychoanalytical movement in Britain and many years later was voted number 96 in the list of top 100 Welshmen of all time.

Perhaps more importantly, Ernest Jones wrote and produced the definitive biography of the great psychoanalyst Sigmund Freud – a work that even now, over fifty years after it first appeared, is still regarded as a classic text.

Jones was born in Gowerton, just outside Swansea, on 1st January 1879. Educated at Llandovery College, he went on to study at University College Cardiff and University College London. In 1901 he was awarded a First Class Honours Degree in medicine and obstetrics. He followed this with an MD and, in 1903, membership of the Royal College of Physicians.

Ernest Jones specialised in neurology and, in his early years in practice, worked mainly in hospitals in the London area. Appalled by the brutal, almost inhuman treatment of people then termed "insane", he began experimenting with hypnotic techniques. Then, in 1905, he read an article by Sigmund Freud in a German medical journal and became fascinated by the Austrian's theories.

Concepts and terms such as the ego and libido were soon second nature to the young man. However, the medical profession, and the whole medical establishment of the time, were opposed to Freud and his treatments and Jones faced considerable opposition from people who disliked the Freudian approach. So much so that in 1906 he faced a charge of abusing a girl in his care. The charge was subsequently dropped but it undoubtedly hurt his professional standing.

Jones encountered Carl Jung, Freud's pupil and fellow professional, in 1907 and this brought him first-hand information about Freud's work.

Then in 1908 he met the great man himself for the first time, at a Psychoanalytical Conference in Salzburg. Nothing daunted, Ernest Jones promptly followed Freud back to Vienna after the Conference and the pair carried out in-depth discussions on psychoanalytical practice – it was a period that helped form the personal and professional relationship between Freud and Jones, a relationship that lasted until Freud's death in 1939.

In 1908 Ernest Jones ably demonstrated that repressed sexuality was the underlying problem with the paralyzed arm of a young girl who had come to him for treatment. Her parents, however, were appalled at the suggestion and promptly complained. Jones had little option and resigned from his position at the hospital.

Following his resignation, Jones moved to Canada where he taught at the University of Toronto. For the next five years he taught, wrote and organised conferences, even bringing Freud across the Atlantic for a lecture tour.

Ernest Jones returned to the UK in 1913 and set up in private practice as a psychoanalyst. In 1917 he married the Welsh composer Morfydd Llwyn Owen but it was destined to be a short period of happiness as she died eighteen months later after what was thought to be an apparently routine operation for appendicitis.

Jones re-married just after the war, this time to Katherine Jake, a woman who had been at school with Freud's daughters. Although Ernest Jones had taught himself German in order to better understand Freud's writings, it was his wife's command of the language that later helped him when he was compiling documents, arranging letters and writing his biographical masterpiece.

Following the Anschluss of 1937, when Hitler's Germany annexed Austria, Freud, as a Jew, found himself in a parlous position. Ernest Jones promptly flew to Vienna and helped to negotiate the release, or the evacuation, of Freud to Britain. It was a brave thing to do as anyone who, even at this early stage of the new regime, was connected with Jews was immediately suspect and liable to very severe treatment.

The major achievement of Ernest Jones's final years was the gathering together of Freud's papers and letters and then writing his three-volume biography of the man. The volumes were published between 1953 and 1957 to immediate acclaim – an acclaim that has lasted until the present day.

Always hugely proud of his Welshness, Ernest Jones was a member of Plaid Cymru and remained inordinately fond of the Gower Peninsula. He was one of the first to spot the disagreement between Freud and Carl Jung, a disagreement that would, eventually, split the world of psychoanalytical treatment and thought in two.

Perhaps his greatest contribution to the profession, however, was in recognising and developing the concept of "rationalisation" – the excuses that people make for things that make them uncomfortable or unhappy. That and, of course, his magnificent biography of one of the greatest men produced by the late nineteenth and early twentieth centuries.

77 – Amelia Earhart Flies the Atlantic

Just after noon on 18th June 1928 inhabitants of the coastal town of Burry Port in Carmarthenshire caught the heavy drone of aircraft engines. Looking skywards they were soon able to pick out the graceful lines of a small orange aeroplane, making its way along the coast from the direction of Tenby and the far west.

The aircraft, soon identified as the seaplane "Friendship", was flying low across the water. She circled the Loughor estuary and just after twenty minutes to one touched down on the choppy waters at Burry Port. Inside the aeroplane was Miss Amelia Earhart and by landing at this small south Wales port she had became the first woman ever to fly across the Atlantic Ocean.

Amelia Earhart was not the only person on board. With her in the plane were the pilot Wilmer Stultz and mechanic Lou Gordon. In fact, Amelia was rated only as "Assistant Pilot" for the trip – yet such was the novelty of a woman taking on the challenge of the Atlantic that Stultz and Gordon have now been all but forgotten.

After landing and mooring their aircraft to a buoy just off the town, the three flyers went ashore in a motorboat, braving the throngs of people who came racing to the area from Swansea, Cardiff and many places beyond. Before the day was out a seaplane and a traditional aeroplane landed at Swansea with parties of reporters, photographers and special correspondents.

They came to note a remarkable achievement, the "Friendship" having left Newfoundland only twenty hours before. Bill Stultz was well aware of what he and the others had achieved, commenting to a reporter from the *Llanelli Mercury*:

> "We encountered fog almost all the way, and there was considerable rain as well. Most of the way I was flying blind because of the fog and rain. We had no idea where we were, as we had not seen Ireland. We landed here in South Wales because we were short of fuel."

Such was the enthusiasm of local people and the press that telephone lines were blocked and reporters who came hurrying to the area from London found it difficult get their stories away. The flyers had intended to leave Burry Port that same night, heading on to Southampton, but bad weather forced them to postpone their departure and they were obliged to spend the night in the Ashburnham Hotel.

Amelia must have maintained a low profile as several dignitaries, who came to congratulate her on her achievement, failed to locate the intrepid woman flyer. Among these would-be visitors was the aviator Sir Arthur Whitten Brown, then living in nearby Swansea. He was an airman of some note, having been the first man to fly the Atlantic, along with Sir John Alcock:

"When I arrived the crowds were so dense," he said, "that I could not get near the machine. I searched Burry Port for some considerable time but failed to find them. I know the wonder of their achievement and would have liked to have offered my personal congratulations."

One person who did manage to speak to Amelia Earhart was the reporter from the *Llanelli Mercury*. He managed to get his interview early on the morning after their arrival, before the three flyers took off again. According to him Amelia admitted that during the historic flight she ate only two oranges and six malted milk tablets:

> "How lovely your country is," she said. "The stillness and the silence brings back again the almost awesome feeling which came to me as, hour after hour, we pushed forward through the thick clouds and fog. It was as if we were alone in the world. To think that 48 hours ago I was in America and now I am in Wales!"

Amelia Earhart did not take the controls of the "Friendship" during the trans-Atlantic flight but she has gone down in history as the first woman ever to fly across the ocean. And she and her colleagues landed in South Wales, a remarkable end to a remarkable achievement.

78 – Peerless Jim Driscoll

Wales has produced many great boxers over the years but none was more respected and loved than Peerless Jim Driscoll, the Cardiff featherweight who once gave up the chance of winning the world title because he had made a promise to take part in a charity show for his local orphanage.

Jim Driscoll died on 25th January 1925, aged just 44, and as his funeral cortege wound its way towards Cathays Cemetery over 100,000 people stood silently on the streets of Cardiff to pay their last respects to a man who had captured their hearts.

Jim Driscoll was born in Cardiff on 15th December 1880. His father was Cornelius Driscoll, his mother Elizabeth, and like many children of the time Jim's early life was one of deprivation and more than a little hardship.

Jim used his skill as a boxer – despite his frail appearance and diminutive size – as a way out of the "poverty trap". From an early age he fought in the boxing booths that most fairgrounds ran in those days, knowing that the only way to make a little money was to stay out of the way of the big "haymaking" punches of his opponents and therefore win in the ring. His reputation began to grow and spread.

He fought his first professional fight in 1901 and despite his reputation as a superb defensive fighter he actually won his first ten fights by knock out. Standing at just five feet four inches, Jim Driscoll knew that, even as a featherweight, it was speed and consistency of punching, rather than the weight of his blows, that were going to win him fights. And win he did.

Out of a total of 77 fights in a career that lasted eighteen years, he won 58 and lost only three. This was in the days when the "no contest" rule was in place – in other words, no knockout, no result. In 1910 Jim Driscoll became the first featherweight to win a Lonsdale Belt and then decided to try his luck in America.

Despite the scepticism of the American sporting press, most reporters considering him too slight and frail to succeed, Driscoll had nine fights in the USA and won seven of them. The other two were no contests. The Americans took him to their hearts.

In 1910 he fought Abe Attell for the World Featherweight Title. With the "no contest" rule in place it was always going to be a difficult ask for the 28–year-old Welshman, whose style was based on skill and speed rather than the brawling and heavy punching that were commonplace in American professional boxing at the time. And so it proved. He totally outclassed Attell but despite winning 7 of the scheduled 10 rounds (two of the remaining three being judged draws) he could not knock out his opponent and the match was ruled a no contest.

The statue of Peerless Jim Driscoll in Cardiff.

The day after the fight Jim Driscoll took a boat for home. He had been offered a re-match with Attell but, having already pledged to make an appearance at the Nazareth House Orphanage Charity Day in his home town of Cardiff, Driscoll knew he could not let the youngsters down. “I never break a promise,” he declared. The chance to fight for the World Championship never came again.

Jim Driscoll, having come out of poverty, loved the party lifestyle. He enjoyed the trappings of fame, although he never allowed his success to turn his head. There are those, however, who say that the partying and good times were contributory factors in his early death but this has never been proved, one way or the other.

Driscoll’s boxing career was exemplary – apart from one occasion. This was when he was matched against Freddie Welsh. The spoiling tactics of Welsh so infuriated Driscoll that by the tenth round he had totally lost his composure and head-butted his opponent. Quite rightly, Jim Driscoll was disqualified.

The advent of the First World War interrupted Driscoll’s boxing career. Like thousands of others he joined up and was employed as a PTI during the war years. After the war he attempted to re-start his career but ill-health was already dogging him. He fought only three more times, finally retiring in 1919.

Driscoll never forgot his roots and remained inordinately fond of his home town. He used to train at the Cardiff Boys Club at the bottom of St Mary’s Street (for many years there was a statue of him on the site) and was a great supporter of the Nazareth House Orphanage.

In the years after the war he contracted consumption and his final days were a desperate battle against this dreaded disease. It was a fight he was to eventually lose, dying on 25th January 1925. Peerless Jim Driscoll, as he was known throughout the boxing world, remains one of the great Welsh sporting heroes.

79 – Evan Morgan of Tredegar House

Of all the great characters in Welsh history – and there are many – none is more unusual, more fascinating and more downright bizarre than Evan Morgan, the last Viscount Tredegar.

Evan succeeded to the title in 1934 but by then his reputation for outlandish behaviour had been well established. Born in 1893, by the beginning of the First World War Evan Morgan was abroad in society. Over the next thirty years he created the myth of wildness and extravagance that has lasted until today.

A second-rate poet and painter, he was nevertheless appointed as adviser on art to the Royal Family. He dabbled on the artistic fringes of society and Queen Mary referred to him as her favourite bohemian. He was also something of a favourite with Lloyd George and was a great influence on Brendan Bracken, Churchill's right-hand man. Those were the more acceptable sides to his character and behaviour.

At his palatial Tredegar House, just on the edge of Newport, he kept a menagerie of wild animals, including a boxing kangaroo and whole flocks of birds that easily and effortlessly did his bidding. More often than not the animals lived inside the house rather than outside. His friends included writers like Aldous Huxley and GK Chesterton, artists such as Augustus John and, above all, the great "black magician" Aleister Crowley.

Known as "the Black Monk", Evan was an expert in the occult and even built himself a "magik room" – the spelling was deliberate – at Tredegar House. Crowley visited him many times, and declared the room the best equipped he had ever seen. Crowley, known throughout Europe as the "Great Beast", took part in many weird and perhaps terrifying rituals at Tredegar Park and christened Evan "adept of adepts". Sometimes those rituals frightened even Crowley.

During the Second World War Evan was a high ranking officer in MI8, his particular responsibility being the monitoring of carrier pigeons. When he foolishly and carelessly let slip the departmental secrets – to two girl guides, would you believe – Evan was court-martialled and was lucky to get away without a term of imprisonment – or even the firing squad.

In retaliation Evan Morgan called Aleister Crowley to Tredegar House to take part in a cursing ritual on his commanding officer. Whatever Evan said or did it frightened Crowley so much that he left before the process was complete. And, amazingly, Evan's CO soon concocted some mysterious illness and nearly died!

Despite his openly acknowledged homosexuality Evan was twice married, to actress Lois Sturt and to the Russian Princess Olga Dolgorouky. Neither marriage was a success and Evan continued to flaunt and entertain his male lovers in hotel bedrooms across Europe.

As if that was not enough, he was able to put his obsession with the occult on hold for a short period while he converted to Catholicism, becoming Chamberlain to Popes Benedict XV and Pius XI. He went to study at the English College in Rome – although the amount of studying he did was limited in the extreme – and was soon a well known figure around Rome, driving through the city in a Rolls Royce that had a portable altar in the back.

The stories of Evan Morgan's behaviour are legendary but perhaps the most mysterious and intriguing episode in his life came in 1932. That year he was invited to a small private dinner and meeting at a restaurant in Bad Wiesse, just outside Munich. Nothing unusual in that, you might say – except that you then look at the other guests. They included Rudolph Hess, the deputy of what was fast becoming the most significant political party in Germany, right-wing British artist Sir Francis Rose, Ernst Rohm – head of Hitler's SA or Brownshirts – and his deputy Edmund Heines.

What was discussed at the meeting will never be known but all of the diners were ferociously right-wing in their politics. Many of them were gay and a large number were fascinated by the occult. This was the period just before Hitler came to power and it would not be stretching things too far to suggest that the emergent Nazi party was trying to find out how things were run in Britain, perhaps by courting one of the wealthiest aristocrats in the country.

Evan Morgan continued to maintain distant links with the Nazis. Some years later Hermann Goering was on the Isle of Capri for a meeting with Italian dictator Mussolini. In the room next door was none other than Evan Morgan. Evan's parrot, a bird that used to sit obediently on his shoulder as he walked around, apparently bit Goering on the nose – much to the displeasure of the portly German.

During the war, after he had parachuted into Britain in an attempt to end the conflict, Rudolph Hess was imprisoned at Abergavenny, not too many miles distant from Tredegar House. If Hess and Evan knew each other – however slightly – they would surely have met.

Hess might even have come to Tredegar House as he was given a fair degree of freedom and latitude to journey around eastern Wales. Was Evan Morgan one of the people Hess was hoping to use as an intermediary in his bid to end hostilities? It is a fascinating speculation.

Unfortunately, it will remain just speculation. Like so much that went on in his life, we will never know what was really going on in the mind of Evan Morgan. He remains one of Wales's greatest and most memorable eccentrics.

80 – The Mumbles Railway

There are many significant dates in Welsh history, moments that we should remember and celebrate, but one that seems to have slipped under the radar – at least for lots of people – is 25th March. For on that momentous day in 1807 the Mumbles Railway opened, the first fee-paying passenger railway service in the world.

Wales had already seen the advent of the first steam locomotive service. That was in 1804 when Cornish engineer Richard Trevithick built and ran a steam engine that was used to draw iron from Merthyr Tydfil to Abercynnon. This was, however, clearly a goods line and passengers never came into the picture, not as far as Trevithick was concerned nor the owners of the iron works.

Trevithick's engine was not a major success and he soon left Wales to return to his native Cornwall but his efforts at Merthyr Tydfil earn him an important place in the history of railway transport, not just in Wales but the whole world.

The Mumbles Railway was built under an 1804 Act of Parliament, authorising the removal and carriage of limestone from the quarries at Mumbles to the docks area of nearby Swansea. From there the limestone would be sent to all corners of the world. Construction was completed in 1806 and services began. There was no formal opening ceremony and, to begin with at least, it was industrial product rather than people that was the important factor.

However, as Patrick Thornhill has written, the thrill of an illicit ride on this early railway soon became a natural part of the games of children from the area:

> "What could be more fun for the children than a coach ride along the shore to Mumbles? One hears the thud of the horses' hooves, the gritting of sand between rail and wheel, the thunder and swish of breakers."
> (Quoted in *Railways for Britain.*)

At this stage the operation was known as the Oystermouth Railway, only later acquiring the correct name of the Swansea and Mumbles Railway – or the Mumbles Railway as it was soon being called. There was no road link between Swansea and Mumbles and, when they looked at the children hitching rides on the trams, it did not take local entrepreneurs long to realise that some form of passenger service, for people who wanted or needed to make the trip, might just result in something of a goldmine.

In 1807 permission was given for the line to carry passengers. Benjamin French, one of the early investors in the project, paid twenty pounds for the right to run the line and carry passengers. The concession was for one year only and on 25th March 1807 the world's first passenger railway began operations. It was a huge success, so much so that French and his partners quickly upped their offer to twenty-five pounds a year in order to continue with the arrangement.

It was an amazing achievement for small investors from South Wales. George Stephenson did not open his Stockton and Darlington Railway (the first public railway to use steam-powered locomotives) until 1825 and by then the Mumbles Railway had been running for nearly twenty years.

Despite the ground-breaking achievement of Trevithick's steam engine at Merthyr, the first passenger wagons on the Mumbles Railway were actually drawn by horses. Over the years several other means of transportation were tried, ranging from a short-lived attempt at sail power to steam and electric – more means of transportation than any other railway ever attempted.

However, towards the end of the 1820s a Turnpike Road was built between Swansea and the Mumbles, the road actually running parallel to the railway line. The success of this road deprived the Mumbles Railway of much of its traffic and Simon Llewellyn, who was then running the railway, decided to stop carrying passengers after 1826 – by sheer coincidence, at the very moment when Stephenson's Stockton and Darlington Railway was gathering force and momentum.

For some years the line was almost derelict although it was still used for occasional deliveries of coal from mines in the Clyne Valley. Then, in 1855, George Byng Morris decided to take a hand and invest in the railway. He replaced the plates on which the original wagons had run with edged rails and installed standard gauge lines (four foot, eight and a half). A horse drawn passenger service was duly reintroduced.

Steam power replaced horse-drawn vehicles in 1877 although, for a number of years, horses were still used as a dispute between the railway and the Swansea Improvements and Tramway Company (which owned the locomotives) rumbled on.

The line celebrated its centenary in 1907 and was electrified in 1928. A full "tram" service began in 1929 with eleven double-decker trams, the largest ever built in Britain, being delivered for use on the railway.

After the Second World War it quickly became clear that the age of the tram car was nearly over as modern buses, more effective and efficient than trams – but not nearly so atmospheric – began to be introduced in cities right across the United Kingdom. In 1958 the Mumbles Railway was bought by the South Wales Transport Company. They ran coaches and buses in the Swansea area and it soon became clear what they had in mind.

On 5th January 1960 the last tram left Swansea for the Mumbles and the railway, which had run for over 150 years, finally closed down. At the time of its closure the Mumbles Railway was the longest-running railway in the world but that meant nothing to the businessmen who were concerned solely with efficiency and with profit.

There have been many talks about re-opening the railway/tramway but these have never got beyond the discussion stage. Wales – and Swansea and the Mumbles – can be proud, however, because this railway line will always be remembered as the first passenger railway service in the world.

81 – The Death of Lloyd George

David Lloyd George, the only Welshman to have become Prime minister of Great Britain, died on 26th March 1945. By then his glory days were long past and although still a member of Parliament during most of the war years, he rarely attended the House of Commons during that time and took no part in the debates.

When the offer of an earldom came from Winston Churchill on the morning of 18th December 1944, Lloyd George was, at first, undecided as to whether or not he should accept. He had, after all, always regarded himself as a man of the people.

However, after sleeping on the problem he finally cabled back the simple message "Gratefully accept". He was to become 1st Earl Lloyd George of Dwyfor but, in the event, did not live long enough to enjoy the honour.

David Lloyd George, one-time Prime Minister of Britain, seen here playing golf. The game was something of a passion for him but he did not play it particularly well.

Lloyd George and his second wife, Frances, had moved into his house Ty Newydd outside Llanystumdwy in September 1944. He was old and ill, clearly suffering from cancer. He had, in effect, come home to die.

David Lloyd George had been born in Manchester on 17th

January 1863. The family moved to Pembrokeshire when David's father, William George, became ill and, after his death, moved again, this time to Llanystumdwy in North Wales. Here the young David fell under the influence of his uncle Richard Lloyd – so strong was the relationship that the young man even added his name, Lloyd, to his own.

He qualified and worked as a solicitor and, almost inevitably, moved into the political arena. On 13th April 1890 he became Liberal MP for Caernarvon Boroughs, winning the seat by just 19 votes. He made his political name by his opposition to the Boer War, being instinctively on the side of any small nation that was in danger of being oppressed by a larger one.

Soon the Liberal Party realised that it was safer having this charismatic and wonderful orator on the inside, rather than waiting on the fringes where he could cause any amount of political carnage. Consequently, he was brought into the Cabinet, becoming President of the Board of Trade in 1906. When Herbert Asquith became Prime Minister, Lloyd George replaced him as Chancellor of the Exchequer.

Lloyd George, of course, is famous for his People's Budget of 1909. Contrary to popular belief, he did not introduce old age pensions (that had already been done by Asquith) but he was responsible for the introduction of state support for the sick and infirm.

During the First World War he was, by turns, Minister of Munitions, Secretary of State for War and, finally, in 1916, Prime Minister. In each of those roles he was hugely successful, a dynamic and thrusting leader who, by his example and energy, did much to actually win the war.

He had much to contend with during his years as leader of the wartime Coalition Government, not least representing Britain at the Versailles peace talks of 1919. It was, in no small degree, thanks to him that the Treaty of Versailles was not a great deal more vindictive in its terms. Desperate to achieve peace in Ireland, Lloyd George also presided over the Anglo-Irish Treaty when the Irish Free State was created. In hindsight it was a flawed solution but in the immediate post-war years it is hard to see what else could have been done.

Lloyd George's political life was one of huge success and a fair degree of scandal. He was accused of "insider dealing" during the Marconi Scandal of 1913, when he was at best economical with the truth in his responses to Parliamentary questions. And, of course, the taint of selling honours in return for funds for the Liberal Party followed him to the grave.

As the 1920s progressed Lloyd George and a Liberal Party that was, in no small degree due to the man himself, split into warring factions, gradually lost power and influence. By 1944 he was clearly "yesterday's man" as the growing Labour Party pulled away so many working men and left-wing intellectuals. Always something of a ladies' man, however, Lloyd George retained his charisma and appeal right to the end.

Barbara Jones was, in 1944 and 1945, a Wren, serving in the naval base at Pwllheli. On their days off she and her friends would go to the river close to Llanystumdwy where they would sit and throw stones into the river:

> "Sometimes this rather short man with grey hair would come and chat to us, ask us where we were from and what not. He used to wear a black trilby and a black cape – it had seen better days, that cape. He was our little old gentleman. Then we heard that Lloyd George had died. All the photographs were in the papers and we thought 'Oh gosh, that's our little old gentleman.'"
> (Quoted in *Wales at War* by Phil Carradice)

It had been announced, in January 1945, that Lloyd George would not be present in the House of Commons for some time because of a severe case of the flu. He was eighty-two years old and the announcement fooled very few. His cancer was growing – it could only end in one way. On 26th March it soon became apparent that the end was near and, with his family by his bedside, Lloyd George slipped into unconsciousness and died.

The funeral was a memorable affair. Lloyd George had always said he did not want to be buried in a cemetery or church yard and the spot chosen was the bank of the River Dwyfor, a place he himself had selected back in 1922. As Barbara Jones remembers:

> "Those of us who used to talk to him went to the funeral. The coffin came up on a farm cart, pulled by an old dray horse. It had trails of leaves coming right over the cart, coming down over the coffin. I remember the colours because on the other side of the river there were

two fields and they were a mass of colour. People were singing hymns. It was absolutely gorgeous."
(Quoted in *Wales at War* by Phil Carradice)

Lloyd George was far from a conventional politician. He made mistakes but he achieved much during his long lifetime. And he is still the only Welshman to have ever risen to the supreme post in the British political system.

82 – Harry Grindell Matthews – the Man who Invented the Death Ray

Think of it, the classic eccentric inventor, the man who designed and built a Death Ray and a Sky Projector for flashing messages on to the clouds – Batman or what? – and he's just moved into a house situated outside your home town. That's what happened, not in some Californian hideaway, but on the hills of south Wales between Clydach and Ammanford in the closing years of the 1930s.

Harry Grindell Matthews was born in Gloucestershire on 17th March 1880. After serving with the South African Constabulary during the Boer War (and being twice wounded) he became an electrical engineer at Bexhill. The humdrum life of an ordinary engineer was not for him, however, and Harry Grindell Matthews soon began to turn his hand to what, in the early twentieth century, were known as "inventions".

In 1911 he invented a device to transmit radio telephone messages between the ground and aeroplanes – and this at a time when aircraft had been around for fewer than a dozen years. On 12th September the noted early pilot CB Hucks, flying at a height of 700 feet, received a message from Matthews, standing on Ely Racecourse in Cardiff, the first time such communication had ever been achieved.

When the government asked for a demonstration of the device, however, Matthews objected to several of their engineers exploring the insides of his machine. He promptly packed up all the equipment and stormed off. Newspapers of the time were all behind the new inventor but the War Office, desperate not to lose face, promptly announced that the tests had been a failure.

Undaunted, Matthews continued to work. In 1914, with war declared against Germany, the government offered a grant of twenty-five thousand pounds to anyone who could come up with a way of defending the country against zeppelins or other remote controlled weapons of war. Harry Grindell Matthews created a system using selenium cells and this time demonstrated his invention to the Admiralty. He got his twenty-five grand but, strangely, his device was never used.

The list of Matthews's inventions is long and varied – an early version of the mobile phone, a system for making talking pictures (long before *The Jazz Singer*) and, above all, a Death Ray that would stop the engines of cars and motorbikes, even planes, from a great distance away.

In 1924 the government asked for a demonstration of this Death Ray but, always prickly where authority was concerned, Harry Grindell Matthews refused. Instead he showed how it worked to journalists, igniting a charge of gunpowder from many feet away. Once again the British press took him to their heart.

Matthews refused to say how his Death Ray worked, simply stating that the device sent out a beam or ray that stopped the magneto in any car or motorbike engine. Clearly there was some substance to his invention, several of his assistants having been knocked out when passing too close to the beam and Matthews himself claimed to have lost the use of an eye during one experiment.

For a brief while Harry and his Death Ray were headline news in all the papers, particularly when the government – mindful, perhaps, of his petulance some years before – refused to buy it. Matthews declared that it was his invention and he would sell it to a foreign government if necessary. There was even a High Court injunction to stop this happening but when he did finally demonstrate the Death Ray to the Air Ministry in April 1924 officials were unimpressed and strongly suspected a confidence trick.

Harry Grindell Matthews next spent some time in America, working for a time for Warner Brothers, before returning to the UK with his next invention, a Sky Projector. In December 1930 he threw up the image of an angel and the message "Happy Christmas" on to the clouds outside London.

Despite this the Sky Projector was not a commercial success and by 1931 Matthews was close to bankruptcy. Part of the trouble was that he enjoyed the high life, dining in fancy restaurants and staying in the best hotels, and that was where most of his sponsors' money actually went.

Somehow Harry Grindell Matthews managed to survive – his relationship and later marriage to Ganna Walska, a wealthy American opera singer may have helped – and in 1938 he moved to a house he had built for himself, Tor Clawdd on the hills above Clydach in south Wales. It was not just a house, he also created a laboratory and carved out an airstrip for himself on a shelf of land at the back of the building.

Matthews continued to invent, creating, amongst other things, a machine that was able to detect submarines. The locals around Ammanford and Clydach did not quite know what to make of the man. They listened to the strange noises from his workshops, noted the powerful lights at night.

Some even told stories about how their motorbike engines would suddenly cut out when they were riding on the mountain road – "Mr Matthews and his machine again," they would say.

Although the British government remained wary of his ideas they were sufficiently concerned about the safety of this wayward inventor that when war came in 1939 they were happy to provide electric fences and, for a while, troops to guard his property.

Harry Grindell Matthews died suddenly, from a heart attack, on 11th September 1941. His funeral was a low-key affair. Virtually nobody came and with the war raging against Germany people had other things on their minds – a sad end to a man of undoubted genius? To a man who hoodwinked the nation's press? To a confidence trickster of the highest order? You pays your money and you takes your guess!

83 – Dr Merlin Pryce and the Discovery of Penicillin

Most people remember Sir Alexander Fleming as the man who, on 3rd September 1928, discovered penicillin. Yet the part played in the discovery by his friend and colleague Merlin Pryce, a Welshman from the Merthyr area, should never be underestimated. Indeed, there are many who say that it was Pryce who actually discovered penicillin, not Fleming at all.

Merlin Pryce had been employed as research assistant to Fleming but in February 1928 moved on to work in other areas.

According to Mrs Hilda Jarman, Pryce's sister, Fleming went on holiday that summer and Merlin, calling in to say hello on what should have been Fleming's first day back at work, noticed blue-green mould on one of the petri dishes in the laboratory. Lab assistants should have cleared the dishes away but, for some reason, they had been left untouched.

Merlin Pryce drew the attention of Fleming to the petri dish, noting that no bacteria surrounded the mould. Something, as yet unknown, in the dead cells that lay apart from the mould had caused the bacteria to die. The rest, as they say, is history.

But one thing is sure – if Merlin Pryce had not noticed the mould and drawn it to the attention of Alexander Fleming penicillin would not have been discovered for several more years and, quite possibly, it would not have been available for the treatment of wounded soldiers during the Second World War.

While it is clear that the discovery of penicillin owes much to the work of other men, apart from Fleming – notably Florey and Chain who were responsible for developing the antibiotic and bringing penicillin to the hospital ward – Merlin Pryce, from the very beginning, played down his part in the affair. He was a modest man who insisted that credit for the discovery should rest solely with Dr Fleming.

Born at Troed-y-Rhiw in Merthyr, Merlin Pryce was educated at Pontypridd Boys Grammar School before moving on to the Welsh National School of Medicine when he was just seventeen years old. He then left Wales to study at St Mary's Hospital in Paddington, London and in 1927 was appointed to a Junior Research Scholarship under Fleming.

In the years to come Merlin Pryce enjoyed a successful and distinguished career in medicine, remaining devoted to St Mary's all his life. He became, after the war, first Reader and then Chair of Pathology at the hospital. He retained his affection for and relationship with Fleming right to the end, always maintaining that Sir Alexander was rightly honoured as the man who discovered penicillin.

Only twice did he ever break that stance – once, many years later, at an after-dinner speech to the West Kent Pharmaceutical Society and, for a second time, in an aside to Fleming's widow. After a joint interview with himself and Lady Fleming by Andre Maurois, Fleming's first biographer, she hissed at Pryce, "Anybody would think you discovered the mould." Pryce's response was a simple statement that summed up everything – "But I did."

At this distance – and without written evidence – it is hard to deduce quite why Merlin Pryce should actively seek to play down his part in the discovery.

He was, undoubtedly, a modest man and his devotion to St Mary's (as well as his relationship with Fleming) are perhaps indicators of the reasons for his stance. He would do nothing that would damage the reputation of either.

Merlin Pryce died on 8th February 1976, his reputation as a doctor and as a teacher unblemished. He could have been remembered for much, much more – if he had had the inclination to tell the world about the part he played in one of the most significant discoveries of the twentieth century.

84 – The Boys' Clubs of Wales

Many people across the country have cause to be grateful to the Youth Clubs that provided – and still provide – activities and education, in the broadest sense, for young people. In later years many of these clubs were funded and run by Local Authorities but at the beginning of the twentieth century the foundation of a Boys' Club Movement in Wales gave youth care a decided boost.

Founded by Captain J Glynn-Jones and David Davies of Llandinam – Wales's first millionaire and the builder of Barry Docks – the first Boys' Club was opened in Treharris in 1922.

Glynn-Jones, as Welfare Officer of David Davies' Ocean Group of Collieries, was faced by the problem of how to help and support adolescent collier boys who, after their shifts in the mines, found themselves with little to do apart from hang around street corners and get into mischief. His solution was to create a series of clubs where boys could be given something positive to occupy their minds – and hands.

The original Treharris Boys' Club was quickly followed by others in Nantymoel, Ton Pentre, Treorchy, Wattstown and Nine Mile Point:

> "They were led by full-time youth workers on a scale unparalleled elsewhere in Great Britain, even during a time of economic depression. Captain Glynn wanted every boy to be a member of a club which provided healthy exercises, cultural activities and discipline."
> (Quoted from 'Timeline, A History of the Boys' Club Movement in Wales'.)

Realising the need for greater unity, the various clubs formed themselves into The South Wales Federation of Boys' Clubs in August 1928 and in due course the organisation grew to include St Athan Boys' Village and, after the Second World War, the Abercrave Adventure Centre. These two establishments began to offer week-long activity programmes, specifically geared to the need of young people – no longer just collier boys.

In 1947 the organisation extended its operations across the whole of Wales, rather than simply the Welsh industrial valleys, becoming The Welsh Association of Boys' Clubs.

The changing needs of society caused serious financial difficulties in the 1980s and this resulted in the Association of Boys' Clubs having to change its role and even its name. The St Athan and Abercrave sites were sold off and the Welsh Federation of Boys' and Girls' Groups was came into existence in 1992.

"We held a meeting at Bettws Boys' Club in October 1991," says David Allen-Oliver, the first Chief Executive of the new organisation. "Eighty-four clubs joined the new organisation which was recognised by the Charity Commission the following year. And since then it's gone from strength to strength."

The new organisation has developed and grown and has now become one of the most important voluntary youth organisations in Wales. Just as the original organisation did back in the 1920s it continues to offer opportunities for young people through a wide range of educational, sporting, social and cultural activities. Captain Glynn-Jones's vision is still alive and, more importantly, still working.

85 – Murray the Hump, Welsh Gangster

Say the words "American gangster" and your mind inevitably turns to criminals like Al Capone, Pretty Boy Floyd or John Dillinger. But one of the most successful of all gangsters – perhaps because he lived to a ripe old age – was actually a man of Welsh descent.

His real name was Llewellyn Morris Humphreys and for many years, under the assumed name or nickname of Murray the Hump, he was one of the most powerful men in the whole Chicago underworld.

Murray the Hump's parents came from Carno, a few miles outside Newtown, having been married in the Methodist chapel at Llanidloes. However, the final years of the nineteenth century were difficult for the small Welsh farming community and the young couple found it difficult to make a living on their isolated hilltop farm. As a result they decided to emigrate to America in the hope of "making it big" in the New World. Their son, Llewellyn Morris Humphreys, was born in their first American home on North Street, Chicago in the year 1899.

Conditions in Chicago were not much better than in Carno and by the age of seven young Llewellyn had quit school and was making a living selling newspapers on the street corners. It was a rough and dangerous existence in a city where the newspaper sellers – and even the staff of the papers – fought with fists and baseball bats for the best pitches.

Luckily, Llewellyn found himself befriended by a local judge, Jack Murray, a man who took something of a benevolent and fatherly interest in the mischievous young boy. He soon adopted the judge's name, Murray, instead of Llewellyn – which was probably just as well because nobody in Chicago could even begin to pronounce his real name anyway. And, of course, it let the other paper sellers know that he had powerful "protection".

Murray the Hump, as he became known because of his fondness for wearing fashionable camel-hair coats, had big ambitions and he quickly moved on, out of newspaper selling, into the world of gangsters and hit men.

To begin with he worked as a hired gun – one of his victims was apparently Capone's arch-enemy Roger Touhy, blown apart by a shotgun blast shortly after his release from federal prison.

Nobody was ever able to solve the riddle of his murder and Murray the Hump was certainly not going to tell anyone about his part in the affair.

Forging his way up the ladder, Murray the Hump was one of the planners behind the infamous St Valentine's Day Massacre in 1929 when seven members of Bugsy Moran's gang were lined up against the wall of a garage in North Street, the very street where the Hump was born, and machine gunned to death. He was far too clever and too powerful to be involved in the killings himself but his was the hand that guided the machine gunners.

After that Murray the Hump was clearly destined for the top. He was the man who, when Prohibition was repealed in 1933, decided to channel the mobsters into the semi-respectable world of running bars, keeping saloons and distributing liquor.

He also became involved in controlling the unions and by the early 1950s the mob was making nearly $100,000 dollars a year under his careful and diligent management. The other interests of the mob, prostitution and gambling, the Hump kept to himself.

When Al Capone died in 1947, Murray the Hump succeeded him at the head of the organisation. The FBI were clear that the Hump was a violent and vicious gangster but one who always preferred to use his brain rather than the machine gun. He was, they declared, the gangster who introduced money laundering to the mob, investing money from crooked deals in what were otherwise legitimate businesses. He was the man, they said, who was responsible for the introduction of gambling to Las Vegas.

Violence, however, had long been a way of life for Murray the Hump. It is believed that he murdered the husband of one of his mistresses, stabbing him with an ice pick. He then went on to divorce his own wife, a Native American by the name of Mary, and soon afterwards married the younger mistress.

Murray the Hump never forgot his Welsh roots, so much so that he had a real desire to see what his native country was like. He visited Wales just once, in 1963, travelling to the land of his parents under an assumed name.

He never had the chance to come again as, two years later, at the age of sixty-six, he died suddenly at his Chicago home. It was perhaps just as well for the Welsh gangster as the FBI had just issued a warrant for his arrest and with his violent and murderous past beginning to catch up with him he was certainly looking at a long spell behind bars – or maybe even the death penalty.

86 – A Brief History of Cardiff Airport

These days around 1.6 million passengers use Cardiff Airport every year, flying off to destinations as varied as Florida, the Algarve and the Greek Islands. Most of them hurry through the terminal, eager to board their plane, and give little or no thought to the actual airport itself. Yet the story of the place is fascinating.

The airport's history dates from the early years of the Second World War when the Air Ministry requisitioned land in the village of Rhoose, about 12 miles to the west of Cardiff. Construction work began in 1941 and the aerodrome was officially opened on 7th June the following year. It was a training base, housing No. 53 Operational Training Unit where pilots could gain experience and learn to fly Spitfire fighters before being sent into the turmoil of aerial combat against the German Luftwaffe.

Just a few miles to the west of RAF Rhoose, as the new base was christened, lay the operational airfield of Llandow. Here pilots of the Canadian Air Force also flew Spitfires. Llandow continued to operate as an RAF airfield after the war, being the scene of Wales's worst ever air crash when an aeroplane carrying seventy-five rugby supporters back from the Triple Crown match in Dublin came down just outside the nearby village of Sigginston.

Unlike Llandow, when the war ended in 1945 the airfield at Rhoose was surplus to requirements. As a consequence it was turned over to commercial enterprise. Before the war flying had been the preserve of the privileged few, although for several years there had been a commercial airfield at East Moors outside nearby Cardiff.

Now, however, flying was a mode of transport that was suddenly open to everyone and there was a real demand for more airports. For a while the airfield at Rhoose housed only private flying clubs and a few commercial freight companies.

Then, in the wake of the Llandow air disaster, when it was at last realised that commercial airports required facilities for things like the weighing of baggage, people began to see that Rhoose was able to offer real opportunities for development. Aer Lingus opened a regular service to Dublin in 1952 and a few years later, on 1st April 1954, Cardiff Municipal Airport at Pengam Moors on the eastern side of the city transferred all its flights to Rhoose.

Shortly afterwards a new terminal building was opened and

flights began to operate to places like the Channel Islands, France, Belfast and Cork. By 1962 the new airport was handling over 100,000 passengers a year.

The 1970s saw huge developments with the airport's name being changed to Glamorgan, Rhoose Airport. Concorde landed a few times but in those days the runway was only long enough to take the mighty jet when she was lightly loaded. And she was not able to take off with passengers on board.

The runway was extended by 750 feet in 1986 and this enabled the airport – now called Cardiff - Wales Airport – to cater for transatlantic flights to Florida and Canada. British Airways quickly realised the value of the place and built a huge maintenance hangar alongside the runway, capable of handling the huge 747 jumbo jets that could now also land at Cardiff.

The airport was privatised in 1995 and, as the new millennium dawned, was recognised as the UK's 20th busiest airport. In 2009 came another name change and the place is now known simply as Cardiff Airport. These days flights are scheduled for destinations as varied as Majorca, Malta, Amsterdam (with its world-wide connections), Greece and Ireland.

Perhaps the most interesting recent development, however, has been the air link between Cardiff and Anglesey, planes flying into the RAF base at Valley.

This is the first air link between north and south Wales and though there has been a recent glitch – Highland Airways going into administration – this had little or nothing to do with the north-south Wales link. The route has now been taken over by Manx2 and the experiment looks set to continue.

Cardiff Airport is a vital part of the infrastructure of Wales. It looks set to grow and grow.

87 – People's Poetry of the Second World War

When you look at mainstream poetry of the Second World War it is obvious that, unlike the Great War of 1914-18, the conflict failed to throw up any really great poets. Perhaps Alun Lewis in the forces and Dylan Thomas as a civilian came close but, as far as war poetry is concerned, there was no one of the calibre and quality of writers such as Wilfred Owen, Siegfried Sassoon and Isaac Rosenberg.

However, when you read people's poetry, the poetry or verse written by ordinary men and women during the conflict, there is no doubt that, when taken overall, its quality is markedly superior to that produced by similar men and women in the earlier war. There are many reasons for this.

Universal education had, by 1939, been established for nearly seventy years and the educational system was now able to ensure that virtually everyone had the means and, in many cases, the desire to express themselves in verse.

Poetic experimentation in the 1920s and 1930s meant that there was a growing acceptance of free verse as an art form. So men like Gwyn Elwyn Evans could happily and easily write:

In skies above an alien land
They gave their lives –
By the thousand;
Tens of thousands.

When I am gone
Let it be said of me
'He flew with this illustrious band –
Bomber Command.'

During the Second World War men and women served all over the world – unlike in the Great War when, really, the conflict was limited to France and the Middle East. Their experiences of new and strange places often manifested itself in poetry:

We sat on the dark veranda and drank our beer,
Held by the alien, stifling Nigerian night.
The dank foliage ambushed us, wet and horrid,

Darting the unseen fireflies nervous light.
(John S M Jones)

But, of course, the Second World War was also the first real conflict to involve civilians on a huge, unparalleled scale. And it was, therefore, inevitable that they too should try to recount what was happening to them. Even before the war began local Welsh newspapers like *The Penarth Times* were warning about the dangers of things like gas attacks – and they were doing it, not in long dense leader columns where it would never have been read but in simple and highly accessible verse:

If you get a choking feeling and a smell of musty hay
You can bet your bottom dollar that there's phosgene on the way.
But the smell of bleaching powder will inevitably mean
That the enemy you're meeting is the gas we call chlorine.

Humour, certainly, was more prevalent in the Second World War. The art of subversion, challenging authority and those who felt they had a divine right to rule or lead, reached new heights during the war, arguably becoming something of an art form. It led, inevitably, to the Labour landslide of 1945 and to the anti-establishment satire of the 1950s and 60s. So serving soldiers could write about honour, companionship and death but they were, perhaps, at their best when they stuck their tongues in their cheeks and took a quiet pot shot at the men who had put them into their fox holes, gun turrets or submarines:

It's Churchill's fault we're stuck out here
With all the flies and sand,
While he and all his cronies
Live a life that's grand.
(Ken Burrows)

The thought of imminent death or mutilation often brought out a sardonic and self-deprecating train of humour – you couldn't help the situation you were in, you couldn't change it, but you could laugh at it:

You must remember this
That flack don't always miss
And one of you may die,
The fundamental thing applies
As flack goes by.

And when the fighters come
You hope you're not the one
To tumble from the sky.
The odds are too damned high
As flack goes by.
(Anon)

88 – The Loss of the *Arandora Star*

The sinking of the liner *Arandora Star* on 2nd July 1940 is a story of tragedy and human folly, a disaster that need never have happened.

The *Arandora Star*, previously run as a cruise ship by the Blue Star Line, had been commandeered by the Admiralty in the early days of the Second World War and on 1st July left Liverpool with nearly 1200 Italian and German internees on board. Early the following day she was torpedoed and sunk by U47 under the command of Gunther Prien, the German U Boat ace who, only the previous year, had conned his submarine into Scapa Flow and destroyed the battleship *Royal Oak*.

The roots of the disaster, however, go back many years. Almost every Welsh community in the 1920s and 30s had its Italian café or ice cream parlour. Most of the immigrants came to Wales from the Bardi area of Italy and were quickly integrated into Welsh society. Their cafes were places of refuge and hope, where a little warmth and comfort might be found during the dark days of the Depression.

However, when Mussolini declared war on Britain in June 1940 the Italian community – at least in the eyes of the Government – immediately became suspect. Fear of Fifth Columnists and spies meant that within days of Mussolini's declaration over 4000 Italians, men who had spent the vast majority of lives living in perfect harmony with the people of Britain, were behind bars. It was a harrowing experience. One young boy still remembers how his father had been arrested and interned:

> "They came for him at gunpoint in the night. The policeman hammered on the door as if we were criminals. My father thought something had happened – he hadn't a clue he was going to be arrested – I was a little boy of six and that was the last time I saw my father for eleven months."
> (From *Wales at War*, by Phil Carradice, Gomer Press)

The internees were taken, first, to transit camps and then to specially prepared accommodation on the Isle of Man. The plan was that, from there, all the Italian and German aliens – the term was deliberately used – would be shipped to Canada, well out of harm's way. The *Arandora Star* was the means of transporting them.

The ship did not have Red Cross markings on her side – something that might have warned off any stalking U Boat – as she had previously been used as a troop ship and it is quite possible that Prien mistook her for an armed merchant cruiser. Only one torpedo was fired and the *Arandora Star* sank in just over half an hour.

Over 800 lives were lost, several of the lifeboats either being destroyed in the attack or jamming in the davits:

> "My three uncles were all arrested together. My father went to the Isle of Man but the other three were put on the *Arandora Star*. Of course she was torpedoed and went down. The story is that Uncle Luigi jumped off the ship and survived. But either Guiseppi or Franco, I don't know which, went back to get his false teeth and the other one went with him. They both went down with the ship. Their families were very bitter for a long time with the British government for allowing the boat to sail."
> (From *Wales at War*, by Phil Carradice)

The bitterness was understandable. These were men who had little or no regard for Mussolini and his Fascist regime – they had far more in common with the Welsh – and were certainly not latent saboteurs or secret agents.

And the decision to risk the perils of a U Boat-infested Atlantic was, frankly, ludicrous. After the disaster the plan to send internees to Canada was quickly dropped and most of them sat out the war, until the Italian surrender of 1943, on the Isle of Man.

The interning of Italians during the Second World War was hardly the most glorious episode in British history. The sinking of the *Arandora Star* was equally as damning. July 2nd 2010 marks the 70th anniversary of that terrible event. It is a date we should all remember.

89 – Welsh Children at War – the Early Years

When war was declared against Germany on 3rd September 1939, the children of Wales could have been excused for thinking that, whatever might happen in Poland or France, it would have little or no effect on them. Wales was too far to the west to be greatly influenced or affected, out of range of the German bombers, and well protected by the huge might of the Royal Navy.

And yet, contrary to what they believed, the outbreak of war did have an immediate impact on Welsh children when the government, on the day after the declaration of war, closed all of the schools in Britain for a period of up to a week – and Welsh schools were included in the list of closures.

This extra week's holiday brought great delight for children all over the country but its purpose was both pragmatic and sensible – its purpose, in fact, was pure safety. Nobody knew if air attacks would be launched by Germany and schools, along with cinemas and almost any places of public gathering, could offer great targets. That much had been learned by the German zeppelin and Gotha bombing raids of the First World War when several hundred civilians had been killed and a school in the East End of London destroyed in one of the later raids.

Much better to shut down these places where large numbers of people congregated, at least for a while. That would, at least, keep people safe. No immediate bombing attacks took place, however, and, to the dismay of the children, most schools re-opened within the week, thus making the extra holiday very short-lived indeed.

The other event that had an immediate affect on Welsh children was the arrival of hundreds of evacuees in the towns and villages, even in the cities, of the country. The government had laid out plans for wholesale evacuation of children from large industrial centres like London, Liverpool and Birmingham long before war actually began.

In fact there had already been an evacuation programme in operation during the Munich Crisis of 1938 but once Prime Minister Chamberlain had secured "peace in our time" it was abandoned and all of the children soon returned home.

The Polish Crisis of 1939 was an altogether more serious affair and to government planners and civil servants it was inevitable that, sooner or later, war against Hitler's Germany would break out.

As a consequence, Britain had been divided up into three separate regions or sections – neutral, reception and evacuation. Neutral areas were those parts of the country where there was not any great danger while reception regions were the places where evacuated people could be safely housed. Evacuation areas were those places where danger from bombing was greatest and therefore parts of the country from where the most vulnerable members of society – namely the very young – needed to be removed. Most of Wales was designated as a reception area.

The order to evacuate children was given on 31st August 1939, three days before war broke out. Over the following week almost two million people, most of them children, were sent away from their families in the industrial cities of the south-east and the midlands into the countryside of the west. Many of them went to the rural parts of south and north Wales.

In many cases schools were evacuated en masse, teachers simply moving with their pupils. Very young children were accompanied by their mothers but, in the main, it was a case of simply heading for the station and setting off for places unknown and probably never even dreamed about:

> "I remember a crocodile of little ones having to walk to school. There we were tagged with a luggage label with our name and details. And then we were taken by bus to the station and put on a train."
> (Dennis Barratt in *Wales at War* by Phil Carradice)

The traumatic effect of such uprooting on these young evacuees, being suddenly snatched away from family and loved ones, from everything that was familiar and known, can only be imagined. And of course there was always the fear that, back home in London or Birmingham, bombs might be dropping and destroying people and places while they slept safe and secure in their beds.

For the children of Wales, the sudden and unexpected arrivals of parties of youngsters from Liverpool or Manchester were often moments of high adventure. Local children would stand, staring, as the evacuees disembarked from their trains and follow them along the road to the dispersal centres. The new arrivals were almost exotic for boys and girls who had rarely ventured more than ten miles from their home towns.

In hindsight the evacuation process was far from humane, particularly the way children were herded together in a central location and chosen or rejected, just like cattle at a farmers market. Despite this process, in most cases the evacuees were welcomed warmly enough, although there were always exceptions.

Evacuee children had to attend school along with their Welsh counterparts and in places where the main language was Welsh there were several teething problems. For children from London and other industrial centres, the sights and sounds of the Welsh countryside were, to say the least, unusual. It was effectively the meeting of two cultures and after the initial curiosity had worn off what often emerged were moments of conflict:

> "We were Welsh – they couldn't understand us and we couldn't understand them – We understood some of the words they used – "Daft", we knew what that meant. So we had to have a battle, the whole of Llanllynfni children against the evacuees, by the bridge, down at the bottom of the village."
> (Eluned Giles in *Wales at War* by Phil Carradice)

As the months went on, of course, local Welsh children and English evacuees grew to accept and even like each other. Many long-lasting friendships were formed and each group – English and Welsh – influenced the lives and development of the other.

When the war ended most evacuees returned home. Indeed, many had already gone, having slipped back to the places of their birth once the main German bombing attacks ended in 1943. But many stayed on and made the country their home. Wales, after all, had been one of the most significant factors in their growth from childhood to adolescence.

90 – The Bombing of the Pembroke Dock Oil Tanks

On Monday 19th August 1940 three German Junkers bombers, escorted by two ME109 fighters, flew in over the Pembrokeshire coast and dropped their bombs onto the oil tanks high above the west Wales town of Pembroke Dock. The tanks contained thousands of gallons of vitally important fuel oil and when one of the bombs hit its target it started a fire, the like of which had never been seen in Wales before.

A sheet of flame leapt into the air and the noise of the explosion echoed around the town. Then a huge column of smoke began to billow out of the stricken tank and climb like the sword of Damocles into the sky. The smoke hung there, above the town and the desperate Civil Defence workers who fought to quell the blaze for the next eighteen days.

The Pembroke Dock oil tank fire was the largest fire that Britain had seen since the Great Fire of London in 1666 and the resources to fight it were pitifully few. Initially just one tank had been hit but despite the heroic efforts of Pembroke Dock fire chief Arthur Morris and his team of part-time firemen the flames soon began to spread from one tank to the next.

Hurried appeals were sent out to fire brigades all across the country, asking for men and fire-fighting appliances. Help came from all quarters, from Milford Haven and Narberth and from places as far afield as Swansea and Cardiff. But, at this early stage, nobody quite realised what was facing them. As one Cardiff fireman later said:

> "We'd got as far as St Clears when we noticed the cloud. We didn't realise what was going on until we got a bit further and by then, of course, we were right in the middle of it."
> (Quoted in *Wales at War* by Phil Carradice)

In the end twenty-two fire brigades were involved, over 500 men, from places as far away as Birmingham and Cardiff. The blaze raged for eighteen days and, eventually, eleven of the eighteen tanks were destroyed, their valuable contents just burning, vanishing into the ether or running in a great black river down the road towards the town.

For a while there was a very real possibility that the fire would spread even further than the tank farm and citizens of Pembroke Dock lived in constant fear that the burning oil would set all of their houses alight.

A pall of black smoke hangs like the Sword of Damacles over the town of Pembroke Dock, summer 1940. It remained in the sky above the town and dockyard for three weeks after the oil tanks were bombed.

Dozens of firemen were injured and overcome with exhaustion. Tragically, five Cardiff firemen were killed when the wall of one burning tank just splintered or ruptured and a sea of burning oil engulfed them. Their names are still remembered in Pembroke Dock – Frederick George Davies, Clifford Miles, Ivor John Kilby, Trevor Charles Morgan and John Frederick Thomas – and on a memorial at the site of the inferno.

Molten oil ran out of the tanks, coating the firemen who, in those days, had no specialised equipment or clothing. Sometimes it seemed as if it was raining oil. The men who fought the fire never forgot it:

> "Oh, the flames, they were thirty or forty feet up in the air and you wouldn't believe the width of them. And then the smoke. And oil dropping down. You couldn't

> go too close because it was so hot. What we were doing was cooling the unaffected tanks and the ones on fire. But as one tank seemed to empty another would catch fire."
>
> (Quoted in *Wales at War* by Phil Carradice)

When the fire was eventually extinguished controversy erupted. Arthur Morris, hero of the hour, a man who did not leave the scene of the blaze and had literally slept only in snatches – at the side of his Merryweather Fire Engine – for eighteen days, was passed over in the awards so liberally given out to others – several of whom spent virtually no time at all at the scene of the disaster.

Arthur Morris was never a "yes man", always being regarded as a fireman's fireman. But if he had been critical of the operation then no one ever knew. He remained tight-lipped and took the secret – if secret there was – with him to his grave.

The Pembroke Dock fire was soon to be eclipsed by other fires in London, Coventry and Birmingham as the German bombing offensive gathered momentum.

However, that should never minimise the significance of the disaster and seventy years ago it was a real and terrifying ordeal, not just for the firemen involved but for the whole of the small community of Pembroke Dock.

91 – Rudolf Hess in Wales

Most people know the name Rudolf Hess. Many know the story of his dramatic midnight flight to Scotland in 1941, supposedly in an attempt to broker peace between Britain and Nazi Germany. Yet how many realise that from 1942 until 1945, when he was flown to Nuremberg to stand trial for crimes against humanity, Hess spent virtually all of his time in captivity in Wales?

Rudolf Hess was Hitler's deputy in the Nazi Party and, despite his clear mental fragility, he was a significant figure in the German state. The reasons for his flight to Britain have never really been made clear. Was it a genuine attempt to find a peaceful solution to the conflict? Did he seek just to recover ground and influence with Hitler, ground he had lost to people like Himmler and Goering? And then, there are those who say it wasn't Hess at all, just a duplicate or stand-in.

Whatever his reasons, Hess flew to Scotland on the night of 10th May 1941 in an ME 110 fighter bomber, bailed out over Eaglesham and injured his leg in the process. Arrested by members of the Home Guard – an indignity that irked him greatly, both at the time and in the coming months – he spent several weeks in places like the Tower of London (the last man ever to be imprisoned there) and at Camp Z in Aldershot, obviously undergoing interrogation and debriefing.

Following a supposed Polish plot to assassinate him, on 26th June 1942 Hess was brought to Maindiff Court Military Hospital and POW Reception Centre outside Abergavenny.

Before the war Maindiff Court had been an admission unit for a mental hospital in the town and there were many who thought that Hess – who had already attempted suicide by throwing himself off a balcony in his prison in Aldershot – was well placed.

At Maindiff Court Hess had his own room and there were invariably a pair of guards on duty outside his door at all times. He did, however, have a fair degree of freedom, often being driven about the local countryside, in some style, by his gaolers.

He was allowed to take walks around the grounds, his guards maintaining a close watch from a discreet distance. On several occasions he visited places like White Castle and there are even rumours that he once went to dinner with Lord Tredegar in Newport's Tredegar House.

The British government never tried to hide the fact that Hess was being detained in Abergavenny. Indeed, when he first arrived, the staff of the hospital/centre actually lined up in a formal reception to meet him. And the news did feature in many of the national papers of the time. There was certainly no attempt to play down, or keep low profile, his presence in the quiet Welsh border town. All of this has added fuel to the belief that this was not the real Rudolf Hess, just a double or look-alike, and the publicity was simply adding fuel to the fire. The truth may never be known.

Always supposing that the prisoner in Abergavenny was actually Hitler's deputy, this was not the first connection between the Hess family and Wales. It is possible that Carl Hess, Rudolf's father, actually lived in Cardiff for a short while. Certainly Carl's first wife, not Rudolf's mother, was buried in the parish churchyard at Michaelstone-y-Fedw so there may be a degree of truth in the story.

Hess's sojourn in Wales came to an end in October 1945 when he was taken to Nuremberg where, alongside people like Goering and von Ribbentrop, he was accused of war crimes. Unlike many of his co-defendants, Hess did not face the rope but was sentenced to life imprisonment for his part in creating and administering the infamous Nazi regime.

Rudolf Hess lived out the remainder of his long life at Spandau Prison in Berlin, being the sole occupant of the jail once Albert Speer and Von Schirach were released in 1966. Rumours of him being a double persisted right to the end, an end that came on 17th August 1987.

There are still many people who remember seeing Hess in Abergavenny or at places like White Castle. And despite the rumours most of these are clear – the man kept at Maindiff Court was no double, this really was Rudolf Hess.

92 – Cut in Half Yet She Sailed Again – the Story of the *Tafelberg*

Imagine it. A merchant ship blown in half by a mine and then simply welded together again so that she could continue to play a role in the effort to keep Britain supplied during the dark days of World War Two. That is exactly what happened to the oil tanker *Tafelberg*.

Built by Armstrong Whitworth at Newcastle, the *Tafelberg* was originally a whale factory ship. Owned by the Kerguellen Sealing and Whaling Company, there was such a shortage of ships that she was converted into an oil tanker soon after war broke out in 1939.

The *Tafelberg* made several voyages but then, on 28th January 1941 she struck a mine in the Bristol Channel. The ship was relatively close to shore when the mine exploded and was able to signal for assistance. Several Pilot Boats and five Cardiff tugs – the *Bristolian, Cargarth, Merimac, Standard Rose* and *Blazer* – came to the rescue. The *Tafelberg* was taken in tow and, rather than allow her to sink in what was then a very busy waterway, she was beached on the coast at Porthkerry, to the west of Barry Island.

Unfortunately, the mine had caused serious structural damage and the *Tafelberg* broke in half during the operation. For several months the two sections of the stranded ship lay on the shingle, her active life seeming to be over. She was declared a total loss. For some time her only companions were the wheeling seagulls overhead and the few sightseers who could be bothered to make the journey out to Porthkerry from Barry or Cardiff. But fate still had a hand to play in the life of the *Tafelberg*.

Ships were urgently needed in those days and it was decided that the *Tafelberg* could still be saved. The "wreck" was acquired by the Ministry of War Transport and, after ensuring that they were watertight, the two halves were towed, first, to Whitmore Bay at Barry and then to the docks in Cardiff.

Over the next few months dockworkers and builders laboured to simply join the two halves of the stricken ship back together. It was an amazing job but it was not the first time such an operation had taken place during the war. The *Imperial Transport* had been torpedoed in 1940 and though the front section had sunk, the rear half survived. It was taken into port, a new bow section built and the ship sailed on, surviving another torpedoing and being scrapped in 1958.

The *Tafelberg* was not so lucky, however. Renamed the *Empire Heritage* she was torpedoed and sunk on 8th September 1944 by the U 482. The ship was off Malin Head when she was hit and a large number of crew and passengers went down with her.

The extra space on the old whaling ship meant that she was carrying over fifty passengers and most of these were lost in the disaster. Forty-seven members of her crew and eight gunners also drowned.

The story of the *Tafelberg* is one of fortitude and imagination. It is just sad to think that the ship, welded together with such skill and care, did not survive to see the victory celebrations. Nevertheless, her story does remain an important part of the nautical history of South Wales.

The tanker Tafelberg, shown here ashore at Porthkerry, in two halves, before being towed to Cardiff and welded back together.

93 – Welsh Children at War

Arguably, children – more than any other section of society – should have been aware of the nation's preparations for war during the 1930s. They watched the newsreel features, usually pushed in between the first and second features, at the cinema and read comics that told stories about conflict and the bravery of soldiers. They collected cigarette cards showing things like war planes of the world and Air Raid Precautions. And yet they, like everyone else, were stunned when war finally broke out in 1939.

Welsh children reacted by doing what they did best – they carried on playing. Not, in those days, on computer games or television. Such luxuries lay well in the future. Games for children, in cities like Cardiff or Swansea and in rural areas such as Pembroke and Ruthin, were invariably what you could make up in your head:

> "We had hopscotch and rounders, marbles and 'Mob'. For 'Mob' you shut your eyes, counted to twenty and then you had to find your friends. Indoors, at night, we played games like Snakes and Ladders or Ludo and Snap. We got around by bus or bicycle. Or simply by walking. There was no being picked up by cars – once a year you might have a real treat, to go by train to Barry Island for the day."
> (Sylvie Bailey in *Wales at War* by Phil Carradice)

British toy manufacturers soon cottoned on to a growing or developing market. In pre-war days, many of the best dyecast toys had tended to come from Germany, from firms like Bing who had been making them for years. After the outbreak of hostilities such toys or models were no longer available and British toy-makers had no alternative but to produce their own..

In the early days of the war a whole range of tanks, warships and aeroplanes were produced, many of them from manufacturers in places like Merthyr Tydfil. It was only as the war went on that materials for such luxuries became scarce and from 1942 onwards such toys were in very short supply. Children were forced to jealously guard their old and, by now, rather battered models.

No matter. For the children of Wales there was always the

great outdoors. Racing across the fields, building hides and dens, even playing in the wrecks of crashed aeroplanes, these were what mattered. To the mind of a child, the destruction going on overhead or overseas meant very little. The imagination was all-powerful.

Even the impedimenta of war provided the opportunity for play. Gas mask cases made excellent goal posts while the masks themselves were sometimes the source of unexpected fun, as one man from Newport remembered:

> "Every now and then the teacher would call out 'Gas', in which case we had to get our masks out and put them on. We soon realised that by blocking the intake and then blowing, air was expelled from the sides of the mask. And very realistic farting sounds were made. You'd hear the muffled laughter from inside the masks."
> (Bryan Hope in *Wales at War* by Phil Carradice)

Shrapnel collecting was one of the most popular activities, particularly in places such as Swansea and Barry, towns that – once France had fallen and, therefore, the range of German bombers extended – were heavily attacked on a regular basis.

On the morning after a raid, parties of children would roam the streets searching for the largest or most interesting pieces of shrapnel. Sometimes the shrapnel – the odd pieces of anti-aircraft shells or bombs that were scattered across the place – was still hot. Shrapnel collecting was an activity that both boys and girls enjoyed and long and intense were the discussions in the school playground over who had acquired the best bits.

Many children belonged to organisations such as the Boy Scouts and Girl Guides. During the war years these groups quickly turned their activities towards helping children and young people do their bit for the war effort. Collecting metal to turn into planes and erecting Morrison Shelters – steel tables in living rooms for people who had no room to build a shelter out in the garden – were just two of the many tasks that the scouts carried out.

The creation of the Air Cadets soon offered another outlet for activity and ATC Squadrons came into existence right across Wales.

Above all, however, there was the cinema. During the war years the popularity of cinema-going reached its zenith as men, women and children queued around the block to watch the latest Hollywood epic and the cartoons that were universally adored. To lose yourself in a cowboy film or a classic like *Gone with the Wind* was an opportunity, brief as it might be, to forget the troubles of the war for a few short hours. It was something that everyone enjoyed.

It would be wrong to say that the children of Wales – just like children across Britain – enjoyed the war years. But they endured them and, quite simply, made the best out of a very bad job.

94 – American GIs in Wales

During the Second World War nearly three million American soldiers and airmen were sent to Britain, most of them arriving in the years 1943 and 1944, prior to the D Day landings in France. Wales housed more than its fair share of these exuberant and sometimes brash young men who were, in the opinion of many, "over-paid, over-sexed – and over here!"

The "over-sexed" comment was, perhaps, appropriate as there were over 70,000 GI brides in Britain by the end of the war. Even a small south Wales town like Barry produced no fewer than 56 of them!

There was virtually no part of Wales that did not see American troops and the constant children's cry of "Got any gum chum?" was heard on streets in towns as varied as Aberystwyth, Haverfordwest, Abergavenny, Swansea and Cardiff.

And it was not just chewing gum that the Yanks gave away – the Americans were incredibly generous, wherever they were stationed. As D Day approached they happily presented the locals with cans of chicken, sides of beef or ham and tins of coffee, giving them out almost to anyone who needed it. For the people of Wales, who had been suffering from food rationing for several years, they were welcome gifts.

Barry, then an important port, became a huge hub for American servicemen, over 40 ships eventually leaving the port to take part in the D Day landings. They built a camp in the part of the town known as Highlight and used to take children from Cadoxton to picture shows, picking them up in their enormous six-wheeled army lorries – never mind the cinema, for many of the Welsh children this journey was the highlight of the whole affair.

It was not all fun and games in Barry, however, and the ugly spectre of racism did rear its head on a number of occasions. Thompson Street in the town was eventually placed "out of bounds" after an American complained that he had seen a black soldier being served in one of the clubs in the area. The club owners and the town council, well-used to serving men of all races and colours – this was a dock area, after all – refused to ban black soldiers and the American senior staff took exception and refused their soldiers permission to even walk down the street.

Mostly, however, relations between the Welsh and the

Americans were much more cordial. Sometimes entertainment provided for the Americans was a little bizarre. As one Artillery Officer, stationed for a while in Denbigh, later recorded:

> "Constant entertainment was provided in a public hall in the town or at a mental hospital on the outskirts."

The idea of holding a dance at a mental hospital seems now to be a strange one but back in the 1940s these huge edifices were communities in their own right and the staff had, for years, organised their own entertainment. In Abergavenny things were a little more straightforward, as Christine Jones remembers:

> "Abergavenny was full of Yanks, every night. They all wanted to know where the dances were being held. We used to have concerts every Sunday night in the Town Hall and there were dances every Saturday. In the Angel they used to have a place called a Doughnut Dugout."
> (Quoted in *Wales at War* by Phil Carradice)

Those who knew who and what to look for sometimes spotted famous faces. Rudolph Hess was regularly seen around the countryside, being driven out by his two armed guards, but he was a German and therefore nowhere near as interesting as some of the visiting Americans. Christine Jones was working as a telephone engineer:

> "I went to Gilwern Hospital one day and was on this ladder against a pole. I was putting in the wire and Jimmy Cagney walked by. James Cagney! I lodged in Abergavenny at the time and the children where I was staying said 'Why didn't you get his autograph?' But he hadn't seen me and just walked by with two soldiers each side. I never thought of it until I got home and the children asked."
> (Quoted in *Wales at War* by Phil Carradice)

Haverfordwest hosted an equally famous American, one Rocco Marchegiano, better known as World Heavyweight boxing champion Rocky Marciano.

Rocky was stationed in the area and while his boxing career

only took off after the war, locals from the town still talk about fistfights between Rocky and his Welsh counterparts. The nearby town of Pembroke Dock had an even more famous visitor when, on 1st April 1944, General Dwight Eisenhower – later President of the USA but then Supreme Allied Commander – paid an unexpected visit to the American 110th Regiment in the town's Llanion Barracks.

Eisenhower arrived in Tenby by train and was then taken by fast military convoy, complete with howling sirens and motorbike outriders, to Pembroke Dock. Despite chilly, damp weather he climbed into the back of a jeep to address the men, promising to have a drink with them on the day they crossed the Rhine.

Famous visitors were one thing but for most American GIs the brief period they spent in Wales was an interlude before the real business of war began in earnest. It was an experience most of them never forgot.

95 – Follow in the Footsteps of Welsh Writers

Writers have always been fascinated by people and places. The individuals who inspired the great writers of the past, who acted as role models for their fictional characters, are long dead and therefore beyond our reach. But it is not the same with places.

We can still get in touch with the lives of great writers – and thereby gain greater insight into their literary creations – by visiting locations that meant something to them. It might be a place they wrote about, somewhere they visited or stayed, or a landscape that impinged itself in their subconscious.

But, in particular, the houses where they lived, either as children or during their adult lives, invariably had a huge effect on their development. In Wales we are lucky. So many of the houses where our literary heroes lived are still in existence and, equally as important, are still accessible.

In the footsteps of writers – Dylan Thomas's Boat House.

Dylan Thomas, of course, has several houses. His place of birth and home during the most fertile writing period of his life is

Cwmdonkin Drive in Swansea. It sits just opposite Cwmdonkin Park – the park, like the house, features in many of his writings, poetry and prose alike, and is easily accessible for those who want to experience a little of the atmosphere that inspired him.

The Boat House in Laugharne is, perhaps, Thomas's most famous residence and is open to the public most days. Yet he lived in this "sea girt" house for only four years, from 1949 until his death in America in 1953. Visitors to Laugharne can also wander past Sea View, another house where Thomas had earlier lived, and stare at the Pelican, in the main street – where his parents stayed and his father died – or enjoy a drink, just like the man himself, in Brown's Hotel, almost directly over the road.

Laugharne was also home to another author, Richard Hughes, who wrote *A High Wind in Jamaica* and, incidentally, the world's first radio play – set in a coal mine. He lived in part of Laugharne Castle where Dylan and Caitlin Thomas would lie waiting for him to leave before helping themselves from his copious wine cellar.

T E Lawrence – Lawrence of Arabia – was born in what is now called Lawrence House in Tremadog, Caernarfonshire while nearby, just outside Porthmadog, is Plas Tan-yr-Allt where the romantic poet Percy Bysshe Shelley lived from 1812 to 1813.

Prohibited from taking the "Grand Tour" in Europe because of the Napoleonic Wars, Shelley decided to settle for a while in mountainous north Wales. The house is now a very up-market guest house so you can actually stay there, too, if you wish.

The Welsh language poet Hedd Wyn (real name Ellis Evans) came from Yr Ysgwrn at Trawsfynydd. His nephew will happily show you around the farmhouse where Hedd Wyn's bardic chairs are on display, including the famous Black Chair that he won at the National Eisteddfod of 1917, six weeks after his death at Passchendaele.

There are many other writers who once lived in Wales. And there are questions to be answered.

Where, for example, did Dickens stay when he came to write about the *Royal Charter* wreck off Moelfre in 1859?

For literary detectives the Welsh houses of famous writers could be very fertile ground.

96 – The Great Snows of 1947, 1962 and 1963

Most of us have an idealised version of our childhood years. In our memories the sun shone all summer long and it was always light until 10.00 or 11.00 at night. It rarely rained apart from when there were thunder storms, the intensity of which has never been repeated.

In particular, it snowed every year, crisp white snow like balls of cotton wool – and always at Christmas. As Dylan Thomas said, "There was always snow at Christmas."

That might be, mainly, how people fantasise about their past. Yet there are elements of truth in those dreams. Three years, in particular, have impinged themselves on the imagination of everyone who experienced them. They were, for many, the snowiest months this country has ever seen.

First there was the winter of 1947. It was just two years after the end of the Second World War and Britain was certainly not prepared for such an onslaught of harsh weather conditions. The snow began on 21st January and within hours roads and railway lines across Wales – across the whole of Britain, come to that – were totally blocked.

Coal was already in short supply, the mining industry not having recovered from the privations of the war years, and now trains and lorries struggled to get what limited stocks that were available through to the power stations. Many of these power stations simply ran out of fuel and were left with no alternative other than to shut down. And that, of course, meant power cuts, at a time when people really needed their electricity.

Reluctantly, the government was forced to cut domestic electricity supplies to just 18 hours a day. It was a hugely unpopular move and the Labour Party was to suffer dearly for the restriction in the elections of 1950. That was not all, however. Radio broadcasts were severely limited and the new TV service, so recently reinstated after being suspended for the duration of the war, found itself once more being shut down until the crisis had passed.

Newspapers were reduced in size and many magazines, being regarded by the government as hardly essential, were totally closed down. Shops and schools were shut – the latter to the great delight of children across the country. For them the prospect of sledging and snowball fights were far more inviting than boring lessons in cold, drafty classrooms. For their parents, however, it was a time of deprivation and considerable concern. As the weeks of snow and cold dragged on there were even fears of food shortages as farmers could not tend their crops and livestock. Vegetables were simply frozen into the ground.

On the Denbighshire hills there was 1.5 metres (five foot) of snow with drifts of over twenty feet in some places. Men and women did not walk down lanes, they simply walked over them, and their flanking hedges, as the snow lay so deep and thick. Public transport simply could not run, particularly in the rural areas of Wales, and with whole villages cut off for days on end the RAF was forced to make vital food drops to the stranded populace.

Manny Shinwell, the government minister in charge of the country's economic situation, became the most despised man in the country. He even received death threats and had to be given a police escort. It was not until the middle of March that the snow eventually began to thaw. But when it did it did so very quickly – with the result that in many parts, with the ground beneath the snow so frozen, there was nowhere for the water to go and severe flooding began to occur.

The snow of 1962/63 (the Big Freeze as it is sometimes known) was not so severe as that of 1947 but it certainly lasted much longer. For nearly three months icy, barren wastes of snow lay across the land and the only way of travelling around was on foot as buses and cars found themselves marooned in deep snow drifts. Roads were death traps that only the most desperate or foolish would even try to use. That winter has been recorded as Britain's coldest period since 1740.

Snow began to fall on Boxing Day 1962, followed by a severe blizzard over south-west England and Wales on 29th and 30th of December. Power lines were brought down and, as if the snow wasn't enough, large parts of the country were hit by freezing fog. In February 1963 there was more snow, this time accompanied by gale-force winds, and temperatures in parts of rural Denbighshire fell to minus 18 degrees centigrade.

Lakes and rivers froze and huge blocks of ice were seen on many beaches. It was even reported that, at Penarth in Glamorganshire, the sea actually froze solid and huge lumps of ice – icebergs, in fact – were seen sailing serenely down the Bristol

Channel!

With roads and pavements more like sheets of glass than user-friendly tarmac, miners in the Welsh valleys found it increasingly difficult to reach their pits and many mines actually closed – with the inevitable result that coal supplies ran short. Factories closed and sporting fixtures right across the country were called off.

In the minds and memories of many people it seemed as if the freezing conditions had been here for ever. Finally, however, things began to improve.

The morning of 6th March was the first time since the snow began to fall on Boxing Day the year before that people awoke to a day of no frost. After that a quick thaw set in as temperatures rose and the Great Freeze was finally over.

These days we rarely have snow like that of 1947 and 1962/63. Climatic conditions are different now but there is no doubt that for every person who lived through those traumatic times the great snow falls will never be forgotten.

97 – The End of the *Conway*

The coastline of Wales has seen thousands of shipwrecks over the years but none is more interesting than that of the famous boys training ship *Conway* which went ashore in the Menai Straits on 14th April 1953. It was a shipwreck out of time as the *Conway* was an old wooden battleship, one of many once used to train boys for careers afloat.

The ship involved in the wreck was actually the third *Conway*, the vessels having been changed as they became too tired and dilapidated, but the name was always retained. This third *Conway* was actually the ninety-one gun battleship *Nile* but everyone associated with the training ship knew her only as the *Conway*. From a fleet of over 100 training establishments that were once located around the coast of Britain, ships and shore bases that trained both officers and crew, by 1953 the *Conway* had become almost the last of her kind.

The Training Ship *Conway*, beached and back broken, ashore in the Menai Straits.

Founded in 1859, she was intended to train officers for Britain's enormous merchant fleet. She was, to begin with, moored off Rock Ferry on the Mersey and here 120 young boys came for a two year intensive course of seamanship before beginning their careers as apprentices in one of the great shipping lines.

It was a hard and rugged life. The upper deck had to be scrubbed every day, regardless of the weather, the task invariably being carried out in bare feet. The rope's end across the back was a common punishment if tasks, physical and theoretical, were not carried out quickly or efficiently enough. As you might expect on an old ship full of adolescent boys, a fair amount of bullying took place. As one young trainee later said:

> "I don't think I shall ever forget the stinging clout I got on my head on my first day; and all my toffee was taken from me. There was too much bullying and small new chums were not looked after as they should have been. The result was that I lived to bully other small boys but, thank goodness, I was soon ashamed of myself."
> (Quoted in *Nautical Training Ships* by Phil Carradice)

Amongst famous *Conway* boys were the poet John Masefield (who later wrote a book about the ship) and Captain Matthew Webb, the first man to swim the English Channel – he was not considered a particularly good swimmer while he was training on board.

The *Conway* remained on the Mersey until the dark days of the Second World War when, for safety reasons, she was moved to the Menai Straits and moored, firstly off Bangor and, from 1949, off Plas Newydd on Ynys Mon. The ship was owned by the Mercantile Marine Service Association, continuing to operate as a training ship, despite her old age and lack of modern facilities. Then in 1953 it was decided that, if she was to continue functioning, she required a refit.

The intention was to tow her to Cammel Laird's dry dock in Birkenhead, a task that involved navigating the treacherous Swillies Channel in the Menai Straits. It was a trip that had to be done at high tide but, even then, the clearance between the Devil's Teeth Rocks was a mere four feet.

On the morning of 14th April, towed by the tugs *Dongarth* and *Minegarth,* the old ship left her moorings. All went well until the *Conway* passed the Menai Suspension Bridge and there she was met by the flood tide. A sudden north-westerly wind doubled the strength of the tide and the two tugs simply could not make headway. The towing hawser parted and *Conway*'s bows swung helplessly round towards the Caernarfonshire shore.

Under the gaze of thousands of enthralled spectators, there was a roar like a million pebbles being washed along the beach and ship ploughed up onto the foreshore.

An inspection soon revealed that her hull was badly buckled and strained – there was little hope of refloating her, at least not immediately. During the very next high tide, however, the *Conway* flooded aft and before anyone could do anything about it she had broken her back.

The *Conway* was abandoned and lay for many months on the foreshore. She provided an interesting attraction for the tourists and the locals alike, most of whom had never seen an old woodenwall in the flesh, so to speak.

The ship's trainees were educated, for a while, at Plas Newydd, the house of the Marquess of Anglesey, but the great days of the British mercantile marine were already coming to an end. There was, quite simply, no longer any need of an establishment like the *Conway*.

Declared a total loss, it was decided that the *Conway* should be broken up where she lay. This was duly done, the remains of the hull being finally destroyed by fire in October 1956. It was a sad end for a once proud ship, a vessel that had provided thousands of officers for the merchant navy – and more than a few for the Royal Navy, too.

In the wake of the disaster Captain Eric Hewitt, who had been on board at the time, was much criticised. However, the responsibility for the tow rested with the towing master, not *Conway*'s Captain. Knowing the strength of the tides in the Menai Straits, Hewitt had asked for three tugs but had been told that two were more than enough for the job – as they sometimes say, hindsight is the only exact science.

98 – Welsh One-hit Wonders

Who was the first Welsh man (as opposed to the first Welsh woman – that was Shirley Bassey) to top the UK singles charts? Tom Jones? Shakin' Stevens? Good guesses but both wrong. It was actually Ricky Valance who hit the No 1 spot in September 1960 with "Tell Laura I Love Her".

Ricky's cover version of "Tell Laura" spent three weeks at No 1 and sold over a million copies. These days the singles charts mean very little; albums are what count now. But back in 1960, when teenagers horded their pocket money to buy those desirable pieces of vinyl, to top the charts was a major achievement. "Tell Laura I Love Her" was an instant hit, despite the disapproval of the BBC who considered it (and all "death ballads") in bad taste.

Unfortunately, Ricky – real name David Spencer, from Ynysddu outside Newport – was unable to repeat his success. Although he went on to have further hits in Austria and Scandinavia he never featured in the UK charts again, a true Welsh one-hit wonder. He now lives in Spain and still performs on the cabaret and "nostalgia" circuit.

Another Welsh one-hit wonder was Maureen Evans. Her first recordings were released by Embassy Records, the Woolworth's budget price label that, really, produced only quick cover versions, but it was in 1962 that she hit the big time with "Like I Do". The song was based on a piece of classical music, "Dance of the Hours" – just like Alan Sherman's later comedy record "Hello Muddah, Hello Fadduh".

Maureen's song climbed to No 3 in the charts and was a regular play on Radio Luxembourg, in the days before Radio 1 and 2. She was never able to repeat her chart success, even though she competed in the British heats or trials for the 1963 Eurovision Song Contest. She finished third, crooner Ronnie Carroll being given the chance to sing for the UK that year. He didn't win!

Born in Cardiff in 1940, Maureen Evans continued to sing professionally throughout the 60s and 70s. She still lives in the city and runs a dance and acting school.

Yet another Welsh one-hit wonder was Tammy Jones from Bangor. Although she shot to fame after winning the Hughie Green talent show *Thank Your Lucky Stars* for six consecutive weeks, Tammy had already achieved considerable success in

Wales, regularly appearing on TV and radio.

Tammy's song "Let Me Try Again" reached No 5 in the charts and she was voted the best-selling female artist for 1975. Yet, like Ricky Valance and Maureen Evans before her, she was never able to repeat her chart success. She later moved to New Zealand for several years but eventually decided to return to her native Wales.

Ricky, Maureen and Tammy may not have been able to build on their initial success but their songs remain popular, regularly played on the radio programmes that specialise in songs from the past, and certainly give people a feel of the 1960s and 1970s. They all qualify for the term Welsh one-hit wonders.

99 – The Death of the British Pub

It's a sad fact that upwards of 30 public houses are disappearing, closing down, every week in Britain. Other countries might have their taverns, beer halls or bars but the humble British pub has always been something of an institution, an establishment unique to this country.

Every town or village once had one and the public house was, for many years, the social centre of community life. All that, however, is changing as people now buy cheaper alcohol in supermarkets and are more than happy to sit and drink at home. The cosy chat around the pub fire or bar counter is rapidly becoming a thing of the past.

It might seem as if the pub has been around for thousands of years but, in fact, the public house, as we know it, is not as ancient as we sometimes think.

As far as Wales is concerned, purpose-built pubs only came into being in the last 300 or so years. Inns, for the comfort of needy travellers, had been around for some time – Chaucer's pilgrims in *The Canterbury Tales* began their journey from just such an establishment and there were many examples in Wales. But pubs? These were a different species.

The public house, a place just to drink and talk, arrived in Wales in the early 1700s. To begin with they were beer houses, the name summing up their origins. Quite simply people opened up their houses and sold beer in their front rooms or parlours. In rural areas these beer houses might be located in farm houses – in towns they were just as likely to be terraced properties, surrounded on both sides by the dwellings of ordinary men and women.

To begin with these places had no bar counter – such refinements did not come into being until the middle of the nineteenth century. The beer (and it was, normally, just beer that was sold) was stored in the pantry and was fetched to your seat or, if you were lucky, to your table by the landlady or landlord, being poured from a jug directly into your glass. Most of these early pubs or beer dens had only one room, chairs being set around an inglenook fire or lined along the walls.

These early pubs were well used and provided valuable income for the owners. In many cases they were run by women, the men continuing to work on the farm or foundry during the day and either lending a hand at night or simply sitting and partaking in the entertainment.

It was very much a working-class clientele as the upper echelons of society would either use well-established inns or drink in the comfort of their own homes. But for men coming home from the pit, quarry or steel works these public houses provided much-needed refreshment after a working day that would probably kill or maim most people in this day and age.

Beer was also safe to drink. It was, for the most part, relatively clean and unlikely to carry disease. And that was more than could be said about the water in Welsh towns or villages until well into the twentieth century.

By the middle years of the nineteenth century towns in Wales boasted huge numbers of public houses. By 1840, even a relatively small place like Caernarfon had no fewer than two inns, two hotels, five spirit dealers and 27 taverns or beer houses. The town of Monmouth had the staggering (perhaps literally!) ratio of one pub for every 85 people while in the ship-building community of Pembroke Dock there were over 200 drinking dens. Newport had an amazing 390 pubs, inns and beer houses – at a time when the town's population was less than a third of today.

Just like the long-established inns, after a while the pubs began to acquire names for themselves. In many cases these names were linked to the signs that hung outside their doors. To display a sign advertising their wares had been a legal requirement for anyone who sold alcohol since Roman days – names such as the Bush or Ivy Bush can certainly be traced back to this era. Places like The Royal Oak or the King's Arms soon became commonplace while after the Crimean War, as soldiers began to return home, pubs began to adopt names such as The Alma or Odessa. Other names, such as the famous Cow and Snuffers in Cardiff elude explanation.

The story of the public house – particularly in Wales – cannot be separated from the Temperance Movement. Despite the fact that, in the early days, many religious groups used the pubs and taverns as meeting houses, during the Victorian age the supporters of "temperance" gained ground, railing about drunkenness and portraying the pubs as "gateways to Hell".

Perhaps the crowning glory of the Temperance Movement came in 1881 when the Sunday Closing Act was passed. It might have seemed to be a victory for the supporters of temperance but, in fact, the Act led to a century or more of ingenious law breaking as would-be Sunday drinkers continuously found loopholes in the law.

The simplest way of getting around the Act was to leave the back door open but there were also more sophisticated ways of buying a drink on Sundays. For a long while, for example, anyone travelling seven miles or more could claim a drink in another town – although quite how people were able to prove or disprove that fact remains a little unclear.

Late Victorian and Edwardian Wales produced some staggeringly beautiful pub buildings. And many of them still remain. The Golden Cross in Cardiff, the Waterloo in Newport and The Ivy Bush in Pontardawe are just three superb examples, survivors of an institution once found in many working-class communities.

However, with pub closures taking place right across the country, the future of all our public houses has to be in question. As someone once said about the local corner shop – use it or lose it. The pub remains part of our heritage, envied by visitors and tourists the world over. Use it or lose it.

100 – How Public Was the Public House?

It's a little known fact but the good, old-fashioned public house was, for many years, far less public than most of us ever imagined. Half of the population of Britain was actually banned from many of these establishments, purely on the grounds of gender, and of the other half a large proportion was excluded from certain parts of the building because of social class.

For a long time many Welsh pubs had "Men Only" bars. Until as late as the 1970s women, if they came to the pub at all, were usually sat in the snug or the lounge. They rarely entered the hallowed portals of "the bar" and their men folk – very few women ventured into the pub alone – would bring them drinks as the evening progressed. The men remained, resolutely, standing at the bar.

It had not always been like this and such a situation was actually something of a regression. In the Victorian era you would often find women in public houses but these ladies were not always the kind of girl you would be happy to take home to your mother! Pubs like The Eagle in Cardiff – later, perhaps appropriately, re-named The Spread Eagle - doubled as brothels and many establishments were actually run by women.

When you study the various Directories of Welsh towns and villages in the 1880s and 1890s you find that, maybe, 40% or even 50% of them had women landlords.

There were famous characters in most Welsh towns, drunkards who regularly appeared in court on charges of being drunk and disorderly. Many of these were women and some, like Ellen Sweeney of Swansea had over 150 convictions! No sign of discrimination by gender there, then!

As the twentieth century unfolded, the insidious discrimination towards women developed and became accepted as the norm. In the smaller towns and rural areas the taboo against women in pubs was rigorously enforced and remained firm and constant until well after the Second World War. Pubs often had a small hatch, perhaps at the rear of the building, where women might come to fill up a bottle or a jug but they rarely went inside the pub itself.

Only when the "swinging sixties" unleashed a social and cultural revolution – and, subsequently, the greater freedom that came about as a result of the Women's Lib movement – were some of the more bizarre prejudices of society finally smashed away. The attitude of men towards women in pubs was one of the first taboos to go.

There was also, for many years, a very clear social divide in the pubs. Working men used the bar; the "better class of person" – the town doctor, solicitor or police sergeant – drank in the snug or lounge. And never the twain would meet. Of course there was a charge of two pence extra on all drinks bought in the lounge but, for most members of the middle- or even upper-classes, that seemed to be preferable to drinking with your workers or servants.

Sometimes the working men in the bar had to face yet another form of discrimination. Many pubs expressly forbade the wearing of working clothes. Others allowed it in the early evening, for men on their way home from work, but if they wanted a drink after 9.00 p.m. they had to be properly attired in jackets, shirts and trousers.

These days there is no sense of discrimination in our pubs. The law of the land would not allow it and, anyway, attitudes have changed out of all recognition. The public house has evolved along with the rest of society and if it wants to survive it will have to continue to change, many times, in the months and years ahead.

101 – The Collapse of the Cleddau Bridge

Anyone who drives up the A477 from South Pembrokeshire to the northern part of the county will pass over the magnificent structure of the Cleddau Bridge. They will wonder at the glorious views down Milford Haven towards the sea but they will probably never realise that this was the site of the last major bridge disaster in the United Kingdom.

It happened during the construction process. The bridge was – and is – of a box-girder design. In other words it was built in sections or self-contained boxes that were trundled out along the partially completed bridge and simply lowered onto the front of the construction.

On 2nd June 1970, as one of the box girder sections for the bridge was being positioned and lowered into place, there came a deafening rumble and the bridge sections on the Pembroke Dock side of the river plummeted to the ground. Four workmen were killed and five more were injured in the disaster.

The fallen Cleddau Bridge with the box girders resting on the foreshore, only narrowly missing the houses beneath.

It could have been so much worse. The bridge passed virtually over the top of Pembroke Ferry, a tiny village on the southern shore of the River Cleddau, but when it collapsed the debris and the falling box girder sections missed the houses by a matter of just a few feet. It was a very lucky escape.

The River Cleddau has always divided the county of Pembrokeshire into two and before the bridge was built there were only two ways of moving from one part of the county to the other – either by driving the long way round through narrow lanes and B roads or by taking a ferry boat across the often choppy waters of the river.

From the mid 1850s the Admiralty, who ran the dockyard at Pembroke Dock, agreed to allow steam-driven ferry boats to dock at their jetty and fitting out berth of Hobbs Point. These ferries would then take people – dockyard workers amongst them – across the river to Neyland. The ferry boats ran for many years, the County Council taking over the process in 1950. The ferry boats became famous on both sides of the river, vessels like the *Alumchine, Lady Magdalene* and *Cleddau King* plying their way across the water at all times of the day and night.

When the Admiralty closed the dockyard at Pembroke Dock in the years after the First World War part of the establishment was taken over by the RAF as a flying boat base – at one time the largest flying boat base in the world. The huge Sunderland aircraft that lay moored out in the river for many years provided something of a hazard for the ferry boats, particularly when they were taxiing for landing or take off.

As the twentieth century progressed it became clear that the ferries, despite their interest and sentimental appeal, could not hope to cope with the growing density of traffic and in the mid 1960s it was decided to build a bridge across the Cleddau.

Actually there were to be two bridges, the first one crossing the main waterway and a smaller one spanning the creek at Westfield Pill in order to link to the main A477. The contract for construction was awarded to the firm of AE Farr and the estimated cost was to be 2.1 million pounds. The aim was to complete the building process by spring 1971.

The collapse of the bridge and the trauma of the event brought construction to a sudden halt. An inquiry was immediately called. After much deliberation it was decided that the disaster had been caused by inadequate supports on the pier that was lowering the box-girder section into place. There was also, apparently, a failure of organisation and communication on the building site itself.

As a result of the disaster and the subsequent Inquiry, new British Standards for the design and construction of box-girder bridges were brought in. These seem to have been effective as there have been no further disasters involving box-girder bridges – and, it is hoped, there never will be.

The Cleddau Bridge was eventually finished at a cost of 11.83 million pounds, rather more than had been originally foreseen. It was opened to traffic on 20th March 1975 and the ferry boats that had, for so many years, plied their trade across the river, were duly towed away for scrapping.

In the first year of operation it is recorded that 885,900 crossings were made on the new Cleddau Bridge – considerably more than would ever have ventured on to the ferry boats. The bridge is now a crucial part of the infrastructure of south Wales but we should never forget the cost of its creation, in both financial terms and, more importantly, in human life.

Select Bibliography

There are hundreds, even thousands, of excellent books about various aspects of Welsh history. The readers must make up their own minds regarding what they want to read or study. The following, however, have been particularly useful in writing the blogs and in compiling this book:

Terry Breverton	*100 Great Welshmen* (Wales Books)
	The Secret Vale of Glamorgan (Glyndwr Publishing)
	An A to Z of Wales and the Welsh (Christopher Davies Publishing)
Giraldus Cambrensis	*The Journey Through Wales* (Penguin edition)
Phil Carradice	*Wales at War* (Gomer)
	Nautical Training Schools (Amberley)
	Pembroke: For King and Parliament (Pembroke Town Council)
	Penarth Pier (Barracuda Books)
	The Last Invasion (Village Publishing)
Phil and Trudy Carradice	*Golf in Wales* (Amberley)
John Davies	*A History of Wales* (Penguin)
Deb Fisher	*Princes of Wales* (University of Wales Press
	Princesses of Wales (University of Wales Press)
Dilys Gater	*The Battles of Wales* (Gwasg Carreg Gwalch)
Kate Marsh	*Writers and Their Houses* (Hamilton)
John May	*The Yearbook of Welsh Dates* (Privately Printed)
Graham Smith	*Headlines From Wales* (Countryside Books)
Patrick Thornhill	*Railways for Britain* (Methuen)

David Webb	*The Battle of St Fagans* (Stuart Press)
David Williams	*Modern Wales* (John Murray)
Herbert Williams	*Davies the Ocean* (University of Wales Press)
	Come Out, Wherever You Are (Gomer)

Index